10 0572822 7

D1152542

Contemporary Political Studies Series

Series Editor: John Benyon, *University of Leicester*

Published

DAVID BROUGHTON
Public Opinion and Political Polling in Britain

JUNE BURNHAM and ROBERT PYPER
Britain's Modernised Civil Service

CLYDE CHITTY
Education Policy in Britain

MICHAEL CONNOLLY
Politics and Policy Making in Northern Ireland

DAVID DENVER
Elections and Voters in Britain

JUSTIN FISHER
British Political Parties

ROBERT GARNER
Environmental Politics: Britain, Europe and the Global Environment; 2nd edn

ANDREW GEDDES
The European Union and British Politics

WYN GRANT
Pressure Groups and British Politics

WYN GRANT
Economic Policy in Britain

DEREK HEATER and GEOFFREY BERRIDGE
Introduction to International Politics

DILYS M. HILL
Urban Policy and Politics in Britain

RAYMOND KUHN
Politics and the Media in Britain

ROBERT LEACH
Political Ideology in Britain

ROBERT LEACH and JANIE PERCY-SMITH
Local Governance in Britain

PETER MADGWICK
British Government: The Central Executive Territory

ANDREW MASSEY and ROBERT PYPER
Public Management and Modernisation in Britain

PHILIP NORTON
Parliament and British Politics

MALCOLM PUNNETT
Selecting the Party Leader

Forthcoming

CHARLIE JEFFERY
Devolution and UK Politics

Contemporary Political Studies Series

Series Standing Order ISBN 978–0–230–54350–8 hardback
Series Standing Order ISBN 978–0–230–54351–5 paperback

(outside North America only)

You can receive future titles in this series as they are published by placing a standing order. Please contact your bookseller or, in case of difficulty, write to us at the address below with your name and address, the title of the series and one of the ISBNs quoted above.

Customer Services Department, Macmillan Distribution Ltd
Houndmills, Basingstoke, Hampshire RG21 6XS, England

Britain's Modernised Civil Service

June Burnham
and
Robert Pyper

University of Nottingham
Hallward Library

palgrave
macmillan

© June Burnham and Robert Pyper 2008

All rights reserved. No reproduction, copy or transmission of this publication may be made without written permission.

No paragraph of this publication may be reproduced, copied or transmitted save with written permission or in accordance with the provisions of the Copyright, Designs and Patents Act 1988, or under the terms of any licence permitting limited copying issued by the Copyright Licensing Agency, 90 Tottenham Court Road, London W1T 4LP.

Any person who does any unauthorised act in relation to this publication may be liable to criminal prosecution and civil claims for damages.

The authors have asserted their rights to be identified as the authors of this work in accordance with the Copyright, Designs and Patents Act 1988.

First published 2008 by
PALGRAVE MACMILLAN
Houndmills, Basingstoke, Hampshire RG21 6XS and
175 Fifth Avenue, New York, N.Y. 10010
Companies and representatives throughout the world

PALGRAVE MACMILLAN is the global academic imprint of the Palgrave Macmillan division of St. Martin's Press, LLC and of Palgrave Macmillan Ltd. Macmillan® is a registered trademark in the United States, United Kingdom and other countries. Palgrave is a registered trademark in the European Union and other countries.

ISBN-13: 978–0–333–94532–2   hardback
ISBN-10: 0–333–94532–8   hardback
ISBN-13: 978–0–333–94533–9   paperback
ISBN-10: 0–333–94533–6   paperback

This title is designed as a replacement for *The British Civil Service* by Robert Pyper (1995).

This book is printed on paper suitable for recycling and made from fully managed and sustained forest sources. Logging, pulping and manufacturing processes are expected to conform to the environmental regulation of the country of origin.

A catalogue record for this book is available from the British Library.

A catalog record for this book is available from the Library of Congress.

10   9   8   7   6   5   4   3   2   1
17   16   15   14   13   12   11   10   09   08

Printed and bound in China

1005728227

Contents

List of Boxes, Figures and Tables

Boxes

Figures

Tables

List of Abbreviations

AM	Assembly Member (Wales)
CCSU	Council of Civil Service Unions
CIPFA	Chartered Institute of Public Finance and Accountancy
CMT	Community Management Tool (Canada)
CPRS	Central Policy Review Staff
CRE	Commission for Racial Equality
CSD	Civil Service Department
CSR	Comprehensive Spending Review
DEFRA	Department for the Environment, Food and Rural Affairs
DERA	Defence Evaluation and Research Agency
DES	Department of Education and Science
DETR	Department for Environment, Transport and the Regions
DfES	Department for Education and Skills
DfT	Department for Transport
DH	Department of Health
DoE	Department of the Environment
DSS	Department of Social Security
Dstl	Defence Science and Technology Laboratory
DTI	Department of Trade and Industry
DVLA	Driver and Vehicle Licensing Agency
DWP	Department for Work and Pensions
EEC	European Economic Community
EFTA	European Free Trade Area
ENA	Ecole National d'Administration
EO	Executive Officer (Civil Service)
EP	European Parliament
ECSC	European Coal and Steel Community
EU	European Union
Euratom	European Atomic Energy Authority
FCO	Foreign and Commonwealth Office
FDA	First Division Association

FMI	Financial Management Initiative
FO	Foreign Office
FoI	Freedom of Information
FTE	Full-time equivalent (staff)
GCHQ	Government Communications Headquarters
GFS	graduate fast stream (Civil Service recruitment)
HMSO	Her Majesty's Stationery Office
IMF	International Monetary Fund
IMO	International Maritime Organization
IND	Immigration and National Directorate
IRA	Irish Republican Army
IT	information technology
ITU	International Telecommunications Union
JMC	Joint Ministerial Committee
MINIS	management information system for ministers
MoD	Ministry of Defence
MP	Member of Parliament
MPO	Management and Personnel Office
MSP	Member of the Scottish Parliament
NAO	National Audit Office
NATO	North Atlantic Treaty Organisation
NFU	National Farmers' Union
NHS	National Health Service
NICS	Northern Ireland Civil Service
NID	Northern Ireland Department
NIO	Northern Ireland Office
NPM	New Public Management
ODA	Overseas Development Administration
OECD	Organisation for Economic Co-operation and Development
OGC	Office of Government Commerce
ONS	Office for National Statistics
OPSR	Office of Public Services Reform
PAC	Public Accounts Committee
PCS	Public and Commercial Services Union
PFI	Private Finance Initiative
PII	Public Interest Immunity
PIU	Performance and Innovation Unit
POA	Prison Officers' Association
PPM	Public Performance Measure
PPP	Public Private Partnerships

PRP	performance-related pay
PQ	Parliamentary Questions
PSA	Public Service Agreement
QT	qualifying test (civil service)
SAE	stamped addressed envelope
SASC	Senior Appointments Selection Committee
SCS	Senior Civil Service
SNP	Scottish National Party
SO	Scottish Office
TRL	Transport Research Laboratory
UK	United Kingdom
UN	United Nations
UNSCOM	United Nations Special Commission
USA	United States of America

Acknowledgement

Crown Copyright material in Boxes 2.1, 2.2, 2.3, 5.1 and 5.2 is reproduced with the permission of the controller of Her Majesty's Stationery Office under click-use licence CO1W0000276.

Introduction: Mapping the Territory

The title of this book makes clear our view that the British civil service has been 'modernised'. It means that the service has been subjected to a series of reforming measures and processes that enable it to respond better to the demands, needs and expectations of the government of the day and of contemporary society. Despite its many imperfections, identified in the following chapters, the British civil service, in the bald terms of dictionary definitions, comes closer to being 'organised in a manner which matches today's needs', and to having been 'given a modern form, adapted to current techniques', than the civil services of many other liberal democracies or, indeed, its own old self of the 1960s.

Indeed, in the opinion of some of the critics we cite later, the British civil service has become *too* modernised in recent years, abandoning the traditional characteristics and patterns of behaviour that had given it worldwide standing as a well-oiled and superior 'Rolls-Royce' machine. It changed involuntarily in the 1980s and early 1990s, when it was forced to adapt to the 'economy, efficiency and effectiveness' agenda of the 'New Right' governments led by Margaret Thatcher and John Major. Then, after 1997, civil service leaders adapted – too eagerly, the critics might say – to the 'New Labour' government's desire for a more informal, personalised style of administration; they wanted to show that they had not taken on 'Thatcherite' values, and could still serve any government equally loyally.

Paradoxically, the British government gained an international reputation in the late 1980s for its modernising reforms, despite being one of the few European governments at the time not to have proclaimed a 'modernisation programme for the public sector' (for Britain, that came in 1999 during the government of Tony Blair, as we shall see), and despite some other countries, notably in Britain's former anglo-phone colonies and in Northern Europe, having already adopted similar reforms, usually grouped under the heading of 'new public management' (NPM). However, the modernisation of the British civil service attracted greater attention than those elsewhere, perhaps because the more conflictual policy process in Britain (as personified by Mrs Thatcher) gave the reforms a radical tone, perhaps because texts in English are more widely accessible than those in Scandinavian languages, or perhaps simply because Britain is larger with a greater presence on the international stage: it has more politicians, officials and academics to promote or explain the changes taking place. During the Major government of the early 1990s, officials from the Office of Public Service liked to astonish their counterparts in European Union (EU) meetings with news of the latest reform, and the Foreign Office issued publicity brochures on the 'Citizen's Charter' project, while the British Council was made responsible for spreading information abroad about the Charter and other public service reforms.

British academics, because of their greater familiarity with the context and details of the modernising reforms, have been more restrained in their praise, especially when comparing the outcomes with the grand ambitions announced by ministers. Yet the continuing interest from abroad could not have been sustained without real changes having been achieved. The international Organisation for Economic Co-operation and Development (OECD), has since the 1980s, in its Public Management Development and Public Sector Modernisation reports, consistently included the United Kingdom among its top examples, whether concerning organisational change, managing senior civil servants, performance-related pay, increasing managerial autonomy, or the outsourcing of services. The reports of the OECD and others have generated a good deal of permanent interest abroad in the workings of the British civil service. However, the OECD has a market-orientated world view, and tends to focus on managerial reforms to civil services that it considers will help the economic and financial performance of its member countries. One reason that Scandinavian public sector reforms received less international attention was that they stressed the transfer of power to local governments and user boards rather than budgetary savings (there were no moves towards democratic decentralisation in Britain until the Labour government's devolution of power to Scotland and Wales in 1999). Yet there is much more to a civil service than the impact of its wages bill on public expenditure and the general economy. A large part of the purpose of this book is therefore to put the story of successful public-sector modernisation into a wider context.

The big-picture story of success also needs to be examined in more detail before an informed judgement can be made. Even within the relatively narrow focus of public management reform, have the projects gone according to plan and achieved the results confidently predicted? Furthermore, what have been the impacts on other characteristics of the civil service? For example, there has been a drive to open up the higher civil service and bring in people from the private sector, with different talents, experiences and ways of working; but what consequences does this have for the cohesive civil service culture that aids interdepartmental communication, or on the relationship between public officials and the private-sector contractors with whom they do business? How has the increase in managerial autonomy affected the coordination of government policies or the accountability of officials to ministers, and of ministers to Parliament and citizens? What mechanisms have been put in place to counteract these potential problems? For those analysts who regard such questions as being at least as important as efficiency and effectiveness, the evaluation of the British civil service must include an assessment of these issues. Indeed, those who have had the strongest criticisms of the 'modernisation' reforms do so on the grounds that they have harmed in a very fundamental way the finest characteristics of the traditional service: high ethical standards, impartiality and willingness to 'speak truth unto power' (officials giving ministers an honest opinion, including a polite 'No').

As the raising of such questions implies, there are several features of a civil service that are easily left out when a discussion of 'public-sector management' draws too close a parallel with 'private-sector management'. A civil service organisation inevitably differs from a large private company. Even firms who are 'good corporate citizens' with strong ethical codes must ultimately act in the interests of shareholders, while civil servants are required to act in the public interest – as defined, constitutionally, by Parliament and the ministers it supports, and to demonstrate that they have done so. Recent efforts to modernise the British civil service have stressed improvements in serving the citizen as a customer or a client of public administration, and thus lessons from the private sector have often been highly appropriate. However, in other respects, such as parliamentary accountability, public policy formation, freedom of information, merit-based systems of recruitment and promotion, and the need to deal with all citizens and their affairs impartially, the civil service has constraints and duties that go beyond the idea of a 'generic management'. Yet developments in these aspects of the British civil service are not so widely known; they deserve a full treatment, which we try to give them in subsequent chapters, and to be put alongside the improvements in the realm of NPM.

It would be wrong to imply that the civil service of the past was a stagnant, unchanging element of the political system. The modernisation processes undoubtedly accelerated from the 1980s, resulting in profound changes to the structure and management of the organisation. They stemmed from reforms introduced within the civil service itself (for example, the structural changes leading to the creation of semi-autonomous executive agencies, or the adoption of more flexible pay and recruitment systems), but also from external developments that had serious implications for the civil service (most notably devolution). Nevertheless, the historical development of the British civil service has been based on a steady, gradual accommodation of change, and organic growth, even if the sheer scale and volume of changes during the last years of the twentieth century and the early part of the twenty-first were without precedent.

It is perhaps ironic that 'modernisation', as a governing principle, has a long history. For example, in the UK, the Liberal–Tories of the 1820s and 1830s, their Peelite successors, and the radicals in the Liberal Party were 'modernisers' in the sense that they favoured judicious social, economic and constitutional reforms as means towards their aim of modernising the state progressively to meet the challenges of the time. The political heirs of these groups could be seen at work in the more advanced parts of local government (running progressive administrations in cities such as Birmingham and Glasgow) during the second half of the nineteenth century, and then in the reforming Liberal governments of 1905–15, pursuing the policies that represented the emergence of an embryonic welfare state. In the USA, the early part of the twentieth century saw modernisers, in the guise of Progressives, taking control of city and state administrations, and influencing the political programmes of Presidents Theodore and Franklin D. Roosevelt, to give just two examples. Modernisers, in the historical context, often had particular views about the processes and structures of bureaucracy. For example, US President Woodrow Wilson, in the pre-political phase of his career, wrote extensively about the principles of public administration and argued strongly in favour of a modern approach to government that recognised the professional nature of the civil service and shielded it from political corruption. Modernisation therefore has a long association with progressive change in systems of government, and with improvements to the administrative elements of these systems.

In order to map out the territory for our study, the remainder of this Introduction will outline the key historical themes in the development of the civil service, provide some basic facts and figures about the civil service, and establish some benchmarks for comparing the British civil service with administrative systems in other states. Finally, we shall set out the broad structure and content of the rest of the book.

Key historical themes

The civil service is both a component and a product of the UK's constitutional system. It has evolved as state systems and structures have changed and grown over the years. Organic growth and incremental change have been the characteristic modes of development, rather than sudden, dramatic changes (although the following chapters will explore the extent to which the modernisation drive of recent years has marked a departure from this rule of thumb). In contrast to most other nations, there is no 'founding statute' or basic civil service law setting out the purpose, function and responsibility of this vital arm of the state (although, as we shall see later in this book, the idea of introducing a Civil Service Act has been voiced increasingly loudly since the 1990s). Instead, in line with the broader constitutional framework in the UK (which, again unlike most other nations, is an uncodified collection of certain Acts of Parliament, court decisions, conventions, customs and learned works deemed to be of constitutional significance), the work of the civil service is to be understood with reference to an array of statutes, codes, memoranda and time-honoured procedures. The most significant of these documents and customary procedures, linking the civil service to the 'constitutional conventions', will emerge in the following chapters. For example, when we discuss issues of accountability in Chapter 5, we shall stress the importance of the convention of ministerial responsibility, which governs the way in which civil servants account for their work.

The origins of the UK's civil service lie in the sets of courtiers surrounding the early monarchs of the nations of Britain that themselves had yet to crystallise. The evolution was slow and hesitant. As Box I.1 shows, it took from the ninth century to the sixteenth for the increasingly refined organisation of the English Crown's records to distinguish between the monarch's 'household' finances and national finances, and for staff to be appointed to administer 'government' affairs. Even then, there was no formal distinction between ministers and officials, or between administrators and parliamentarians, as illustrated by the case of Thomas Cromwell, variously MP, solicitor, Principal Secretary to the King, and Lord Privy Seal (now a ministerial title). All were servants of the Crown, remaining in post for as long as the monarch decided. Well into the nineteenth century, ministers had time for administrative tasks, and officials were often their political supporters, or young relatives of their political supporters, who would leave with their minister when he resigned or was dismissed. The 'story' of the early development of the bureaucracy can be seen in terms of financial administration, and thus of the supremacy of Treasury concerns. In the nineteenth century too (see Box I.2), the Treasury often took the lead in improving administration and building the civil service into a unified organisation, and its strong role was to persist into the twenty-first century (Hennessy, 1989, 1990: 17–30; Drewry and Butcher, 1991: 39–41).

On the other hand, another important and ancient source of control over civil service matters derives from the 'Privy Council', comprising a monarch's religious, official, judicial and political advisers. In modern times, Privy Counsellors are appointed by the Queen, but are chosen by the government from among ministers, opposition party leaders, top officials, judges, archbishops and other senior figures, either simply as an honour, or to enable them to be told in confidence sensitive intelligence 'on Privy Council terms'. From the Privy Council derived a number of constitutional and organisational arrangements.

First, the inner circle of the Privy Council (the monarch's closest advisers in his private *cabinet*) eventually became today's Cabinet government. By the early eighteenth century it had become the Cabinet of government ministers, whose role was to advise the Crown. They found it safer to reach a private consensus before giving that advice ('better to hang together than hang separately'), thereby nurturing the concept of collective – and confidential – Cabinet government. By the end of the eighteenth century the Cabinet of ministers, led by the prime minister, exercised power, provided it had the support of Parliament, but it acted in the name of the Crown (a Cabinet minister is still 'Her Majesty's Secretary of State'). There was little administrative

---

***Box* I.1   The modernisation process: the civil service emerges**

870–1066   Clerics and household servants, including the *thesaurarius* (treasurer), keep records and look after the royal money ('treasures') for Anglo-Saxon kings

1086   Henry, *thesaurarius* to the Norman King William the Conqueror, appears in the Domesday Book; the first Treasury officer identified by name

1232–33   Peter de Rievaulx, finance adviser to Henry III, reforms the record-keeping

1340   Parliamentary control over Crown finances is recognised in statute

1485–1524   Henry VII and his Treasurers introduce more efficient financial accounting

1529   Henry VIII takes over Cardinal Wolsey's house and names it Whitehall

1533–40   Thomas Cromwell gives the Privy Council a departmental structure, separating Royal household administration from national government administration

1572   Burghley, Lord Treasurer and Principal Secretary to Elizabeth I's Privy Council, appoints staff (clerks, messengers) to administer government matters

1668   An Order in Council gives the Treasury control over revenue and departmental expenditure, and the right to scrutinise all staff appointments

1696   William III creates a Board of Trade & Plantations. As the Board of Trade from 1786, its high-calibre officials campaign for civil service reform in 1855

1707   Act of Union of England and Scotland; the Privy Council of Great Britain combines the functions of the two Privy Councils

1780   Speech of Edmund Burke on 'economical reform' stimulates Parliament to examine the administration of public offices

1782   The Home Office (Crown, Irish and colonial affairs) and Foreign Office (FO) are created from the Southern and Northern Departments of the Principal Secretary of State. The FO develops as a separate, aristocratic bureaucracy

1786   Act requiring the East India Company to administer the Indian Empire as a Crown subsidiary; it calls its staff 'civil servants'; Trevelyan joins in 1826

1810   Act providing a pension scheme for the staff of 'public departments'

1848   Parliamentary Inquiry on Miscellaneous Expenditure told by Trevelyan that the Treasury would need fewer staff if they were recruited on competence

1853–54   Northcote–Trevelyan *Report on the Organisation of the Permanent Civil Service* prepared and published

---

***Box* I.2   The modernisation process: building a unified
civil service**

1855   Order in Council sets up the Civil Service Commission
1859   Officials with a Civil Service Commission certificate qualify
for a non-contributory pension scheme of the 'permanent civil
service of the State'
1870   Order in Council gives Civil Service Commission general control over recruitment, to Treasury rules; open competition
becomes the norm
1876   Civil service unions form because of discontent with unequal
conditions; Order in Council creates a common, service-wide
'Lower Division'
1890   Order in Council reconstitutes Higher Division as 'First
Division'; women, scientific and technical staff now recruited
in significant numbers
1916   Prime Minister Lloyd George sets up Cabinet Secretariat (later
Office)
1919   Fisher becomes Treasury Permanent Secretary and Head of the
Civil Service; Treasury introduces common pay scales for all
but the top two grades; Whitley Councils set up for employer–
staff bargaining on conditions of service
1920   Prime Minister, advised by Treasury Secretary, to approve top
appointments; Order in Council confirms Treasury responsibility for regulating the service
1921   Partition of Ireland and creation of Northern Ireland Civil Service
1929–31 Tomlin Royal Commission on the Civil Service provides the
classic definition of the British civil service, in the absence of
statutory provisions
1945   Prime Minister Churchill makes the Cabinet Secretary also the
Treasury Permanent Secretary and Head of the Home Civil
Service (without FO)
1946   Women no longer have to leave the civil service if they marry
1947   Prime Minister Attlee keeps the Treasury Secretary as Head of
the Home Civil Service, and another official is Cabinet Secretary
and joint Treasury Secretary
1952   Government agrees to equal pay for women civil servants; this
is implemented in the non-industrial civil service in 1955, and
in the industrial civil service in 1970
1956   Treasury Secretary retires; Cabinet Secretary becomes Head of
Home Civil Service and Second Permanent Secretary in the
Treasury
1961   Plowden Report questions the managerial competence of the
civil service
1962   Return to a separate Cabinet Secretary in the Cabinet Office,
and a Head of the Home Civil Service who is also Treasury
(Second) Permanent Secretary

help to support Cabinet government until the First World War, not even to keep records on what ministers had decided when they met in Cabinet. When Lloyd George became prime minister half-way through the war, the Cabinet Secretariat (which became the Cabinet Office), was created to serve his War Cabinet, using the staff and the coordinating techniques of the inter-departmental secretariat already serving the Committee of Imperial Defence. The continuation of the Cabinet Office after the war was opposed by the Treasury and by Conservative politicians keen to abolish what they saw as Lloyd George's 'empire-building'. However, the incoming Conservative prime minister (Bonar Law) had seen at first hand, as Lloyd George's deputy, the usefulness of the Cabinet Office, and the Cabinet Office and its Cabinet Secretary stayed. The Cabinet Office and the Treasury have remained traditional rivals for the role of being 'the centre of government', including control of the civil service (Box I.3 charts the complicated history of the transfer of civil service functions between these two institutions and the short-lived Civil Service Department).

Second, decisions by the 'King/Queen in Council' have remained a valid way of making law long after Parliament became the main source of legislation. The Queen still assents to 'Orders in Council' at a meeting of four or more ministers who are 'Privy Counsellors'. Most of the early monarchs' former areas of competence have transferred to Parliament, but those powers that the Crown still retains (the 'Royal Prerogative' powers), such as agreeing to international treaties, dissolving Parliament before holding new elections, and being head of the armed forces, are exercised in practice by ministers, usually the prime minister. An Order in Council is one way in which these executive powers are exercised. The many examples of these Orders in Boxes I.1–I.4 show how useful this instrument has been for making changes to the organisation of the civil service without the need to persuade Parliament first. Paradoxically, the short Civil Service (Management Functions) Act of 1992, delegating personnel functions from ministers to top officials, aroused considerable suspicion from Parliament just because it was so unusual for MPs to be asked to give their consent on civil service matters.

Third, managing the civil service is a prerogative power of the Crown, exercised by the prime minister. The *Civil Service Management Code* (that is, the set of rules and regulations that govern the recruitment, promotion, conduct, transfer, retirement or dismissal of civil servants) reaffirms the historic principle: 'Civil servants are servants of the Crown and owe a duty of loyal service to the Crown as their employer'

Box I.3   The modernisation process: managerial reorganisation and reform

1966–68	Prime Minister Wilson orders and publishes the Fulton Report
1968	The Treasury's civil service functions transfer to a Civil Service Department (CSD), whose Permanent Secretary is Head of the Home Civil Service
1969	Order in Council sets out the criteria for employing 'outsiders'
1970	Civil Service College set up in London, Sunningdale and Edinburgh; Prime Minister Heath's White Paper, *The Reorganisation of Central Government*, proposes (and introduces in a small way), management reforms, including 'super-departments' and 'hiving-off' discrete functions to agencies
1979	Labour government abandons civil service pay policy after mass strikes
1981	Long strike against Thatcher Government's abolition of pay agreements; CSD is abolished; pay functions go to Treasury; rest to Management & Personnel Office (MPO) attached to Cabinet Office; Treasury Permanent Secretary and Cabinet Secretary become joint Heads of the Home Civil Service
1982	Financial Management Initiative on budgetary control and performance
1983	Cabinet Secretary appointed Head of the Home Civil Service
1987	MPO abolished; some functions go to Treasury, others to Cabinet Office
1988	*Improving Management in Government: the Next Steps* (the Ibbs Report) leads to the creation of 116 Executive Agencies by 1998
1991	Prime Minister Major launches *The Citizen's Charter* before the 1992 election; Treasury White Paper, *Competing for Quality*, on market testing, is issued; Order in Council replaces Civil Service Commission with Office of the Civil Service Commissioners (outside professionals) and makes departments and agencies responsible for recruiting staff, except for senior officials
1992	Civil Service (Management Functions) Act enables responsibilities for most personnel functions to be delegated to civil servants as heads of departments; Treasury announces the Private Finance Initiative (PFI) to bring private-sector loans and project management into public investment
1994	Treasury's *Fundamental Review of Running Costs* leads to transfer of remaining civil service functions back to the Cabinet Office; Cabinet Office White Paper, *Continuity and Change*, announces more training, performance pay, and open competition and contracts for senior jobs

(Cabinet Office, 2006; para. 4.1.1). This declaration is followed by a statement of the contemporary practice: 'Since constitutionally the Crown acts on the advice of Ministers who are answerable for their departments and agencies in Parliament, that duty is ... owed to the duly constituted Government' (para. 4.1.1). Modernising reforms are easier in Britain than in nations where the public service is the subject of a special statute and Parliament has to be involved in reform projects. British governments have substantial powers to reorganise the service, as seen in Boxes I.3 and I.4, because it is still, in principle, the administrative staff of the monarch, and the vestigial powers of the monarch can be used to make new laws on its reorganisation.

Two Orders in Council during the Blair Government show the range of this power. In 2007, the *Civil Service Management Code* was 'issued under the authority of the Civil Service Order in Council 1995'. It gives power to the Minister for the civil service (the prime minister), 'to make regulations and give instructions for the management of the Home Civil Service, including the power to prescribe the conditions of service of civil servants' (para. 1). In contrast to this wide-ranging control, a carefully-focused Order in Council of 1997 gave a new power to the prime minister by permitting the appointment of up to three special advisers (temporary political appointees), who could give orders to permanent civil servants: Blair's 'chief of staff' (Jonathan Powell) and his press secretary (Alistair Campbell) were appointed under this unusual provision. The Privy Council is no longer important in itself, but it provides a powerful tool for a British government trying to reform its civil service.

Fourth, government departments such as Trade and Education originated as committees of the Privy Council. The Board of Trade, which was created in a permanent form in 1786, is particularly significant in the evolution of the civil service because it was organised on the basis of a clear distinction between its government ministers, on the one hand, and its small staff of officials on the other; it introduced a clear differentiation between ministers and civil servants on functional grounds (Pyper, 1995: 6). At about this time ministers were also starting to act as a single government and resign together, so that it became administratively convenient if those junior officials who were not identified closely with their minister's politics stayed to serve the incoming government. It was the emergence of formal departmental structures that led to the development of a permanent, official dimension of the state in the UK. However, the myriad collection of departments and boards being set up in the early nineteenth century barely merited the name 'civil service', although a form of common pension scheme for officials was introduced under Treasury auspices in 1810. Even the term 'civil servant', used first by the East India Company (a Crown agency) in the eighteenth century to categorise those employees who were not military personnel, was not much used in Britain until late in the nineteenth century, when it came into use to describe 'permanent' officials – that is, those who remained when ministers changed. It took the first wave of modernisers (or, in the parlance of the day, 'administrative reformers') to counteract the nepotism, inefficiency and corruption by imposing common recruitment and promotion systems, working practices, and a collective ethos on the growing bureaucracy.

Individual reformers, such as the early monarchs Alfred the Great and Henry vii, and the Principal Secretaries, Thomas Cromwell and Lord Burghley, made significant contributions to the initial development of the central administration. Cromwell's employer, Henry viii, made an unwitting contribution to administrative language when he took over the area of London between Parliament and today's Trafalgar Square, which now houses many government buildings and turned it into a palace he called 'Whitehall', which became the 'shorthand' term for the central bureaucracy, just as Parliament and its associated political institutions around the Palace of Westminster are collectively called 'Westminster' (see Chapter 1). Although these individuals and many others played a part in transforming the civil service into a corporate entity, the special part played by two top Treasury officials – Charles Trevelyan in the mid-nineteenth century, and Warren Fisher between the two World Wars – cannot be ignored. The recurrent interest of Parliament in cutting back on expenditure had stimulated a special parliamentary inquiry in 1848. Trevelyan, Secretary to the Treasury, advised it that one way to reduce the growth in the bureaucracy would be to recruit officials on the basis of competence (rather than on giving favours to friends and relatives of ministers and parliamentarians), and to use more productively the junior officials with higher qualifications. Trevelyan already had a great interest in reforming the British civil service, which was poorer in quality than the East India Company, for which he had previously worked. His ideas gained the support of W. E. Gladstone (then Chancellor of the Exchequer), who asked for a report from Trevelyan and Stafford Northcote (one of Gladstone's young aides), on how to ensure that qualified people were recruited and then encouraged to work hard.

The Northcote–Trevelyan Report of 1854 (see Box I.5), recommended:

- A division of the civil service into superior, 'intellectual' work and lower, 'mechanical' tasks;
- Recruitment through an open, competitive examination, conducted by an independent Board;
- Promotion on the basis of merit; and
- Moving staff between departments to make use of them where they were most needed, and to create a more unified service.

The reformers clearly expected resistance to their proposals from the 'powerful interests' of those who benefited from the old system, or were aghast at the idea of 'being displaced by middle-class, meritocratic clerks' (Drewry and Butcher, 1991: 44). Gladstone could not assist because he was (temporarily) out of government. Yet the administrative incompetence demonstrated in the Crimean War boosted the case of the civil service reformers. Furthermore, educational reformers were pressing for outlets for students coming from the progressive public schools and the universities of Oxford and Cambridge ('Oxbridge'). Thus, in 1855, the Civil Service Commission was created to examine candidates put forward by departments. The Commission was given practical support by the 1859 Superannuation Act, which offered a generous pension to civil service recruits who had been approved by the Commission. In 1870, with Gladstone now prime minister, and with Robert Lowe a reforming Chancellor of the Exchequer, open competition was established as the norm, though the Home Office and Foreign Office were still slow to join in. Some other elements of the Northcote–Trevelyan recommendations, such as the functional separation into two divisions, also took place, but other proposed reforms, notably actions to reduce departmental fragmentation, were still not in place by the end of the First World War despite more Reports endorsing them.

Endorsement was one thing; implementation was another. It was not until Warren Fisher was appointed Permanent Secretary (top departmental official) to the Treasury in 1919 that a genuine corporate identity took shape and the unitary nature of the organisation became clearly established. Fisher, who wanted the civil service to have the same status as the armed services, was designated 'Permanent Head of the Civil Service'. On the one hand, the move could be seen as reinforcing Treasury interests in controlling expenditure on personnel: an Establishments

---

Box I.5   The Northcote–Trevelyan Report

A summary of the recommendations

- Recruit young people – it is easier to train than to retrain
- Make promotion depend on hard work and ability
- Recruit through examination, followed by a short probation period
- For senior appointments, have centrally-organised competitive examinations, open to all; a literary examination, to select the fittest persons; but can also recruit for special skills
- For lower class of appointments, local examinations – cheaper for candidates
- Appointments to lower class, mechanical work, at 17 to 21 years
- Appointments to superior class, intellectual work, at 19 to 25 years
- Reduce fragmentation with uniform salary scales to help mobility and transfers
- Improve responsiveness to changes in workload by recruiting some staff to 'supplementary posts', who can move between offices
- Annual pay increments to maximum in class; further increases to depend on promotion
- Promotions on merit are to guard against favouritism by a system of regular reports on performance sent to the head of the office, for reference when vacancies arise
- Pensions to be granted only after a report on the work done by the official

Northcote and Trevelyan's own summary

- Provide, through examinations, a supply of efficient officials
- Encourage hard work and foster merit by offering officials a promotion system that rewards people according to the quality of their work
- Reduce fragmentation by uniform first appointments, transfers and mobile officials
- An Act of Parliament is needed to ensure these changes are implemented – because 'the existing system is supported by long usage and powerful interests'

Sources: S. H. Northcote and C. E. Trevelyan (1854) *Report on the Organisation of the Permanent Civil Service* (Eyre & Spottiswoode for HMSO); for the outcomes, see Hennessy (1990: 31–51) and Drewry and Butcher (1991: 39–46).

Branch was set up in the Treasury and soon organised common pay scales for all but the top tiers of officials. On the other hand, the appointment was thought to be a way into bringing about 'Treasury' or general classes of civil servants at the different hierarchical levels who could be deployed across departments, and it gave the holder the authority to issue guidance to the permanent secretaries of other departments, and thus developing common conventions (Lee *et al.*, 1998: 141). The Cabinet decided in 1920 that the prime minister (then David Lloyd George) would have the final say in the appointment and dismissal of all senior civil servants. Warren Fisher then used his position as Head of the Civil Service and chief adviser to the prime minister in the latter's guise as First Lord of the Treasury to put forward names in a way that encouraged officials to seek inter-departmental transfers and work in more than one department on their way towards the top.

Fisher implemented the 1854 Report during the inter-war period, but the Northcote–Trevelyan prescription for 'intellectuals' to perform the 'superior' tasks was interpreted narrowly as a requirement for generalist administrators recruited through the 'literary' examinations at which Oxbridge arts graduates excelled. During Fisher's long tenure at the head of the civil service, the number of senior officials with specialist knowledge or outside experience fell dramatically. His personnel policy was to have serious repercussions as government intervention in social and economic affairs became an established fact of political life in Britain, and the issue of 'generalist' versus 'specialist' expertise was a significant theme of the next big inquiry into the British civil service, by the Fulton Committee.

In sum, the full effect of the Northcote–Trevelyan Report of 1854 was not felt for some decades after its publication, but it was the defining stage in the emergence of a modern civil service (see Greenwood *et al.*, 2002; ch. 4; Hennessy, 1989; ch. 1). By the early part of the twentieth century, a corporate, unitary civil service could be discerned. It was characterised by local recruitment to the lower-level posts in departmental offices, but also by a standardised system of national recruitment of university graduates for the top posts. This central control over higher-level recruitment, coupled with inter-departmental staff transfers for officials moving into the senior ranks, a centralised pay system, and common approaches to the administrative tasks faced by all government departments, led to the emergence of a coherent organisational entity. The functions of the civil service expanded far beyond its nineteenth-century regulatory role, as government became involved in managing pensions, national insurance, health and social care systems, employment offices, and, in time, industries and transport systems.

Whitehall's structures and processes, while essentially inward-looking, were exposed to fresh ideas and new personnel during both the First and the Second World Wars, as 'temporary' civil servants from a range of business, scientific and academic backgrounds took up posts in government. However, even as Whitehall reverted to its traditions in the 1950s, concerns were already starting to emerge about the civil service's fitness for purpose as the UK's relative economic performance declined and the institutions of the state came under scrutiny.

The twentieth-century equivalent of Northcote–Trevelyan was the Fulton Report of 1968. While the administrative reformers of the 1850s had been inspired by elements of Britain's imperial adventure (especially the initiatives introduced in the Indian Administrative Service), by the educational elitists' promotion of the public schools and Oxbridge, and by the municipal 'improvers', Fulton and his prototype modernisers were influenced in large measure by the corporate and strategic management revolutions sweeping through the business world: the major US corporations believed they would be more efficient and profitable with greater integration of the manufacturing process. 'The report was based on collectivist assumptions about "big government", emphasising the need for management expertise in an era of rising expenditure, the expansion of government activities and large departments' (Theakston, 1995: 90). The inquiry also fitted into a wider reforming programme by the Labour government of 1964–69, with other committees examining the case for corporate management in local government, larger local government areas, economic planning regions, and reforms to the National Health Service.

The recommendations of the Fulton Report have, like those of the Northcote–Trevelyan Report, continued to be debated for many decades, whether implemented or not, and form a point of reference for other chapters in this book. The main points of the Report are listed in Box I.6, and here we need note only that the agenda for change set out in the Fulton Report was extensive, and that much of it fell by the wayside. Successive governments lost interest in the detail of civil service reform in the face of serious economic crises, and top officials successfully neutralised the parts they saw as most damaging to the civil service they knew, even if younger officials, especially those with technical qualifications, had rather looked forward to the new management opportunities that were proposed. Nevertheless, some significant changes were introduced by the early 1970s, including a rationalisation of the staff grading system to give more opportunities for specialist administrators at senior level, the beginnings of managerial training for officials (spearheaded by the

***Box* 1.6   The Fulton Report**

A summary of the recommendations (Vol. 1: 104–6)

- Civil service to be managed by a Civil Service Department, under the control of the prime minister (Civil Service Minister), and headed by the Head of the Home Civil Service
- Fusion of generalist and specialist classes into a single unified grading structure, with civil service jobs evaluated to determine the grade
- Recruitment to take into account relevance of university studies to future work [a 'majority' recommendation – some Committee members did not agree]
- Administrators in early years to specialise, such as in economics, financial or social affairs; those without these qualifications to receive training
- Specialists should receive training in administration and be able to reach the top
- Civil Service College to provide this training and post-experience management training
- More movement in and out through late entry, temporary appointments, secondments, and transferable pensions
- Make managers responsible and accountable for performance; adapt government accounting; investigate whether work could be 'hived-off' to non-departmental bodies
- Introduce departmental policy planning units, reporting directly to the minister, to ensure that decisions are taken in the light of possible future developments
- Investigate how unnecessary secrecy can be removed
- The government should review the progress made in implementing the Report – for example, by an annual report to Parliament for the next five years.

Sources: Fulton, Lord (1968); for the diagnoses, recommendations and views of the outcomes of the Report, see Garrett (1980), Hennessy (1989, 1990) and Greenwood *et al.* (2002).

new Civil Service College), a few experiments with executive agencies, and the advent of new accountable management, planning and budgeting systems.

The half-hearted introduction of Fulton's recommendations, which were already rather restricted by the Committee's official terms of reference (for example, it did not examine the machinery of government or ministerial responsibility), coupled with a growing concern about the quality and efficiency of the Whitehall machine, left the civil service exposed as being 'behind the times' when the Thatcher Government came to power in 1979 armed with a set of preconceptions about the role of the mandarins as props for a discredited system of 'big' government and state intervention. The impact of the resultant modernisation drive, which was taken on by Thatcher's successors, John Major and Tony Blair, is the subject of this book.

Scope and size

There is no single, precise and unambiguous, legal definition of 'a civil servant'. The most frequently cited definition is that proposed by the Tomlin Royal Commission (1931): 'Servants of the Crown, other than holders of political or judicial offices, who are employed in a civil capacity and whose remuneration is paid wholly and directly out of moneys voted by Parliament', though this definition would also include members of the Queen's household. As a working definition, the civil service encompasses officials who are employed, in various capacities, by UK central government departments and the devolved administrations in Scotland and Wales (see Greenwood *et al.*, 2002: 73).

The Diplomatic Service in the Foreign and Commonwealth Office has maintained its separate identity from the 'Home Civil Service' since 1782, when the Southern and Northern Departments of the Principal Secretary were reconstituted at the Home Office and the Foreign Office. It was formally separated when the various parts of the civil service dealing with Britain's overseas relations were grouped together in 1943. The separation was consolidated when Prime Minister Winston Churchill made Edward Bridges, already holding the onerous post of Cabinet Secretary, both Treasury Permanent Secretary and Head of the *Home* Civil Service. The Northern Ireland Civil Service has been separate from the 'British Civil Service' since partition in 1921, but the small number (approximately 150) of officials who work for the Northern Ireland Office (in London and in Northern Ireland) are part of the Home Civil Service because their department, under the Secretary of State for Northern Ireland, is an element of the Whitehall system. (These separate services and the devolved administrations are explored further in Chapter 3.)

As we point out below, when making some comparative observations, the staff employed by local authorities (including education services), the National Health Service (as opposed to the Department of Health), and police authorities are not part of the civil service. On the other hand, prison officers working for the Prisons Agency (but not for the small number of privately-managed prisons) are civil servants. Figure I.1 illustrates graphically the fact that the civil service is only a small part (10 per cent) of the public sector, which itself accounts for one-fifth (20 per cent) of all employment in Britain. In recent years the numbers of jobs have increased in both the public and private sectors, but the growth of the public sector (13 per cent, 1998–2005) was double that of the private sector (6 per cent), as a result of Labour government policies (Office for National Statistics, 2005: 477). Most of the increase was in health, social work and education, which are not delivered directly by the civil service, but civil servants are strongly engaged in preparing the policies and budgets for these services.

In Table I.1, the breakdown of civil service staff across the full range of government departments is provided. The 'headcount' and 'full-time equivalent' figures refer, respectively, to the total numbers of people employed, and to aggregate figures once part-time posts have been combined for the purposes of calculation. The entry for Her Majesty's Courts Service exemplifies the complexity of determining the exact boundaries between civil servants and non-civil servants, because it includes staff of the former Magistrates' Service, who had been local authority employees until the previous year. Figures and, more important, the careers of individual staff, are in constant flux as governmental reforms change the status of components of the administration (see Chapters 4 and 6).

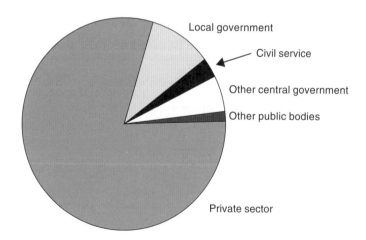

Figure I.1   Civil servants in the public sector
Source: Data for June 2005 from Office for National Statistics (2005: 479).

The chart in Figure I.2 shows the departmental locations of civil servants at the end of 2005. The comparative 'weight' of a ministry in the total varies over the years (see Chapter 4). The Ministry of Defence has experienced the biggest reductions since the 1980s, first because its manufacturing and maintenance work was privatised, and then because of the end of the Cold War. The departments that expanded most during the Blair Government were HM Revenue & Customs (because of the working family tax credits introduced by Gordon Brown as Chancellor of the Exchequer) and the Home Office (increases in its Immigration Directorate and the Prison Service), though many staff in the Home Office were transferred in 2007 to Constitutional Affairs

Table I.1   Civil service staff by department (December 2005)

Department	Headcount	Full-time equivalent
Attorney General's Departments	9,820	9,210
Cabinet Office	1,820	1,760
Other Cabinet Office Agencies	750	730
HM Treasury	1,220	1,200
Chancellor's other departments	5,860	5,560
Charity Commission	540	500
Constitutional Affairs	24,010	21,900
Culture, Media and Sport	650	640
Defence	91,320	89,230
Education and Skills	4,680	4,460
Environment, Food & Rural Affairs	14,210	13,560
Export Credits Guarantee Department	320	320
Foreign & Commonwealth Office	6,220	6,150
Health	6,510	6,310
HM Court Service	11,980	10,990
HM Revenue & Customs	107,810	99,690
Home Office	73,700	70,930
International Development	1,870	1,830
Northern Ireland Office	160	150
Office of the Deputy Prime Minister	6,120	5,940
Office for Standards in Education	2,560	2,440
Scottish Executive	16,380	15,700
Security & Intelligence Services	5,110	4,900
Trade and Industry	11,470	11,060
Transport	19,390	18,390
Welsh Assembly	4,300	4,050
Work and Pensions	134,210	121,610
Total	**562,980**	**529,200**

Source: Extracted from data published by the Office for National Statistics (2006).

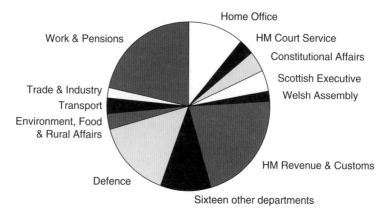

Figure I.2   The comparative size of departments
Source: Data for December 2005 from Office for National Statistics (2006).

(itself a remodelling of the Lord Chancellor's Department during Blair's term in office), which became part of a new Ministry of Justice.

Table I.2 sets out the civil service staffing trends since the election of the Major Government in 1992. It is clear that there has been no dramatic variation in the size of the organisation over the period as a whole, but there was a steady reduction in staff of about 3 per cent a year during the Major Government and the first years of the Blair Government, followed by increases of about 2 per cent a year until 2004. The desire by successive governments to be seen to be controlling the scale of the state bureaucracy has prompted periodic bouts of serious concern about the numbers of officials, coupled with the announcement of 'efficiency' drives and targets for reducing the size of the civil service. On occasion, it has appeared as if the political importance of the numbers themselves, rather than the work carried out by civil servants, has driven the debate. In Chapter 4 we analyse the Gershon review of 2004, which was the Blair administration's bid to take control of this issue.

Taking a broader historical perspective on the growth of the civil service, we can see from Figure I.3 that it has expanded more or less in line with the growth in government involvement in society and the economy (note that, in another example of the effect of reorganisation on civil service numbers, the graph excludes throughout the huge number of Post Office workers – civil servants until the change of status of the Post Office in 1969 as a public corporation). Thus, for example,

Table I.2   Size of the civil service (1 April each year)

Year	Headcount	Full-time equivalent
1992	588,410	587,700
1993	579,380	578,700
1994	559,400	561,410
1995	537,070	535,140
1996	514,820	514,580
1997	495,830	494,660
1998	484,210	480,930
1999	480,690	476,370
2000	497,640	486,720
2001	506,450	494,950
2002	516,040	502,780
2003	542,770	520,930
2004	554,110	534,400
2005	550,010	529,200

Notes: Headcount is the total number of permanent industrial and non-industrial officials full-time and part-time). The full-time equivalent figures (taking into account the proportion of full-time hours worked) includes not only these permanent officials but also casual staff (those officials on a contract of less than a year).
Sources: Data for 1992 to 2004: Cabinet Office, *Civil Service Statistics: A history of staff numbers* www.civilservice.gov.uk/management/statistics/reports/2004/history/index.asp accessed 29 March 2007; data for 2005: ONS (2006).

the gradual shift from laissez-faire to a more active state in the course of the nineteenth century saw civil service numbers fluctuate between 17,000 in the early 1840s and 80,000 in the 1890s (these figures and those that follow *do* include the Post Office, which expanded greatly from 1861, when Gladstone gave it the task of running a savings bank). The social reforms of the 1905–15 Liberal governments saw the civil service double in size to around 282,000, while the impact of the First World War and the inter-war expansion of the state brought further increases in numbers of officials. By the eve of the Second World War, the civil service total was 374,000, and rose to nearly 670,000 by 1945. The Attlee Government's programme of social reform (including the establishment of the National Health Service) and nationalisation of key industries saw the civil service swell to over one million employees by the early 1950s. Thereafter, governments struggled intermittently to cut the size of the organisation, with varying degrees of success. At the height of the UK's crisis of wage and price

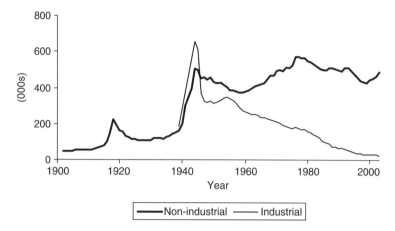

Figure I.3　Historical changes in the number of civil servants
Note: This chart refers to permanent officials (full-time equivalents). It excludes Post Office officials throughout.
Source: Data from Cabinet Office, *Civil Service Statistics* (Cabinet Office, various years) – (1993, 2004, 2005); HM Treasury (1993) *Civil Service Statistics 1993* p. 46 (HMSO); Cabinet Office (2004) *Civil Service Statistics 2004* (Cabinet Office website); Cabinet Office (2005) *Civil Service Statistics 2005* (Cabinet Office website).

inflation, and economic stagnation, in the mid-1970s, the civil service employed nearly 750,000 people. During the period of the Thatcher Governments, from 1979, as public expenditure came under consistent pressure, civil service numbers fell, slowly, but fairly steadily, to below 600,000, while Margaret Thatcher's successor, John Major, finally succeeded in getting the numbers down below 500,000. The pattern of growth and decline differs between non-industrial and industrial civil servants ('white-collar' versus 'blue-collar'), especially after 1960 (the Macmillan Government). While the number of industrial civil servants has since 1954 been in constant decline (barely 20,000 of them remain), the number of non-industrial civil servants varies more erratically around a mid-point of around half a million (for discussions of the historical trends in civil service numbers, see Hennessy, 1989, ch. 1; Pyper, 1991, ch. 2).

Some comparative reflections

When comparing the British civil service with those in other systems of government, it is useful to make reference to some basic benchmarks, against which the comparisons can be framed. The first relates to the constitutional setting. The British civil service is an intrinsic element of a political and governmental system characterised by an adherence to unwritten codes, doctrines and conventions, and functions without a single codified constitution. As we noted earlier, the management and operation of the civil service is guided by an array of legislative and non-legislative documents, but, despite a long-standing commitment on the part of the Blair Government, there is no Civil Service Act to collate the powers, duties and responsibilities of the organisation. All of this sets the British civil service apart from the administrative systems found in comparable liberal democratic states, where codified constitutions, precise legislative frameworks and civil service statutes are the order of the day.

A second point of comparison relates to the non-partisan, permanent, career nature of the British civil service. This British tradition can be contrasted, most obviously, with the civil service system in the USA, within which the senior and middle-ranking posts are subject to political patronage. In France too there is a great turnover of senior officials when the political colour of the president and/or National Assembly changes, such that French analysts complain of a waste of talent, with only half the set of senior officials in active work in the top posts while the other half wait for the political majority to change (Mény, 1992: 110). The implications and the debates about 'politicisation' are discussed further in Chapter 2.

A range of issues concerning the educational background and training of officials can be used as further points of comparison. In spite of successive reform programmes, dating back to the Fulton Report of 1968, the senior ranks of the British civil service remain disproportionately composed of people with 'liberal arts' backgrounds supplemented by relatively small amounts of 'professional' training (Chapter 6 sets out the current debates about this dimension of human resource management). Obvious comparisons here would be with the European (especially French) tradition of intensive and highly specialised training for future civil servants in the *grandes écoles* even if other 'northern' countries besides Britain also favour 'on the job' training.

The scope of the bureaucracy offers a further benchmark for comparison. In the UK, the civil service encompasses only those working for central and devolved government departments and their executive agencies. In other civil service systems (especially in Europe) all elements of the state machine (not just central government but also local government, education systems, police authorities, health services, and even some industries) can form part of the civil service.

The experience of the British civil service as it has engaged with the various facets and components of the 'new public management' (including the adoption of performance measurement regimes, the proliferation of targets, devolved budgets, creation of chief executive posts, contracting-out, 'consumer-orientated' and service delivery agendas, and so on) can also serve as a point of comparison. The experience of civil service systems since the 1980s or so in Scandinavia, the UK, the USA, Canada, Australia and New Zealand, where there has been an increasing obligation to engage with 'NPM' (variously defined), can be contrasted with the more selective, limited and less comprehensive embrace of managerialism in central and southern Europe.

Europe provides an additional possible benchmark for comparison. There is a clear contrast between the prevailing civil service culture in many European states in which there is a strong basis in constitutional law (and the work of civil servants focuses to a significant extent on drafting laws and implementing legal codes) and the much more policy-orientated and service delivery civil service culture to be found in the UK (and, arguably, the USA).

The literature on comparative approaches to analysing civil services is rapidly expanding, and can be exploited as a way of shedding further light on the features and characteristics of the British civil service (see, for example, Zifcak, 1994; Bekke *et al.*, 1996; Flynn and Strehl, 1996; Verheijen, 1999; Bekke and van der Meer, 2000; Burns and Bowornwathana, 2001).

The book

Having mapped out the territory of our subject area, we should now do the same for the book itself. Of course, 'modernisation' is a contested concept, and its precise meaning is unclear. The Labour governments in the period from 1997 adopted 'modernisation' as the unifying theme for their various reform programmes and legislative initiatives. In Chapter 1, some of the key debates about the nature and extent of civil service modernisation will be discussed, and the components of the Whitehall institutional model will be examined. Proponents of this model see it as being subject to forces, including organisational fragmentation, privatisation and devolution, that are eroding its importance. Others argue that 'Whitehall' was always much less homogeneous than had traditionally been assumed, and that it was even characterised by fragmentation and the need to deal with a network of 'actors' and interests (a theory of 'governance' and a 'hollowing-out' of the central state as opposed to the more direct hierarchical control by 'government'). Yet others would argue that the modernisation agenda (including managerial reform, devolution, the focus on delivery and performance, concerns with user satisfaction, diversity in HR policies and practices, and so on) has had positive consequences that balance the aspects of 'decline', and may be viewed as simply another stage in a continuously evolving civil service. The chapter explains these three different general perspectives on the recent development of the civil service ('decline', 'hollowing-out, networks and governance' and 'modernising or progressive') from the viewpoint of their proponents. None of these approaches addresses all the questions we would like to ask about the civil service (their proponents would not themselves make such a claim), but each can illuminate some aspects and provide some answers, while failing to fit what seem to be the observed facts in other areas. In the later chapters we therefore use one or more approaches in that spirit of illumination and interpretation, and in the conclusion we make some evaluation of the relative validity of each of these different perspectives on the civil service.

Chapter 2 deals with policy issues and processes at the heart of government. The changing role of the civil service in policy-making, the extent to which 'politicisation' has become a serious issue for officials, and the functioning of the civil service within the complex array of departments, units and offices at the heart of Whitehall, will be examined here. The traditional policy advice role of the higher civil service will be set out, and attention will be given to questions about the extent to which this has been challenged and perhaps undermined by: (1) the extended period of Conservative government, and the alleged creation of a limited 'mindset' in the higher civil service; (2) think tanks and special policy advisers; and (3) the influx of special advisers and spin doctors under New Labour.

Chapter 3 examines the impact of multilevel governance and the differentiated polity on the civil service. The emergence of a network of 'civil services' at the levels of Whitehall, Brussels, Edinburgh and Cardiff will be set out and analysed. The challenges and opportunities presented by the emerging 'multi-layer democracy' will be set against the threat of 'Balkanisation'. Can the unified civil service hold firm in the face of the development of new modes of policy work and differing accountability regimes in this diverse system? To what extent are the new civil service realities in Edinburgh, Cardiff and Brussels transferable to Whitehall? This chapter examines the consequences for the civil service of changes in the constitutional framework from a unitary sovereign state to a devolved state that is also a member state of the European Union (EU). The discussion is set within the contrasting perspectives of the Whitehall model of a unified civil service that fitted and supported a unitary conception of the Constitution, and the multilevel governance model of complex policy-making, implementation and accountability in a quasi-federal system.

The theme of Chapter 4 is the link between civil service restructuring and the objectives of enhanced efficiency, ministerial control and service delivery. This chapter deals with the restructuring and redefining of internal and external boundaries of the civil service: (1) for cost-efficiency reasons; (2) so that ministers can in principle understand what officials are doing and control policy direction without getting bogged down in day-to-day executive detail; and (3) to improve service delivery by putting it in the hands of specialised executive agencies, privatised companies or regulated services. While the Wilson and Heath Governments made some moves on these issues, the long terms of office of Thatcher, Major, and then Blair, produced an astonishing array of 'initiatives'. The chapter gives detailed coverage of the more substantial reforms: the Thatcher Government's Efficiency Scrutinies, Financial Management Initiative, *Next Steps* Report, and the post-*Next Steps* experience of agencies; Major's *Citizen's Charter*, privatisation, and the Private Finance Initiative; and the Blair administration's Public Private Partnerships, Service First, Gershon efficiency drive, and the Public Service Agreements and Public Expenditure Reviews promoted by Gordon Brown. It emerges that, under the Conservatives and New Labour, there were common twin themes of fragmenting and devolving to service delivery units, leading to the question of whether the state has been hollowed-out or whether the government has retained and made the unitary Whitehall model more effective.

Civil service modernisation has involved adapting to the challenges and implications of changing regimes of accountability, freedom of information and open government initiatives, and these issues are analysed in Chapter 5. We examine the 'Whitehall' tradition of internal and external civil service accountability, the 'managerial' controls of Agency Framework Documents and the 'consumerist' accountability offered by Citizen's Charters. How has accountability been affected by 'multilevel governance' (creation of new audit regimes in Scotland and

Wales) and the newer forms of direct accountability to individual citizens represented by the Parliamentary 'Ombudsman' and the Freedom of Information Acts (in the year 2000 in England and Wales; 2002 in Scotland)? Accountability, freedom of information and open government are all constrained by the conventions of the traditional British model of a confidential relationship between ministers and civil servants. The role of civil servants as forces for and against change will be considered, as well as the implications of greater freedom of information for the functioning of the civil service. Analysis will include the civil service dimensions of the Armstrong Memorandum (and its incorporation into the *Civil Service Code*), the 1989 Official Secrets Act, and the initiatives from Major to Blair on access to government information, with its different outcomes in Westminster from those in Edinburgh or Cardiff. All these issues are illustrated with examples from the various *causes célèbres* in this sphere (including the Ponting prosecution, the Scott Inquiry on Arms to Iraq, and the Hutton Inquiry's exposure of Whitehall decision-making), which suggests that more is learned about civil service procedures from decisions that have unintended consequences than from formal provisions regarding open government.

Chapter 6 deals with the human and organisational dimension of civil service modernisation. The key themes and debates surrounding matters of pay, recruitment and promotion, training and development, and conditions of service are considered, together with questions about the implications of the modernisation agenda for the roles, management and future direction of the civil service. To the familiar issues about the selection, training and promotion of senior policy officials that relate to the Whitehall unitary model, we add questions about the recruitment, training, management, organisation and work environment of all grades of officials, which came to the fore with the 'new public management' narrative. How are agencies organised and managed to deliver more customer-focused quality services? What capacities do officials have and need in order to deal directly with users, targets, PPP capital procurement systems, and regulated utilities? How have officials, especially through their representative organisations, reacted to the formation and combination of agencies (such as Jobcentre Plus) and/or their privatisation, and to attacks on the personnel policies of their 'internalised' Whitehall model (by performance pay; or the threatened removal of inflation-proofed pensions and early retirement)?

The concluding chapter ponders the prospects for the British civil service by considering the evidence presented on all these aspects of

1

Perspectives on 'Decline' and 'Modernisation'

The civil service of the early twenty-first century retains at least some of the defining characteristics of the organisation that was effectively created as a result of the Northcote–Trevelyan Report of 1854, even if its origins were elsewhere. At the same time, however, it bears the imprint of the series of significant reforms to its structure and management that were put in place during the 1980s and 1990s, and built upon in the first years of the new century. The fundamental question this book seeks to address concerns the extent to which the Civil Service has been transformed positively by the process of modernisation and change, or, alternatively, has been damaged. Some quite different positions on this question are adopted by those who analyse and comment on the workings of the British civil service. The range of answers has considerable importance, beyond the theoretical interests of academics, because the alternative conceptions of what the civil service is, and could or should become, feed into the practical projects of reformers, and indeed the behaviour of civil servants themselves as they interpret and develop their own roles in the organisation.

In order to reach a judgement on this issue, we examine in this chapter the main features of some key perspectives on decline and modernisation, before turning in subsequent chapters to interpret the changes in the civil service in the light of these different perspectives. Other theories have been put forward about particular aspects of the civil service, or public bureaucracies in general, and we consider these in later chapters where topics are addressed for which they seem to have particular relevance. However, the three perspectives explained below are specially pertinent to the British civil service and its constitutional and political context; and they offer contrasting views. These perspectives might variously be described as theories, models, or, in

31

more straightforward terms, as alternative stories or narratives about the British civil service, each of which has supporting evidence, and each of which contains unresolved discrepancies.

The Whitehall model and theories of decline

The Whitehall model is the most well-known analytical tool used to understand the functioning of the British central bureaucracy and its relationship to ministers and Parliament. It still provides the most useful guide to the organisational and even ethical principles on which the civil service was built. It is a normative ideal for many analysts and for some civil service leaders; that is, it is a model of how they think the British civil service should be run, and which civil servants – not to mention their political bosses, the ministers – should aspire to emulate. For some of these people it is also a good general description of the 'traditional' civil service, especially before it was, in their eyes, attacked and sent into decline by the policies of the Conservative governments in the 1980s and 1990s. Until the 1990s, it was the dominant way of explaining the general lines on which the British civil service operated, even if there were always contrary interpretations that noted the ways in which the Whitehall model did not seem to fit all the facts about the contemporary organisation.

It is usually deployed in conjunction with the Westminster model of the constitutional and political system, which provides a basic framework for comprehending the procedures and processes of the British Parliament, the Cabinet, the system of ministerial departments of state and the premiership, even if it is more valuable for telling us what it is important to examine than as an accurate description of the real world (Rhodes, 1997: 4). The Whitehall and Westminster models were effectively 'exported' during the high-growth periods of the British Empire, and the former became the basis for the civil service systems in countries such as Canada, Australia, India and New Zealand, although some of these states later introduced significant changes to their bureaucracies that moved them away from the key features of the Whitehall model, just as they did not adopt wholesale the features of the Westminster constitutional and political model. To a very large extent, the Whitehall model of relations between the civil service and the political world depends on the Westminster model. We therefore need to discuss the Westminster model, and the social or cultural characteristics that underpin it, before turning to the Whitehall model itself.

Table 1.1   The Westminster model of parliamentary democracy

The Westminster model: *majoritarian democracies*	*The consensus model:* *pluralist democracies*
• Executive power concentrated in a Cabinet of members of one party that has won by a small majority	• Executive power shared between all the significant parties that have won seats
• Cabinet is made up of parliamentarians, in principle responsible to Parliament, but in practice dominating Parliament	• Executive power and legislature are separate and independent of each other, both formally and informally
• One-chamber Parliament, or a two-chamber Parliament in which the power is in the chamber of the elected majority	• Two-chamber Parliament, in which chambers have equal power, and at least one gives minorities a strong voice
• Party system dominated by two large parties which are able at different times to win a majority of seats	• Multiparty system, in which no party comes close to majority status in Parliament
• Party system based on a single (usually socio-economic) divide in a homogeneous society or where one culture dominates	• Party system representing multiple divisions (socio-economic, language, religion, regional) in a culturally-divided society
• Plurality ('first-past-the-post') electoral system, where in each seat the candidate with the most votes wins – 'winner takes all'	• Proportional representation allocates parliamentary seats to parties according to their share of the vote – 'fair shares'
• Decision-making is unitary and centralised; local government is weak	• Power shared between national and local or cultural communities
• Parliamentary sovereignty, with no codified constitution to constrain the power of the parliamentary majority	• Written constitution, with minorities able to block changes to the distribution of powers allocated in the constitution
• Representative democracy exclusively exercised by Parliament	• Direct democracy, through frequent referendums by popular initiative

Source: Based on the ideas in Lijphart (1984): 4–36.

As is often the case, it is easier to define the Westminster model by drawing a contrast with its opposite. Lijphart (1984) made the classic distinction between the Westminster model of democracy and what are called 'consensus' or 'consociational' democracies, which occur in peaceful multicultural societies where the different groups have developed ways of sharing power. Table 1.1 sketches the distinguishing features of the two models. 'The British version of the Westminster model is both the original and the best-known example of the model' (Lijphart, 1984: 5) but that does not mean that it is now (or ever was) a perfect example. Similarly, Switzerland is a standard illustration of the 'consensus model', though it too departs from the model on certain points (see Klöti, 2001). It is hard to identify which of the defining characteristics of these two 'ideal-types' are causes and which effects, since all are closely intertwined, but Table 1.1 lists the nine in the order proposed by Lijphart (1984: 4–30).

Lijphart is probably right to put in prime place as the distinguishing feature of the Westminster model the *executive's concentration of power*. In the British case, it is composed of a one-party Cabinet government, formed by the leader of the party that has won the majority of parliamentary seats, but nearly always on a minority of votes (because smaller third parties are also present). In Switzerland, on the other hand, the executive Federal Council systematically shares out its seats between four parties and three linguistic groups in an informal 'magic formula'.

A second distinguishing characteristic is the *relationship between government and Parliament*. In the Westminster system, Cabinet members are also Members of Parliament (MPs) and elected in the same election as other MPs. In the UK's case, some ministers are members of the House of Lords (and appointed as Lords just for that purpose), and in this respect Westminster does not obey the Westminster model! In principle, the government is responsible to Parliament; that is, it must have the continued support of a majority of MPs if it is to remain in office, but in practice MPs need and want their party to stay in power. Therefore government dominates Parliament and the legislative process, and accountability is weak. The greatest contrast is a presidential system, typically that of the USA, where the president is elected separately from MPs, and appoints ministers freely. Yet the president cannot dissolve Congress, which has a veto over presidential policies it opposes. The Swiss system mixes the alternatives in that MPs choose the members of the Federal Council for a four-year term, but they cannot be removed by MPs, even if their policy proposals are defeated. There is a more equal balance between government and Parliament than in Westminster systems. The Swiss executive is also internally balanced in that the president, elected from among the Federal Council for a one-year term only, really is the 'first among equals' which the British prime minister is supposed to be (though some British prime ministers, such as Attlee and Major, were more collegial than Thatcher or Blair): 'A government head with supreme authority who can make policy decisions does not exist in Switzerland' (Klöti, 2001: 27).

Another distinguishing feature is the *balance of power within Parliament*. Westminster systems have usually copied Westminster in having a two-chamber Parliament (the Commons and Lords in the UK), in which one chamber has much less authority than the other, or is even non-existent (as in New Zealand). Consensus systems ensure that minority interests (such as smaller regions) have a strong place in decision-making by making the two chambers equal, and enabling one chamber to represent the minority opinions that are outvoted in elections to the other chamber. Federal systems, such as Switzerland or the USA, give smaller regions an equal voice with larger regions in a Council of States (or Senate), while the people as a whole elect the National Council (or House of Representatives).

A fourth difference is in the *party systems*. The real Westminster political system was constructed during the late nineteenth and most of the twentieth centuries, around a party system dominated by two increasingly tightly-organised parties, one in government, the other in opposition (institutionalised as 'Her Majesty's government' and 'Her Majesty's loyal opposition'). Single-party government is reinforced by and reinforces the two-party system and the subservience of Parliaments in the Westminster model, because the party leadership can hold out the promise of ministerial posts (unlike leaders in a coalition) and warn of the dangers of rebellion. In the multiparty model, in which no party has a majority, governments need the consent of more than one party to have their legislation passed; ministers in these consensual democracies are more likely to negotiate over a long period with all the relevant actors than to try to rush policy fixes through Parliament, as happens increasingly often in Britain.

The different party systems are in great part the reflection of different *social structures*. Two-party systems are more likely to occur where an advanced industrial society is more or less homogeneous, meaning (in political science terms) that there is no strong cultural divide, only the single socio-economic divide between capital and labour (right and left). Many would argue that other political divides have come to the fore in post-industrial societies such as Britain (for example, over green, libertarian or rights-based issues), and that other divides (regionalist, religious) have been artificially suppressed or ignored by the majoritarian structures. Nevertheless, there is no cultural divide in Britain that can rival the multiple religious and linguistic divides in Switzerland, which require that each minister elected to the Swiss Federal Council must fulfil criteria on party, language, region and gender; or those in Belgium that prevent French-speaking socialists combining with Flemish-speaking socialists in one party.

Fifth, the contrasting *electoral systems* typical of the two models not only reflect different cultural views about democracy but in turn maintain the different party systems. In the 'majoritarian' (winner takes all), Westminster-style democracy, the first-past-the post voting system gives the party that comes first in most constituencies a larger number of seats in Parliament than its overall share of votes nationally, and thus a stronger chance of a clear majority of seats and forming a one-party government (as Labour did in 2005 with not much more than a third of the votes). This effect encourages the development of two 'catch-all' and cohesive parties because of the benefits of grouping together to win each seat. In contrast, the consensus countries use proportional voting systems which reflect fairly the weight of different groups in society but also encourage tiny parties to keep standing for election. The outcome of a proportional voting system is therefore more likely to be a multiparty system and a coalition government, but in consensus democracies even a majority party leader may choose to share power and appoint some ministers from minority parties.

The Westminster system is a *unitary system*, which means that power is concentrated in one government rather than being divided between two tiers of authority, each with the right to make laws in specified domains. The USA, with its Federal and State governments is a typical case, but Switzerland, Australia and Germany are other examples. In addition, local government has become increasingly weak in the UK, losing powers and power continuously since the 1930s. Given that substantial power was devolved to Scotland in 1999 (and Wales and Northern Ireland are both accumulating more power), could we say that the UK is becoming a 'little bit federal', with possible consequences for the British civil service(s)? In formal terms, the UK is still a unitary state, because the Westminster Parliament has not abandoned its sovereign authority to decide. In practical terms, the more devolution to Scotland and Wales becomes established the less it would seem likely to be rescinded. Yet the Northern Ireland Parliament at Stormont was suspended by the Westminster Parliament in 1972 after it had been in operation for half a century.

The presence of a formal *codified constitution* that specifies the allocation of power is therefore crucial if the power-sharing system of a consensus democracy is to be maintained. The provisions in the written document would need to be defended by such devices as a Constitutional Court and/or special parliamentary voting rules. Few Westminster systems apart from Westminster have not introduced a Constitution, though New Zealand's Constitution Act of 1952 was like Britain's constitutional arrangements in having as its central principle the unfettered sovereignty of Parliament (Lijphart, 1984: 19). In the Westminster model, any Act of Parliament can be overridden by another Act of Parliament passed by a simple majority vote. Westminster politicians argue that parliamentary sovereignty is of greater democratic value than depending on the interpretation by judges of a written Constitution. Governmental systems can be reformed more easily without the need for specially large parliamentary majorities or the 'double majorities' of both the people and the regions, as required in Switzerland. By the same token, however, rights of devolved authorities and civil servants (such as membership of trade unions), can more easily be taken away if they are not enshrined in a Constitution.

Finally, though more ambiguously, the attitude towards *direct democracy* in the form of popular referendums (those proposed by citizens), can differentiate between the Westminster and consensus models. The principle of parliamentary sovereignty has limited the use of the referendum in Britain, with most MPs arguing vigorously that it is their role to listen to the arguments and decide on behalf of the people. In contrast, Switzerland is well known for its very frequent use of this tool, which has decision-making force (though the government can make alternative proposals). There are 'theoretical' reasons for not associating referendums with consensus models, since minorities can achieve success in a popular referendum on a topic opposed by all parties. There are also 'empirical' objections, since New Zealand is in other ways a Westminster-style democracy yet holds referendums fairly frequently, and some consensus democracies, such as Belgium, do not. Yet the resistance within the real Westminster to having its role replaced by a referendum on 'national' questions (as opposed to regional questions), does seem to encapsulate the centralised and controlling nature of the British political system in contrast to the decentralised and bargaining procedures of the consensus democracies such as Switzerland.

The Westminster model provided the basic set of constitutional doctrines and conventions around which the system of governance in the UK seemed to have evolved. The cornerstones of the Whitehall model were laid down following the Northcote–Trevelyan Report of 1854, but only after the Westminster model of parliamentary democracy was well-established in Britain (see the Introduction and Box I.1

on page 7). Unlike in France, where today's bureaucratic institutions pre-date parliamentary democracy, and which have sometimes had to substitute for failing governments and operate 'in the public interest', almost autonomously of politicians, the evolution of the British civil service has always been confined within the rules of the game defined by the political system. Thus the constitutional conventions regarding the responsibilities and conduct of ministers (whether or not these were followed in practice), were bound to interact with and affect the roles and duties of civil servants. They created a set of conventions about the operating principles of the British civil service that are still incorporated into the written codes governing the conduct of ministers and civil servants today (as we shall see in the next chapter).

Two conventions that are applied to ministers stand out as being crucial to the conventions that the Whitehall model applies to civil servants:

- Ministers of departments are individually accountable, in law and to Parliament, for the work of their departments and the activities of their officials; and
- Ministers are collectively responsible to Parliament for decisions made by the Cabinet, and for the actions of the government. A minister should publicly support government decisions or resign.

The consequences for civil servants of these principles for ministers, put alongside the principles for building an efficient civil service enunciated in the Northcote–Trevelyan Report, constitute the important civil service dimensions of the Whitehall model, as set out in Box 1.1.

***Box* 1.1   The Whitehall model: civil service dimensions**

- A professional, career civil service, governed by impartiality
- Recruitment of generalists, to be trained 'in-house'
- Promotion on merit, mainly from within
- Doctrine of ministerial accountability governs the accountability of civil servants
- Civil servants to be 'faceless', impersonal
- Civil service enjoys a monopoly in the provision of expert policy advice and enables ministers to function effectively in the parliamentary arena
- Civil service implements the policies agreed collectively by ministers
- Civil service to be a unitary organisation, assuring coordination
- Hierarchical structures (government departments) organised on a functional basis, are the mechanisms through which policy is implemented

This model can be described in terms of what the nineteenth-century reformers wanted to see achieved (and which civil servants and experts on the civil service in the first half of the twentieth century thought had been achieved), as follows.

The civil service would be non-political, because based on the principle of a permanent career service and therefore constrained by the requirement that it would have to serve governments of varying political persuasions with equal impartiality. In its recruitment and promotion systems, the civil service would be an avowed meritocracy. The recruitment processes would be open and competitive, with nationally-organised examinations designed to fill the posts that would lead to the most senior positions. Promotion opportunities would be available to the most able candidates. As a career civil service, candidates would generally be recruited at a young age. In line with normal business as well as public-sector practice in Britain, they would be taken on soon after completing their general education and trained in whatever they needed to know by learning 'on the job' or 'in-house'. Apart from the few specialists that would be required, most civil servants would require general administrative skills that would be useful in a wide variety of posts. Appointment and promotion to the senior posts in the civil service would take place mainly internally, with relatively few opportunities for 'outside' candidates to apply for these jobs, except in extraordinary circumstances (for example, the national emergencies of wartime 1914–18 and 1939–45).

The accountability of the civil service was carefully circumscribed by the doctrine of ministerial responsibility. Though officials had to obey the law, like any other citizen, it was not officials but ministers who were responsible for the work done in the department, and ministers were accountable to Parliament for any failures (or indeed good outcomes) of policies and implementation. Officials worked within this framework of parliamentary accountability, knowing that ministers might be called upon to answer questions in Parliament, the courts or the media. Therefore they had to work in an orderly, bureaucratic way, keeping records, checking with more senior officials, and possibly as far as the minister, before making decisions. In simple terms, this meant that lines of accountability ran from officials to ministers, and then to Parliament. For the great majority of civil servants, accountability for their work would be upwards to their departmental superiors and ultimately to the ministers, but not, in any meaningful sense (with the notable exception of the accountability of the department's Accounting Officer – normally the Permanent Secretary – to the

Public Accounts Committee of the House of Commons) to Parliament, let alone to the public.

As a corollary of the doctrine of individual ministerial responsibility, civil servants were expected to be 'faceless' or 'anonymous', self-effacing behind the high-profile personality of the ministers they served. Not only was the minister officially responsible for their acts, but they also had to dissociate themselves personally from decisions or risk losing the trust of a new set of ministers or of society more generally. This behaviour would be required in particular for those small numbers of senior civil servants, operating at the top levels of the Whitehall departments, whose work would involve producing expert policy advice to government ministers (effectively as monopoly providers) and aiding these politicians as they functioned in the parliamentary arena. This role did not derive from the Northcote–Trevelyan Report (which was more concerned with producing an efficient bureaucratic organisation), but from much earlier times (see the Introduction and Box I.1 on page 7) when officials were a monarch's and then a minister's closest confidential advisers (the 'secretaries' who knew the secrets). It was bound to be an equivocal role for civil servants to play – providing politically-aware advice without losing their 'impartial' reputation – and difficult to perform to the satisfaction of not only the ministers they served but also those who would replace them (see the next chapter), but it is an important component of the Whitehall model.

Analysis in terms of the Whitehall model seems often to give undue emphasis to the policy advice role performed by few civil servants in comparison with the larger numbers occupied with tasks and duties that involve, in one form or another, the management of government departments, the implementation of public policy and the delivery of services. No doubt part of the explanation is in the limited direct provision by central government of public services before the Second World War (the larger contribution was being made by municipal councils, district boards, churches and other voluntary bodies). In any case, it is evident that a major function of civil servants would be to implement the policies that ministers had decided. Following from the doctrine of collective Cabinet or ministerial responsibility, the Whitehall model stresses – as indeed did the Northcote–Trevelyan Report – the unitary nature of the civil service that could ensure, through inter-departmental transfers of staff and other mechanisms for inter-departmental coordination, a collective response from the bureaucratic machinery rather than an inefficient and possibly conflictual or 'turf-guarding' segmentation between departments.

Government departments (ministries) are the fundamental structural device in the Whitehall model for organising the civil service – this conventional hierarchical format fitting well with both the requirements of a career bureaucracy in which officials were to be rewarded with systematic promotion on merit, and the long chain of accountability from junior to senior officials, and thence to ministers and Parliament. Government departments were, and are, centred on Whitehall (see Figure 1.1), because in earlier days they served ministers who met each other in Cabinet very frequently, and who attended Parliament almost every day to answer MPs' questions (a practice dropped only in the mid-twentieth century). As services grew, and for other reasons, such as wartime, post-war regional planning, or decongesting London, regional outposts were created. With the exception of the 'territorial' departments (the Scottish Office from the late nineteenth century, the Welsh Office from the mid-1960s and the Northern Ireland Office from the early 1970s) these structures were functional – organised around specific policy spheres such as trade, education, health, defence and so on. The tendency in discussions about civil service issues to focus on the policy work that will always take place close to ministers and around Westminster means that the term 'Whitehall' and the assumptions within the Whitehall model will continue to have value, at least in those discussions. Yet occasionally, such as during the rare strikes at government offices that draw the media's attention to the civil service's delivery work, the revelation that most civil service activity takes place outside Greater London (let alone Whitehall), raises questions about the relevance of the model to the twenty-first-century civil service.

Many observers subscribed to the Whitehall model as a accurate general description of the civil service, and adhered to its implications in a positive spirit, seeing it as a desirable role model. They became increasingly concerned about the impact of civil service reform in the 1980s and 1990s (especially the structural and managerial reforms taken forward under the Thatcher and Major governments) on the key components of this model. Richard Chapman's work epitomised this outlook. A series of articles (Chapman, 1992; Chapman and O'Toole, 1995; Chapman, 1997) charted what was perceived as the decline and fall of the traditional civil service by those who believed it had been encapsulated by the Whitehall model.

Chapman's theory of decline identified the effect of the Next Steps initiative in 1988 as crucial in this process. The Next Steps reform is explained in more detail in Chapter 4 (on restructuring) and in

this function. This approach had been promoted and heralded in the earlier Wilson and Heath Governments but was introduced by the Thatcher Government in a more radical way. It was a 'U-turn' from the century-old effort to make the civil service a unitary organisation (similar grades, pay and titles, and uniform procedures across departments) and to promote inter-departmental coordination. In addition to this break with the principle of unitary management in the Whitehall model, the convention of ministerial accountability to Parliament for departmental actions was also called into question by the announcement that the chief executives (officials), in charge of the agencies would answer MPs' questions about their own agency's work (this procedure was soon modified, but chief executives nevertheless still account directly to Parliament as well as to ministers). In sum, 'agencification' bought about a radical restructuring of the civil service and was used as a catalyst for fundamental changes to the management and accountability of the organisation.

Reviewing the effect of Next Steps four years after its inception, and taking into account other reforms to the recruitment and appointment systems, such as those enabling people to be brought in at senior level from the private sector and other public bodies, Chapman (1992) speculated about whether these managerial reforms might mark 'the end of the civil service', as traditionally understood. Three years later, Chapman and O'Toole (1995: 19) expressed further doubts about the impact of the reform process:

> Undermining some of the best elements of the uniform civil service, emphasising operational criteria, and encouraging the pursuit of private interests in a public context may result in short term savings but longer term dangers. Once the values of the old civil service are undermined, it may be exceedingly difficult to reintroduce them at a later date.

Returning to the subject of civil service reform, Chapman later cast aside any doubt, and declared 'the end of the civil service' in definitive terms (Chapman, 1997). In his view, by this point there had been a fundamental erosion of the core values and functions of the civil service caused by the managerial and structural reforms of the 1980s and 1990s. Chapman now saw the civil service as a reduced, fragmented organisation (or series of organisations), its functions limited partly as a consequence of privatisation, and with a more marginal role in policy-making as a result of creeping politicisation.

In the period since Chapman set out his critique, it might be argued that additional developments, including the proliferation of special policy advisers and think tanks, have further eroded some of the components of the Whitehall model, such as the exclusive reliance of ministers on their trusted civil servants for policy advice. Indeed, in a review of developments within the civil service during 2004, O'Toole analysed a series of policy initiatives and statements from the prime minister and the Head of the Civil Service. Despairing of the 'managerialist approach' and the 'business-is-best language' emanating from the Prime Minister's Office in Downing Street and the Cabinet Office, O'Toole argued that 'the cultural change sought, even if implicitly, will signal the end of the Gladstonian legacy' while the 'references to the business sector, to customers, to strategy, to management, to delivery, to performance, to leadership, and to risk … all … sit at odds with the old ethos of public service' (O'Toole, 2004).

Bevir and Rhodes (2003: 147) locate the perspectives of Chapman and O'Toole within 'the Tory tradition':

> They defend 'the virtues of the traditional British civil service, with its emphasis on accountability, and its almost vocational approach to motivation' against the 'fashionable pursuit of apparently new approaches to management'. The notions of accountability to parliament through the minister and of public duty lie at the heart of their critique. They argue that civil servants must display integrity, never putting private interests before public duty, objectivity and impartiality … Agencies fragment the civil service. Civil servants are no longer socialised into its shared traditions. The principles of the Citizen's Charter replace the public service ethos … we will lose the traditional values unless we protect them. Business-like methods are no substitute for old values.

A similar conclusion was reached by two American observers of the UK polity. Campbell and Wilson analysed 'the end of Whitehall', describing what they saw as the 'death of a paradigm'.

> The role of the permanent bureaucracy in the Whitehall model long seemed unproblematic, as British politicians of both main parties found the service provided by what they often termed a 'Rolls Royce' of a civil service entirely satisfactory … By the 1990s, however, the Whitehall model had come under such stress that its survival seemed questionable. (Campbell and Wilson, 1995: 20)

The stress to which Campbell and Wilson referred emanated, in their view, from a variety of factors, including the reform process that had been criticised so heavily by Chapman, the characteristics and conduct of the Thatcher and Major governments, and more deeply rooted failings and weaknesses in the British constitution.

However, the diagnosis of civil service 'decline' associated with the demise of the Whitehall model needs to be put into perspective. To some extent, it is debatable whether the Whitehall model ever offered a completely accurate account of the functioning of the civil service. For example, the theory that the civil service was the monopoly provider of all policy advice to ministers ignored the reality of ministerial contacts with outside experts and groups, many of which could and did serve to influence ministerial decisions. Furthermore, the strictest interpretations of the doctrine of individual ministerial responsibility tended to underestimate the relatively high profiles of many senior civil servants, even in the historical context (thus belying the requirements of 'facelessness' and 'anonymity'). Adherents of the uncritical traditional view of this doctrine also ignored the extent to which, even in the so-called 'golden age' of this constitutional precept, civil servants would occasionally be 'named and blamed' in order to provide convenient cover for erring ministers (Pyper, 1987). Moreover, as we discuss below, some analysts subsequently cast doubt on the usefulness of the Whitehall model even as a normative account of the functioning of British central government, on the grounds that this approach ignored the complexities of the policy process, such as the involvement of many other actors from outside the boundaries of Whitehall and Westminster.

To sum up, therefore, one set of approaches to understanding the civil service starts with the assumption that the Whitehall model was an accurate and a positive account of the organisation's role and operations, and goes on to chart the demise of this model and the negative consequences for the civil service. However, although these approaches are attractive in many respects, we need to view them with a degree of caution.

Network theory, governance, hollowing-out and the differentiated polity: further visions of civil service decline?

Other analytical approaches, which deploy a set of theories, concepts and models, can be used to examine the factors behind the apparent decline of the civil service. Among the most important of these, linked by the pivotal role of Rod Rhodes (1990, 1994, 1997) in their origins and explication, are network theory, the governance paradigm, the hollowing-out thesis, and the differentiated polity thesis. There are significant connections and areas of overlap across these sets of ideas.

In each case, the analytical approach was developed with a view to making a significant contribution to the understanding of the British state, but in the examples we take here, the authors saw the functioning of the civil service, and the way officials interact with other policy actors, as being at the heart of the problem they were seeking to address. Here, our concern is quite narrow and specific: we seek to identify the extent to which each of these different but inter-linked theories can shed light on the changes taking place in the civil service in the modern period.

Network theory is the oldest and most deeply rooted of these conceptual fields. Among the many differences in its approach from that of the institutional approach that produced the Whitehall model, is that it gives as much weight in its analysis to the linkages between institutions and other actors as it does to the individual actors. It assumes that we cannot understand the actions of an actor unless we take into account the structure of that actor's network of relationships with other actors, because the structure and the place of the actor within the structure affect the perceptions, attitudes and behaviour of each (Knoke and Kuklinski, 1982: 9–21). Just as the Westminster and Whitehall models, whatever their frailties in explaining the real world, signal to us what it is important to look at, so network theory signalled to researchers seeking to explain the complexity of policy-making and policy implementation in the UK, the need to look beyond the actions of the formal actors (civil servants, ministers, Parliament, local government) to the relationships of these institutions with informal actors (business groups, associations of users, service-providers and so on), that is, the quasi-state and non-state organisations.

The work of Rhodes lay at the heart of this conceptual approach, at least in its UK context, although others made significant contributions to the origins and development of the key ideas (see, for example, Richardson and Jordan, 1979; Jordan, 1990; Rhodes, 1990; Marsh and Rhodes, 1992; Rhodes, 1997, ch. 2). There was some debate about the extent to which the British experience could best be viewed through the prism of policy network concepts originating in American political science literature, or in European organisational theory literature. Using very simple terms, the core significance of network theory lies in its assertion that policy-making and policy implementation result from a multiple and complex series of interactions between government departments on the one hand, and arrays of formal and informal interest groups from the public, private and voluntary sectors, on the other. Some of these policy networks are relatively closed, with the key players effectively incorporated within the system. In the USA, such networks were described as 'iron triangles', consisting of government departments or agencies, the relevant Congressional committee and the dominant interest group. The nearest UK equivalent was probably to be seen in the sphere of agricultural policy, where the triangular relationship between the former Ministry of Agriculture, Fisheries and Food; the European Commission's Agriculture Directorate; and the National Farmers' Union (NFU) was the key to policy making and implementation, with UK agricultural policy largely formulated through the close interactions between the Ministry, the European Union (EU) and the NFU, and key aspects of the implementation process (distribution of financial grants to farmers, for example) being handed over to the NFU. Other policy networks were more open and pluralistic in character, and based to a greater extent on personal interactions rather than organisational structures.

A ground-breaking study of UK public expenditure policy-making by Heclo and Wildavsky (1981) examined the interactions between ministers, officials and the key lobbies in the orbit around the Treasury and Whitehall's spending departments; and the work of Richardson and Jordan (1979), with its focus on the extra-parliamentary dimensions of the policy-making process, gave emphasis to these types of network.

> The term [policy networks] refers to those sets of organisations clustered around a major government function or department. These groups commonly include the professions, trade unions and big business. Central departments need the cooperation of these groups to deliver services. They need their cooperation because British government rarely delivers service itself. It uses other bodies. Also, there are too many groups to consult, so government must aggregate interests. It needs the 'legitimated' spokespeople for that policy area ... Policy networks are a long-standing feature of British government ... what is new is the multiplication of networks. (Rhodes *et al.*, 2003: 26–7)

Where the civil service is concerned, the implication of the network theory approach was that the formal Whitehall structures and processes could be viewed as only one element of the policy-making and implementation process. When Jordan and Richardson (1987) described this process in terms of 'arenas' (public, parliamentary, party, cabinet, pressure-group and bureaucratic), only the bureaucratic arena featured the civil service as the major player, even if officials also were involved, in one way or another, in most of the other arenas. As a result of these network approaches to the understanding of the increasingly complex world of public policy-making, civil servants as individuals and as groups, and the departments they inhabited, were placed within a much broader context in which non-governmental bodies, groups and individuals assumed important roles, and officials were required to adjudicate between competing interests, negotiate and compromise to try to secure the outcomes desired by ministers.

Governance is a term and an approach that enlarges the concept of 'government' (the politicians and officials) to encompass these networks of governmental and non-governmental bodies in a more inclusive notion, and at the same time asserts that the role of government is changing towards one of 'steering' policy delivery rather than itself doing the 'rowing'. The steering and rowing analogy came from a book by American public management consultants, David Osborne and Ted Gaebler, that became fashionable within the UK government in the early 1990s; it defined 'governance' rather ambitiously as 'the process by which we collectively solve our problems and meet our society's needs. Government is the instrument we use. The instrument is outdated, and the process of reinvention has begun' (Osborne and Gaebler, 1992: 24).

Historians tend to doubt the novelty of governance. Lowe and Rollings (2000: 100), in research for the 'Whitehall programme' in the late 1990s, concluded that governance was the norm in Britain. The post-war period, in which direct intervention by central government increased, was an exception to which the eventual return to 'steering' was a reaction. Research on local government chief executives found that the 'networking' they must now undertake with Whitehall departments, civil servants in government regional offices, private companies and voluntary organisations had precedents in the work of the clerks to the council, who acted as agents for central government on numerous boards, committees and authorities until after the Second World War (Travers *et al.*, 1997: 2–11). Here, again, straightforward direct 'government' seems to have been a temporary phenomenon. In dictionary terms, 'governance was a core concept at the start of the [twentieth] century. In the 1920s it was classed as "incipiently" obsolete. In the 1960s it was then declared wholly obsolete' (Lowe and Rollings, 2000: 117), before coming back into importance in the 1990s.

Drawing on the work of others (including Kooiman, 1993; Pierre and Peters, 2000), Rhodes synthesised the implications of this change from government to governance in terms of:

- the heightened significance of networks;
- a reduced role for government in some public policy spheres because of the increased use of the private sector for activities formerly provided directly by the state;

- increased attention paid to moral and ethical issues and standards of conduct, as the 'in-house', hierarchical systems of oversight within the civil service were replaced by looser arrangements with outside providers that might not work to the same principles;
- the introduction of a range of initiatives, broadly described as new public management (NPM). These included the transfer of a variety of private-sector management systems and techniques to the public sector, the advent of new structures for the delivery of public services, and the introduction of quasi- (or pseudo-?) markets, contractorisation and consumerism; and
- ongoing programmes of institutional and constitutional reform that would have implications for policies, the political culture, and the governing framework itself.

All these changes were likely to have an impact on the civil service, obliging it to cede some functions to the private sector, enter into partnerships with private and voluntary sector organisations in other spheres, and manage major institutional and constitutional reforms (including 'agencification' and devolution) which would, arguably, undermine the traditional Whitehall structures and ethos.

The *'hollowing-out of the state'* is thought by some authors, notably Rhodes, to be the inevitable consequence of the move (or return) to governance. Simply stated, the hollowing-out thesis (Rhodes, 1994; 1997: 17–19, 87–111; see also Foster and Plowden, 1996) argues that British government has steadily 'lost' policy functions 'upwards to the European Union, downwards to special-purpose bodies and outwards to agencies' (Rhodes, 1997: 17). In fact, the drift 'upwards' involves not only the gradual ceding of power to the EU, but also the continuous process of engagement in the complex interdependencies of international politics and government, via negotiations and compromises with a wide range of state and transnational organisations, including foreign powers, international bodies such as the UN and the World Bank, and multinational corporations (discussed further in Chapter 3). The drift 'downwards' includes dealing with the consequences of privatised and contractualised elements of the system of public services. This involves a constant reconfiguration of the roles and responsibilities of central government in a context in which large areas of public service are delivered through market mechanisms and sub-contracts to a wide array of public and private-sector partner organisations. The drift 'outwards' or sideways refers to the trend towards the deployment of arm's-length bodies, in particular executive agencies, as mechanisms through which policy can be implemented: 'Hollowing out of the state means simply that the growth of governance reduced the ability of the core executive to act effectively, making it less reliant on a command-operating code and more reliant on diplomacy' (Rhodes *et al.*, 2003: 30).

For the civil service, the major effect of these changes was a 'reinvention' of Whitehall, characterised by institutional fragmentation resulting from the creation of scores of executive agencies under the Next Steps initiative. It is argued that the 'hollowing-out' of the traditional Whitehall departments produces significant problems and challenges in relation to the creation and coordination of policy, and to the application of rules governing the accountability of ministers and civil servants (see Chapters 4 and 5). In the hollowing-out thesis, the drift of UK central government functions in the direction of the EU and a range of other bodies, including quasi- and non-state organisations, has had an impact on the civil service in the sense that some traditional Whitehall policy spheres (most obviously those that came within the scope of the various EU treaties) have now become at the very least shared territories. In the domestic context, the emergence of marketisation and contractualisation means that the civil service (largely Treasury officialdom) is required to manage the central elements of the Private Finance Initiative (PFI, see Chapter 4) or the Public Private Partnerships scheme (PPP) as it became under New Labour.

The *differentiated polity* thesis seeks to synthesise the three conceptual approaches outlined above – network theory; governance; and the hollowing-out of the state – and extend it further, paying particular attention to the pre-existing and potential impact of devolution and decentralisation (see Rhodes *et al.*, 2003). It notes that these three approaches have in common an emphasis on specialisation and fragmentation in policies and politics, in contrast to the 'collective' and 'unifying' assumptions and principles of the Westminster and Whitehall models. Policy networks divide the policy-making arena 'vertically' into different policy segments, each focused around a particular department, or even a division of a department (road and rail in the transport department, for example). The 'governance' theme draws attention to the fragmentation of policy programmes between numerous service providers, some in executive agencies still nominally part of the department but split off 'horizontally' from the senior officials, and others connected only by contracts, funding agreements or looser arrangements, but each specialising in its own particular sector. The 'hollowing-out thesis' asserts that, unlike the Westminster–Whitehall portrayal of a well-coordinated governmental system, the picture following the change in the 1980s and 1990s from government to governance is of a very weakened state that struggles to exert a 'joined-up' control over functions that have been dispersed in all directions.

To these three aspects of the way in which the British state is not as strongly controlled and coordinated as the Westminster–Whitehall model would predict (but is divided into different sections, each with its own characteristics – the 'differentiated polity' outlined by Rhodes, 1997: 7), were added after 1999 the distinctive arrangements of the three nations/regions/provinces (Scotland, Wales, Northern Ireland), to which new powers were devolved (or restored). Rhodes *et al.* (2003) demonstrate what the specialists in those areas knew all along – that there was already a significant differentiation between the component parts of the UK.

Rhodes (1997: 6–7) does not reject the Westminster model entirely, and it remains part of mainstream political science, but he proposes the 'differentiated polity' as an alternative: 'It replaces strong cabinet government, parliamentary sovereignty, HM's loyal opposition and ministerial responsibility with interdependence, a segmented executive, policy networks, governance and hollowing-out. The shorthand phrase for this organising perspective is "the differentiated polity".' Adherents of this approach emphasise the new challenges faced by the civil service in an increasingly 'messy' arena of UK public policy:

> The task confronting British government is to manage packages: packages of services, of organisations and of governments. This is not the picture of British government painted by the Westminster model. Its account of Britain as a unitary state emphasises political integration, centralised authority, a command operating code implemented through bureaucracy and the power of the centre to revoke decentralised powers. The differentiated polity narrative highlights political devolution, fragmentation and interdependence, and functional decentralisation. (Rhodes *et al.*, 2003: 32)

In this environment, significant emphasis comes to be attached to the need for the civil service to master the art of coordination and secure 'joined-up government'.

Taken together, network theory, the governance paradigm, the hollowing-out thesis and the differentiated polity thesis can be deployed to paint a picture of an increasingly marginalised, declining civil service, which plays a much less important role in the process of policy creation and implementation than the traditional Whitehall model would have us believe. Alternatively, while making allowance for the special effect of devolution (given particular emphasis in the differentiated polity thesis) a more subtle interpretation of these conceptual approaches would involve arguing that we had an underdeveloped, impoverished understanding of government in the past (hence the prevalence of the more misleading elements of the Whitehall model). In this light, we might consider these concepts less in terms of their contribution to a theory of civil service decline, and more as a set of accurate, realistic and sophisticated means of understanding the proper location of the civil service in a polity that was never as simple and straightforward as we were once led to believe, but which has undoubtedly become increasingly complex in recent years.

Modernisation rather than decline?

In the Introduction, we argued that the concept of 'modernisation' is remarkably fluid and, curiously enough, has fairly deep historical roots. Moving on from our discussions of the Whitehall model, network theory, governance, hollowing-out and the differentiated polity, a further series of analytical and conceptual perspectives can be deployed that set out a case that the British civil service has been undergoing a series of progressive, modernising changes, rather than succumbing to negativity and decline.

In the context of the civil service, those who subscribe to the 'modernisation' thesis fall within two broad groupings. In the first, we can locate those who might be described loosely as coming within the ranks of the New Labour modernisers. This political brand of 'modernisation' is a multifaceted, yet strangely opaque, concept. As Toynbee and Walker (2001: 204) note in their account of the first Blair administration, the new Labour leitmotiv was vague: 'Never explicitly defined, it shaded into democratisation, meaning an effort to breathe new life into participative government by bringing its institutions physically or figuratively closer to the people, making them more accessible, accountable and intelligible.'

'Modernisation' thus came to apply in a range of contexts. Some of its key features, which had particular implications for the civil service, included 'joined-up government', 'evidence-based policy', 'information-age government', 'partnerships' and the 'management/policy dichotomy'. The impact of some of these developments could be felt beyond the managerial sphere, as they brought in their wake challenges to the traditional notions of civil service accountability and ministerial–civil servant relations. Furthermore, at the macro, constitutional level, New Labour's modernisation programme embraced devolution, and the creation of the Scottish Parliament and the National Assembly for Wales, together with their associated executive bodies, heralded an additional set of modernisation challenges for the civil service (for a detailed discussion of the links between modernisation and the civil service dimension of devolution, see Kirkpatrick and Pyper, 2003). As one of the components of modernised UK government, devolution was meant, at least in part, to enhance the accountability of those in power, including civil servants, as well as to improve the efficiency and effectiveness of policy-making and implementation in the sub-nations of the UK polity. As we argue in Chapter 3, the impact of devolution (as one facet of Blairite modernised government) on the civil service has been distinctly variable, with fairly limited managerial and organisational changes, and the implementation of accountability systems that lean heavily on the traditions of the UK polity.

At least to some extent, New Labour's 'modernisation' seemed to be a development and rebranding of New Public Management, which was, in many respects, a similarly disparate and imprecise set of ideas. The relationship between New Labour's 'modernisation' and NPM has been the subject of some debate (see, for example, Minogue *et al.*, 1998; Falconer, 1999; Hughes and Newman, 1999; Newman, 1999, 2001; Massey and Pyper, 2005). Although we are not concerned with the details of this debate, it can be noted that there are certain linear continuities between NPM and New Labour's 'modernisation' programme. Indeed, it might be argued that the New Labour modernisers were effectively carrying forward many elements of the civil service reform agenda that was put in place by their predecessors, who subscribed (in part or in full) to the doctrines of neo-liberalism or Conservative managerialism. Bevir and Rhodes (2003: 149–50) identify some of the main adherents of this early form of radical modernisation, including Geoffrey Fry, 'one of the few academic admirers of Margaret Thatcher's administrative revolution and the economic liberalism that underpinned it'. In a series of works on the civil service (see, for example, Fry, 1981, 1985, 1995), he set out a case for managerial reform in Whitehall as an antidote to bureaucratic inefficiency. Fry's perspectives echoed those put forward by critical 'insiders', including the disenchanted former civil servant Leslie Chapman (1978), who catalogued Whitehall waste and inefficiency; the Thatcherite policy adviser John Hoskyns (1983, 2001), who excoriated the quality of policy advice generated by the senior civil service and, most significantly of all, Derek Rayner. Rayner had served as part of a small team of business leaders seconded to work in Whitehall during the early part of the Heath Government in 1970–2. Rayner returned to head Thatcher's Efficiency Unit in 1979 and to spearhead the drive for civil service managerial reform using approaches borrowed from the private sector (including the concept of efficiency 'scrutinies') which vested considerable responsibility in young, rising officials.

In contrast to the radical fervour evinced by those in the first grouping, the second category of progressive modernisers might best be described as gradualists. Bevir and Rhodes (2003: 150–2) locate some of those in this category within the 'Whig tradition', but, equally, they might be described, in some respects at least, as Fabians, given their gradualist approach. This second category of progressive modernisers is epitomised by Peter Hennessy. His work embraces the concepts of change and modernisation, while expressing a degree of scepticism about the pace and direction of some of the post-1979 developments in Whitehall, on the grounds that the essential ethos and character of the civil service could be damaged by a reform process that moves too quickly. Moreover, through a failure to adhere fully to the traditional norms of Cabinet government and ministerial conduct, it risks undermining the core values of the civil service (see Hennessy, 1989, 1996, 1999).

> Hennessy's core thesis is that, for all his admiration of the higher civil servants as individuals, as a class they have let Britain down. We have inherited a nineteenth-century bureaucracy, which, for all its modifications and refinements, remains ill-suited … to the task of translating political wishes into practical reality. (Bevir and Rhodes, 2003: 150)

Typical of Hennessy's approach is an acceptance of the need for managerial reforms combined with an acute feel for the superficialities of political fads: 'new managerial abrasives in line with Citizen's Chartery, market testing, performance-related pay and the associated jargon and acronymia of sub-management-school babble which will bring so much dry amusement to historians of government' (Hennessy, 1996: 128). Similarly, when examining the work of the senior civil servants charged with the provision of policy advice to ministers, he combines respect for tradition with a healthy disregard for vested interest: 'My defence of a neutral, permanent, career civil service … is not at all the same thing as maintaining that this kind of taxpayer-funded British equivalent of the Dutch Order of the Golden Fleece should enjoy any kind of monopoly supply on the analysis or advice which flows across ministers' desks' (Hennessy, 1996: 132).

The gradualist progressive modernisers would hold to the view that the civil service of the early twenty-first century is the product of a continuous process of organic, evolutionary change, within which there have been extended periods of relative calm, interspersed with periods of frenetic reform (for evidence, see, for example, Pyper, 1991, 1995; Theakston, 1995; Winstone, 2003). Since the early 1980s, periods of reform have been increasingly common. However, it can be argued that the civil service has an almost innate capacity to 'go with the flow' of modernisation and reform, to accommodate new ideas and approaches, and to evolve steadily with the changes without sacrificing its key features and characteristics. The gradualist progressive modernisers would assert that the civil service does not exist in a hermetically sealed vacuum, and its evolution reflects, and has always reflected, changes in the role of government and the state, as well as national and international developments, including the rise of public-sector managerialism.

Conclusion

This chapter has contextualised the debates surrounding the impact of change on the civil service. We set out the basic content of the Whitehall model and the Westminster model within which it is assumed to operate, and showed how the supporters of this view of the position, role and functioning of the civil service, as described by these models, believe that the inherent usefulness of the organisation has been undermined by the succession of managerial and structural reforms in the 1980s and 1990s, to the point where the civil service has entered a cycle of decline.

We went on to examine a set of alternative analytical approaches: network theory, the governance paradigm, the hollowing-out thesis, and the differentiated polity thesis. One interpretation of this collection of models is that they provide evidence to support the view that the civil service in modern UK government is less central and more marginal in the entire process of policy-making and implementation. However, we argued that an alternative and more subtle interpretation of these models would acknowledge their value as reminders that the certainties of the traditional Whitehall model were overstated, and even in its so-called golden era, the civil service's systemic location was always more complex and circumscribed than we were led to believe. In sum, therefore, these models can be seen less as analyses of a civil service in decline, and more as markers towards a more realistic assessment of the place of the organisation in the complex UK polity.

We ended by considering a further set of analytical and conceptual perspectives, which provide evidence to support the view that, rather than declining, the civil service has in fact been moving in the direction of progressive modernisation and adjusting to the realities of modern government. These perspectives encompass the evangelical fervour of the New Labour modernisers (who in turn were at least partly influenced by the neo-liberal and Conservative managerialists who spawned New Public Management), and the more gradualist modernisers who place emphasis on the importance of organic, evolutionary change.

While the approach of those we are labelling as the gradualist progressive modernisers would seem to offer the most productive insights into the broad direction in which the civil service has moved, and continues to move, it cannot be denied that the perspectives that focus on decline and decay can have particular validity in some spheres of civil service work and activity. All the themes we have set out in this chapter will reappear, from time to time, in the rest of the book, as we examine and interpret the different issues, starting with the policy role of the civil service.

2

Policy Issues

The policy role of the civil service has traditionally been described with reference to the work of the senior civil servants who surround ministers, as the official filters and analysts of policy, and as the authors of papers setting out the options available for the political chiefs of government departments. Policy work can be categorised in different ways. One useful approach, adopted by Page and Jenkins (2005: 59–75) describes civil service policy work in terms of 'production' (creating drafts, statements or documents), 'maintenance' (looking after schemes, initiatives or bodies, with no clear end point for the work), and 'service' (providing advice to a person or institution, again on an ongoing basis). The Whitehall model assumes that the civil service exercises (or exercised) a virtual monopoly in the policy business, with ministers reliant on their senior officials as the researchers and writers of policy alternatives. However, as we noted in Chapter 1, other analytical approaches to understanding the civil service (including network theory, the governance paradigm, the hollowing-out thesis and the differentiated polity thesis), would question the centrality of Whitehall and its denizens in the policy-making process; while officials still have an important place in the negotiating networks, the role of the civil service would nevertheless need to be placed in a broader context. We also saw in the previous chapter how important it is to consider the capacity of the civil service to adjust to the new demands of their political bosses, and to the changing institutional context; that is, the realities of modern government in all aspects of civil service work, including the policy dimensions.

The civil service has always faced challenges in relation to policy work, but the terms of the debate have changed. In this chapter we set out the long-standing concerns that exist about 'bureaucratic power';

that is, whether a set of powerful civil servants are imposing their own policy preferences on to ministers. Precisely where the balance of power lies between ministers and civil servants can never be known, but it was likely to move away from civil servants to politicians during the long years of Conservative government as a particular set of ministers became more experienced. We then address the question of politicisation, and its impact on policy-making. It was not unreasonable for the incoming Labour government in 1997 to be worried that almost two decades of radical right-wing government might have schooled civil servants into seeing only a narrow range of options as being worth putting to ministers. How serious were the risks that the civil service had been politicised during the 1980s and 1990s? Could it be relied on to give impartial advice to Labour? And how serious are the risks that it has since then been politicised by Labour? What compensatory actions did the Labour government take to ensure that it received reliable policy advice?

Two alternative challenges to the civil service's role in the policy process have grown stronger since the 1980s. Those who feared bureaucratic power assumed the civil service was a self-confident and close-knit organisation able to develop coherent 'policy lines' and with the capacity to promote them. However, the concern about the civil service's pursuit of its own policy options has evolved into doubt about whether the British civil service had the expertise to develop effective policy proposals in the first place, or to carry them out effectively. One disastrous mistake after another came to light in a variety of policy domains during the Conservative years and continued under Blair (the poll tax; BSE ('mad cow disease'); the Child Support Agency, 'foot and mouth disease' in 2001; numerous IT projects; prisoners who were freed from custody when they should have been deported; the Rural Payments Agency; and the rather special failure of the 'intelligence community' when giving advice on Iraq). Although such policy disasters are not new to British government, some with long experience of Whitehall thought its technical skills and information resources had withered alarmingly since the 1980s (see Foster, 2001), and we tackle that issue in further detail in the chapter on the way that civil servants are recruited and trained.

In addition, Conservative public management reforms (division of departments into agencies, delegation to private firms and other bodies), then the devolution under Labour (to Scotland, Wales and Northern Ireland), as well as the continued internationalisation of policy-making, have increased our awareness that the policy process was and is complex and diverse. That particular challenge to the conventional ideas about civil service policy advice is the context for Chapter 3, about 'multilevel mandarins'. However, we do consider here the Blair government's reaction to the analyses of those who emphasised in the 1990s the fragmentation of the policy process. What attention did the government give in the new millennium to putting it together again?

Perspectives on policy and civil service power

In the Whitehall model of the civil service, it is expected that the state bureaucracy will be somehow 'above' politics, or at the very least insulated from the perceived excesses of party politics. However, in some systems of government, the senior ranks of the civil service are politicised: in the USA, the top levels of the bureaucracy are filled by appointees of the president; and in Germany, one or two posts at the top of each ministry are filled by permanent civil servants who are members of the minister's political party. Defenders of this type of system argue that it has the advantage of providing the executive with senior officials who are openly supportive of the government's policies, and committed to the success of its policy agenda. If the people appointed are experienced civil servants, as in the German system, they have good knowledge not only of the viable policy options but also of how best to implement them with the other actors likely to be involved.

In contrast, the British model of a career civil service operating on the basis of political impartiality is meant to provide for continuity when governments change, facilitate the accumulation of knowledge and expertise within the departments of state, and allow for a more objective and analytical approach to policy-making. A century and a half after its recommendation by the Northcote–Trevelyan Report (see the Introduction), this concept of a wholly non-politicised civil service is deeply ingrained as an ideal within the British civil service and British society. Yet from the perspective of an American observer of many bureaucratic systems (Peters, 1989: 207–8), Britain's lack of a 'counter-staff' (to counter the 'bureaucratic bias' in the advice proffered), meant that Britain was 'perhaps less well served in policy terms' by its belief in an impartial civil service: not, paradoxically, because top British officials did not give political support, but because they were less expert than the specialised policy staffs developed by politicians in other countries.

The traditional Whitehall model of minister–civil service relations tells us that senior officials provide policy advice to ministers and facilitate effective ministerial dealings in the parliamentary arena. The civil service as a whole then implements the policies agreed collectively by ministers. To some extent, this approach can be traced back to the late nineteenth and early twentieth century debates about the nature and scope of public administration and bureaucracy. The key elements of these debates, particularly those concerning the attempts to separate 'administration' from 'politics', is summarised helpfully in Jordan (1994, ch. 3). Jordan points out that Woodrow Wilson's argument in the late nineteenth century, that public administration in US cities, states and federal bodies should be located beyond politics, was an attempt to professionalise and insulate the work of administrators from the wheeling, dealing and outright corruption associated with politics. A few decades later, Max Weber took this approach further by developing the image of government as a machine, within which the bureaucracy makes the process of administration a routine, in much the same way as the factory machine was making production routine. For Weber, the basis for the work of any civil service was rational–legal authority, in which the individual official resembles one replaceable cog in a huge machine. The machinery of government operates on the principle that officials are selected for their posts according to clearly established procedures. There is a system of continuous recruitment and promotion from within, and all the tasks associated with the work of the system are founded on clearly established rules and regulations. The organisation itself is strictly hierarchical. In the British context, an aversion to theories and philosophies of government perhaps led to less emphasis being attached to Wilsonian and Weberian approaches to government than was the case elsewhere, but none the less, the key features of the civil service after the Northcote–Trevelyan Report bore some of the hallmarks of these thinkers. In particular, there was a prevailing belief that the rules and procedures of the Whitehall system somehow served to insulate the civil service from the power struggles associated with policy and politics.

Challenges to these approaches emerged in the course of the twentieth century, as it was realised that civil servants might in fact have power in their own right, and were not merely a collection of inert automatons functioning within a system of rigid rules and regulations, awaiting political instructions on all matters of substance. It began to be understood that civil servants were able to initiate and mould public policy in both its formation and its implementation. Life and work in government is complex, and in this context opportunities arise for the use of discretion, manoeuvring and wielding power, both at the 'street' level and at the level of high policy-making. While there might be arguments about whether it was a good or bad thing, it was undeniably an increasing fact of life in a growing system of government.

Even in its supposed heyday, the view that civil servants were merely the benign providers of policy options to ministers was challenged by close observers of the British system of government, and by participants in the system. Critics argued that the balance of power in the minister–civil servant relationship was tipped in favour of the latter by a number of factors. These included not only those determined by the behaviour of civil servants, such as their capacity for agenda setting (deciding on the range of policy options that should be made available to ministers), but also the imbalance in practical resources, that had tended to move in favour of officials as government grew, independently of the good will of the civil servants. The evidence is rather unsystematic, often relying on ministers' personal recollections, since officials are usually rather slower to rush into print, and more restricted in what they can say. Nevertheless, we can draw up a balance sheet.

Time

Ministers have less time than the permanent officials dealing with a particular item to consider policy issues. They not only have their departmental business (including putting the case for the department's policies in the media, at conferences and in EU meetings), but also their duties in their constituencies and in Parliament, if they are to be re-elected – or even to continue to stay in office when the parliamentary majority is as fragile as in the Major Government of 1992–97. The Scottish Secretary in that government, Ian Lang, noted that on average he dealt each week with 700 items of business – selected by his private office of civil servants from the 1,000 that actually entered the office – leaving him little chance to think about and write down policy ideas of his own (Lang, 2002: 65). Ministers complain about their crowded diaries, and the late nights working through their 'red boxes' of papers to sign. The Scott Inquiry (1996) into why Matrix Churchill was prosecuted for having exported weapons to Iraq, despite ministers having deliberately encouraged it to do so, provides an example. One minister, Tristan Garel-Jones, signed 'in the small hours' a Public Interest Immunity (PII) certificate, asking the judge, 'on the grounds of public interest', not to reveal to the defence lawyers crucial government papers that would help Matrix Churchill's case.

Civil servants had presented Garel-Jones with this demanding material one evening, for signature by the following morning (Scott Report, 1996: G13.21–23).

In part, the problem is within ministers' control: Winston Churchill restricted the size of documents submitted to him to a half-sheet of paper. When the Conservative minister Kenneth Clarke joined the Ministry of Health he told his driver to choose any two of the dozen red boxes his officials had prepared, a warning to staff not to swamp him with paperwork. Michael Heseltine, perhaps because he had dyslexia, perhaps because he was more interested in managing the big themes, read few papers, but considered them carefully. He refused to sign his PII certificate as it stood, believing that documents should be disclosed to the defence as a matter of justice, and agreed to a much weaker version several days later only on the advice of ministers and officials (Scott Report, 1996: G13.52–84).

Yet the more ministers force officials to confine their papers to crucial items, the greater the likelihood that issues ministers should (in retrospect) have dealt with will escape their attention. Inquiries into scandals such as the Scott Inquiry, or the 'Sierra Leone' affair (Legg and Ibbs, 1999) of the Blair Government, routinely include admissions that ministers did not see important documents, and though it can also be a convenient excuse, the odds really are stacked against them. Since the 1960s, when junior ministers were used to 'run errands', according to the former Labour and Liberal Democrat politician, Roy Jenkins, Cabinet ministers now spread the load by giving them sections of the department's work. Though junior ministers are chosen by the prime minister and may not always prove to be harmonious colleagues, they help to ensure that policy orientation is in the direction willed by the politicians.

Size and span

Coupled with the time problem, the sheer size and policy span of some departments can make it difficult for ministers to deal simultaneously with all the fields covered by their domain, as the Home Secretary, John Reid, pleaded in 2006–07, when immigration, terrorism, prisons and identity cards all seemed to reach a critical point at the same time (responsibility for prisons was soon transferred to a new Ministry of Justice). One reason that the Next Steps project initiated in 1988 (see Chapter 4) went relatively smoothly was that it promised ministers and senior officials a lightening of the administrative burden, by 'hiving-off' the more routine work into semi-independent executive agencies, thereby giving those left in the core department more time for elaborating policy. The policy – administration split could never be as clear as the project assumed, and ministers still intervened in agencies when the political imperatives (news headlines) required it, as the Conservative Home Secretary Michael Howard did at the Prison Service Agency when he sacked a governor after the escape of prisoners in 1995. Moreover, it enables ministers to blame officials for poor administration (as in the case of the Child Support Agency, or HM Revenue & Customs' delivery of Gordon Brown's working families tax credits), rather than rethinking the policy itself. However, the exercise of creating agencies and deciding their overall objectives did force ministers and top civil servants to consider the policy goals and implementation targets they wanted to be achieved by sections of their departments that had not previously come to their attention very much.

Expertise

Ministers usually lack expertise in their department's policy area, and may thus be vulnerable to flawed arguments put forward by officials that will not achieve their political goals. Gillian Shephard was said by the leader of a teachers' union at its spring 1995 conference to be the first Education Secretary for many years not to regard her post just as a stepping stone to higher things (though she was soon followed by another teacher, Labour's Estelle Morris). Prime ministers need to take many factors into account when composing their Cabinet, such as balancing party factions. There are even good reasons for appointing people without subject expertise: the appointment of Jonathan Aitken as Minister for Defence Procurement was criticised in case he furthered his business interest as director of a firm trading in weapons; and similar, though more restrained, comments were made in the Labour government during the tenure of Lord Sainsbury at the Department of Trade and Industry. In 1997, Tony Blair did not appoint ministers to jobs they had shadowed while in opposition because they had made promises that would not be fulfilled (Frank Dobson on education; Joyce Quin on Europe; and Clare Short on transport – she had said that Labour would renationalise railways). In general, ministers familiar with the topic may lose sight of the political contribution they should be making to policy development, by becoming immersed in details, as Estelle Morris admitted when she became one of the few ministers voluntarily to resign because her interest in schools made it difficult to see the big strategic picture (it was also said that some unfounded allegations about interference in exam-marking by the Qualifications and Curriculum Agency, plus the frequent intervention in departmental affairs by Blair's adviser on education, Andrew Adonis, were additional triggering factors: Denham, 2003: 292–3).

Transience

Most ministers are temporary, transient beings who move from post to post with an average tenure of approximately two years. Some Cabinet ministers return to a department they have already led with success (for example, Jenkins as Home Secretary and Heseltine as Secretary of State for the Environment) or served in as a junior minister (John Gummer at Environment). But, at the other extreme, there were seven different Secretaries of State for Transport between 1986 and 1995. The reshuffle fever in summer 1999, when the Blair Government had been in power for two years, showed that political reasons for Cabinet change normally override the need for expertise in policy-making. Similarly, Gordon Brown's almost complete change of ministerial personnel in 2007, though more carefully planned than Blair's reshuffles, was more about looking 'new' than 'experienced'.

The contrast often made with the 'permanence' and 'expertise' of top officials is nevertheless exaggerated, since officials close to ministers themselves change posts every two to three years, often from department to department. These top officials are generalist administrators, in their own way as ignorant as ministers about the technical details of the department's work. Their valuable expertise is in knowing Whitehall, its people and its procedures. But one reason for the Conservative government's relative dominance over officials in the mid-1990s was that most Cabinet ministers had been in government for a decade or more. Some of the more effective operators, such as Kenneth Clarke, had learnt how to coordinate with other ministers without the need for officials, such as in brief but frequent conversations in Parliament while waiting to vote. If the Conservative ministers of the 1990s made policy mistakes (the poll tax; the refusal to reinstate a Greater London government; the decision to allow weapons sales to Iraq), they were ministers' mistakes, even if officials carried out the political decisions, and sometimes rather too devotedly, it would appear (see Butler *et al.* (1994) on the poll tax; and the Scott Report (1996) on 'arms to Iraq').

Access to information

However, even newly-transferred civil servants have more access to expertise than do ministers; they are guardians of the rules governing access to information inside government departments (particularly the convention that incoming ministers from one party can be denied access to the files of the outgoing administration). In developing policy ideas and in meetings with ministers, the senior generalist officials are backed up by the department's specialists on the issue under discussion. In the 1970s, ministers improved their systems for information and analysis. The Heath Government set up the Central Policy Review Staff (CPRS) in the Cabinet Office to carry out long-term strategic studies for the government, separately from departments. Margaret Thatcher continued the habit of her predecessors by installing a small policy unit in Downing Street, which expanded after she abolished the CPRS (the more radical of its reports tended to be leaked at embarrassing moments if ministers or departments did not like the contents). The Financial Management Initiative promoted by, first, Heseltine and then Thatcher (see Chapter 4) provided ministers with more systematic knowledge about the staffing and budgets devoted to each policy programme, enabling them to set more informed priorities for their departments. More significant, the Thatcher Governments had their own independent views on policy, which they developed with the help of political advisers and think tanks rather than with civil servants.

The first head of Thatcher's policy unit, John Hoskyns, has written graphically about the tensions between the Thatcher government and Whitehall. Though, like Thatcher, he appreciated the talents of some civil servants with whom he worked, he saw (or thought he saw) examples in which they manoeuvred behind the scenes on individual appointments and on civil service pay awards; he thought they gave policy advice that had a malign effect on the British economy, and were 'defeatist'. After one contretemps with officials in 1979 he felt 'more completely and irrevocably than ever before, that the civil service are the real enemy of hope for the future' (Hoskyns, 2000: 128). There have been many such critics of Whitehall since the 1960s, from both the left and the right, who have argued that civil servants deployed their advantages over ministers to serve as an effective brake on radical policies and a force for centrist continuity.

From the perspective of some on the left, the civil service appeared as a bastion of the traditional establishment, with its senior posts filled predominantly by the products of the public schools and Oxbridge, and its policy outlook geared towards continuity rather than change. Taken to its limits, this logic led to an argument that the social and educational background of senior officials gave them a cohesiveness that enabled them to behave, at least on some occasions, as a dominant force, even a 'ruling class'. The ministerial diaries of Richard Crossman (1975, 1976, 1977), Tony Benn (1987, 1989, 1990) and Barbara Castle (1990), together with other published observations on the functioning of the higher civil service during periods of Labour government (see, for example, Kellner and Crowther-Hunt, 1980; and Sedgemore, 1980), reveal much about the inherent distrust felt towards the civil service by some senior Labour figures during the 1960s and 1970s, and the often volatile working relationships at the top of government departments.

On the other hand, critics from the opposite end of the political spectrum argued that Whitehall had become so intrinsic to the cross-party 'consensus' after the Second World War, with its propensity for interventionist policies in society and the economy, that the senior civil service was now averse to radical policy alternatives coming from the right. This view assumed particular importance during the 1970s and 1980s as the Conservatives prepared for, and then took, power under Thatcher. Thatcher's disdain for the civil service has been examined by a number of observers (see, for example, Hennessy, 1989, ch. 15; Richards, 1997; and Young, 1993; ch. 9). To some extent, the Thatcherite perspective was based on the theories of Niskanen (1971), who argued that bureaucrats generally attempt to pursue their own interests in order to enhance their status and pay, and this leads them to seek larger departments, with the expansion of the bureaucracy becoming an end in its own right, and policy advice to politicians being filtered through this dominant agenda (see Chapter 4 for some empirical development of this thesis). This basic premise strongly influenced the approach of the 'New Right' towards government, both in the USA and the UK during the 1970s and 1980s.

It is important to understand that these leftist and rightist critiques of the civil service policy role were not shared universally, even within the senior membership of the Labour and Conservative administrations. Indeed, some ministers on both sides of the party divide viewed their colleagues' carping about civil service 'power' as excuses for their own failures in office. None the less, the more recent issues and debates surrounding the policy role of the civil service should be viewed in the broader context of these perspectives that were strongly held by some political leaders.

When the Labour Party returned to power in 1997, its attitude towards the civil service was influenced, on the one hand, by the historical experience of the party and the distrust it felt when it was last in government and, on the other, by two more recent developments: the long period of Conservative dominance, and the Labour Party's own process of 'modernisation'. The historical or traditional wariness of Labour towards the senior civil service, as a bastion of the 'establishment', was amplified in 1997 by these two factors. First, Labour feared that the eighteen years of Conservative government between 1979 and 1997 had undermined the conventional impartiality of the civil service. In the course of this extended period in opposition, concerns had grown within the Labour Party about the extent to which the top ranks of the civil service had been affected by the experience of working with the Conservatives over four consecutive terms in government. Informal briefings by senior officials of leading Labour figures were held in the period before the 1997 general election and signalled a positive tone, yet the party remained concerned that the Whitehall 'mind-set' had perhaps been conditioned by the need to provide a certain limited range of policy options to Conservative ministers. The second factor stemmed from a particular aspect of the Labour Party's modernisation process. During the period of Tony Blair's leadership, from 1994 onwards, the party's approach to policy-making had become more streamlined, and its media coordination operation, based at the Millbank headquarters, professionalised. The slickness and efficiency of the avowedly partisan 'Millbank machine' was soon contrasted with the more traditional, and apolitical, approaches of Whitehall and the civil service found wanting. Only much later would Labour leaders start to wonder aloud whether, with Millbank, they had prepared well for fighting an election and 'rebutting' negative stories, but had not done enough to prepare the policies and the policy-making systems they would need when in government.

When Tony Blair's Cabinet was formed in 1997, ministers were clearly sceptical of the willingness of officials trained for nearly two decades under a Conservative government to provide the advice Labour ministers wanted. Labour ministers brought in more substantial numbers of advisers of their own, usually an adviser with policy expertise and another with experience in journalism. Blair had a much bigger staff in his office at 10 Downing Street than either Major or Thatcher had recruited (150 staff as against 100). He had a policy unit whose instructions ('Tony wants') the new and untried ministers took more seriously than the more experienced Conservative ministers and advisers ever took Thatcher's or Major's policy unit. In comparison with previous governments, the Blair Government advisers became more dominant in the hierarchy of the department. Ministers paid more attention to young advisers than was formerly the case, and there was more friction between temporary and permanent officials. A number of top officials and departmental press officers left or were transferred.

In the Treasury, for example, Brown's special economics adviser, Ed Balls (who became chief economic adviser before entering full-time politics), and his press adviser, Charlie Whelan, were influential, while the top Treasury official, Terry Burns, retired, and the Treasury press officer, Jill Rutter, was moved to another post. But neither of these civil servants had been traditional, neutral, anonymous, permanent mandarins. Burns had been an appointee of Thatcher, moving to the top economics role in the Treasury from academia, and Rutter had worked in Major's policy unit, and on devising the poll tax. Whelan himself had to resign in 1999 when his alleged contribution (strongly denied), to the rivalries between Blair and Brown became more newsworthy than Brown's handling of the economy. New Labour's encounters with the civil service would soon lead to renewed debates about 'politicisation', the true risks of which we assess later in the chapter, after looking first at the rules that try to ensure the civil service is impartial but at the same time remains ministers' most trusted policy adviser.

Squaring the circle? constitutional rules on impartiality

The formal rules requiring civil servants to be impartial in the policy context are set out in the *Civil Service Code* (Cabinet Office, 2006b). It was announced by the Major Government in the White Paper *The Civil Service: Taking Forward Continuity and Change* (Cabinet Office, 1995), as an anticipated response to the criticisms by the Scott Inquiry. Indirectly, it was a response to demands by the civil service (notably the First Division Association representing senior officials), Parliament and the public for a document of strong legal status (preferably a Civil Service Act), that would prevent ministers and civil servants from behaving in an unethical manner. The 'Arms-to-Iraq' scandal was only the latest in a series of events in which ministers used officials, and officials allowed themselves to be used, or even colluded with ministers in activities that strayed outside the conventional boundaries of conduct in government. Several incidents in the previous decade were critical to changing public opinion on the conduct of the civil service, to the extent that 'Bagehot' in *The Economist* of 30 April 1994 wrote that 'being Cabinet Secretary is no longer regarded as synonymous with probity and integrity'. They included the following:

- In January 1986, Charles Powell, one of Thatcher's private secretaries in Downing Street, and Bernard Ingham, her press secretary (both civil servants), encouraged a Department of Trade press officer (a civil servant) to leak to the media a confidential letter from the Attorney General to Heseltine, then Defence Minister, to embarrass Heseltine, who held a different position from Thatcher on the sale of Westland (a helicopter firm). The inquiry was unpublished and only held because the Attorney General threatened to call in the police. Thatcher and the Cabinet Secretary, Robert Armstrong, on behalf of ministers, refused to let the officials be questioned by parliamentary committees, who were strongly critical of Armstrong, Powell and Ingham. No disciplinary action was taken.

- In December 1986, the Cabinet Secretary, highly unusually, gave evidence in an Australian court in defence of the government's suppression of the book *Spycatcher*, written by a former counter-espionage officer. Armstrong was 'economical with the truth' (meaning that he had not told the whole story), when trying to square the suppression of this book with the previous publication of similar spy stories; his evidence was treated by the judge as a lie.

- In September 1988, Charles Powell redrafted a speech that Thatcher was about to deliver in Bruges, to give it a very anti-EC tone, which did not correspond to the view of the Foreign Secretary and many leading ministers. The speech had already been worked out carefully between the Foreign Office and Downing Street in the usual way to reflect the collective policy view of the government, but Powell then amended the document unilaterally.

- In spring 1991, the Treasury Permanent Secretary, Peter Middleton, authorised the payment from Treasury funds of £4,700 to pay lawyers handling the press inquiries for the Chancellor of the Exchequer Norman Lamont, in connection with the eviction of a tenant ('Miss Whiplash') from Lamont's London home. Another Treasury Permanent Secretary, Terry Burns, defended this action to Parliament's Treasury and Civil Service Select Committee in 1993, on the grounds that Lamont's private activity might affect the economy.

- As a final example, we come back to the Scott Inquiry, which revealed that officials assisted three junior ministers who encouraged firms to export weapons to Iraq despite government guidelines forbidding it. When MPs asked questions that would have exposed this change of policy, officials from three departments composed answers for ministers to sign that they knew were 'inaccurate and misleading', 'not correct' or 'not true' (Scott, 1996: D.4.25–42). One junior diplomat seems to have resigned from the Foreign

Office rather than continue to write answers that were not true (Bogdanor, 1996: 32), but the support of a dozen other officials for ministers was such that the Matrix Churchill directors would have gone to prison had the judge not agreed that their lawyers should see documents that officials (on behalf of a minister, the Attorney General) had, as we have seen, protected from the defence, and if the minister at the centre of the affair, Alan Clark, had not blurted out the truth in court.

Had officials become too close to ministers, starting to share their political ideals, such that they could no longer give impartial advice? Did officials merely play a supporting role when they saw that ministers had decided that telling Parliament about export licences would raise a public outcry harmful to British trading interests (Barberis, 1997: 17)? Did ministers, fearing political embarrassment, put pressure on officials who feared their career might be in jeopardy if they complained? In 1985, after a number of leaks by officials, Robert Armstrong, as Head of the Home Civil Service, had issued a formal 'Note of Guidance' (see below and Chapter 5), warning civil servants that their duty was owed to 'the government of the day'. As the evidence from the Scott Inquiry started to emerge, the General Secretary of the FDA, Liz Symons, told the Treasury and Civil Service Committee (1994) that civil servants had been required to 'stonewall' or 'withhold the truth' from Parliament, if ministers required it, and that the FDA wanted an official code of ethics for civil servants.

The Government's response to the Committee's report was the *Civil Service Code*, made widely available as a small booklet in 1996. Though it said nothing that had not been said before, Cabinet Office officials said it brought existing principles together 'in a handier form' (Lee *et al.*, 1998: 236). More especially, it gave a new right of appeal to the Civil Service Commissioners to civil servants who thought they were being asked to act in a way that conflicted with the *Code*, though civil servants still had to raise the matter internally first, which most would have found inhibiting. A new version was introduced in 2006, this time with the right to appeal directly to the Civil Service Commissioners, though civil servants were still encouraged to discuss the issue internally first. It applies to all members of the Home Civil Service: those working for the devolved administrations, the Diplomatic Service and the Northern Ireland Civil Service have equivalent codes.

This recent version followed a consultation exercise overseen by the Head of the Civil Service, Gus O'Donnell, and the First Civil Service

Commissioner, Janet Paraskeva. In essence, these rules are designed to ensure that the civil service can play a full and legitimate role in the creation and implementation of public policy, while retaining its essential impartiality. The *Code* is a relatively small document, but its importance is beyond question. For the first time, it was made clear that it was a formal part of the terms and conditions for civil servants, and it is a key element of the contractual relationship between officials and their employer. Section 2 of the *Code* provides working definitions of 'objectivity' ('basing your advice and decisions on rigorous analysis of the evidence') and 'impartiality' ('acting solely according to the merits of the case and serving equally well Governments of different political persuasions').

In Box 2.1, we set out the *Code*'s specific statements on objective and politically impartial behaviour by civil servants. There is a further section on impartial behaviour which deals with the equal treatment of citizens by civil servants when implementing public policy. As a set of rules on civil service conduct (ministers have their own code, issued by each prime minister), its instructions read as a warning to civil servants who are tempted to become politicised or to exercise 'bureaucratic power' (for example, by presenting only facts and advice that fit their own political or departmental views, or slowing down implementation, in the expectation of a change of government). As the FDA implied, it may also aid junior officials to resist pressures from above to act differently.

All the same, there is an essential ambiguity in the instruction to 'act in a way which deserves and retains the confidence of ministers while at the same time ensuring that the same relationship can be established with those they may be required to serve in some future Government' (see Box 2.1). Supporters of the 'Whitehall model' as a norm say that such behaviour is easier to acquire by long socialisation into the values of the civil service, and that such values had been destroyed by the 'enterprise' values imported into the British civil service under the Conservative government (O'Toole, 1997: 92–3). The Scott Inquiry seems, however, to show that officials recruited long before Thatcherism had been socialised into thinking that 'half a picture can be accurate' when accounting to Parliament and the courts, even if the whole picture would tell a different story. However, O'Toole (1997: 93) captures the essence of the problem when he says that: 'The restatement of conventional wisdom, albeit in the elevated form of a "code", may well not be a sufficient substitute for acquiring an appreciation and acceptance of public duty by other means.'

Box 2.1 *Civil Service Code*: standards of objectivity and impartiality

Objectivity

Civil servants must:

- provide information and advice on the basis of the evidence and present accurately the options and facts;
- take decisions on the merits of the case;
- take due account of expert and professional advice.

Civil servants must not:

- ignore inconvenient facts or relevant considerations when providing advice;
- frustrate the implementation of policies once decisions are taken.

Political impartiality

Civil servants must:

- serve the government, whatever its political persuasion, to the best of their ability no matter what their own political beliefs are;
- act in a way which deserves and retains the confidence of Ministers while at the same time ensuring that the same relationship can be established with those they may be required to serve in some future Government;
- comply with any restrictions that have been laid down on their political activities.

Civil servants must not:

- act in a way that is determined by party political considerations;
- use official resources for party political purposes;
- allow personal political views to determine any advice given or actions taken.

Source: Extracted from *Civil Service Code* (Cabinet Office, 2006b).

An important aspect of the system of rules and regulations designed to insulate the civil service from party politics is the question of political activity. As members of society, civil servants have inherent rights to hold and express political views, so the challenge for those attempting to preserve the principles of the permanent, career civil service is to strike a reasonable balance between these rights and the need to secure official impartiality. The formal rules on the political activities of civil servants are set out in Section 4 of the extensive *Civil Service Management Code* (Cabinet Office, 2006a), a document which encapsulates all of the conditions of service issues for the British civil service.

Box 2.2 sets out the general principles on political activity that apply to permanent civil servants. Some general principles and key rules apply to all career civil servants, especially the need to avoid political activity that would seem to criticise the policy stance of the government (or praise that of the opposition), and to keep from the current government the policy papers of previous governments from another party. In Britain the 'national government is an extreme example of closed government', in which the principle of insulating bureaucrats as decision-makers from short-term political pressures has been preferred to the principle of open and accountable government as adopted by Scandinavian systems (Peters, 1989: 256; see also Vincent, 1998; and Chapter 5 in this volume).

The level of restriction placed on the political activities of civil servants depends on their level in the service, with the 4,000 or so civil servants at middle and senior management levels forbidden any national political activity ('politically-restricted'), and with very limited activity (such as behind-the-scenes administrative work) possible in local politics, and then only with extreme caution and permission. Very few officials in this category will even try to seek permission. In contrast, the small numbers of 'blue-collar' industrial civil servants are 'politically-free'. In between these two groups, officials can take part in local council politics with discretion and permission, provided they do not comment on their own ministers or issues affecting their department. The *Management Code* follows up these warnings with more generous instructions to departments (in para. 4.4, annex A) to give permission wherever possible. Nevertheless, senior officials and those hoping to be in those positions one day take care not to demonstrate any political affiliation.

A further key document covers the sensitive issue of civil service evidence to parliamentary select committees (Cabinet Office, 2005a). This set of notes on how officials are to answer questions was first drafted in 1967, after Richard Crossman, as Leader of the Commons, introduced the specialised committees. The 'Osmotherly Rules' (named after the official who compiled the 1980 version) make it clear that civil servants must confine their evidence (oral or written) to matters of fact:

> Any comment by officials on government policies and actions should always be consistent with the principle of civil service political impartiality. Officials should as far as possible avoid being drawn into discussion

Box 2.2 *Civil Service Management Code*: civil servants and politics

Principles

- Civil servants must not ... seek to frustrate the policies, decisions or actions of Government;
- Civil servants must not take part in any political or public activity which compromises ... their impartial service to the Government of the day or any future Government.

Some key rules

- Civil servants must maintain the long-standing conventions that new Administrations do not normally have access to papers of a previous Administration of a different political complexion. The conventions cover, in particular, Ministers' own deliberations and the advice given to them;
- Depending on the status of the civil servant, there may be restrictions placed on his/her right to take part in political activities.

'Politically restricted' civil servants

- Officials who are members of the Senior Civil Service and at levels immediately below the SCS, plus members of the Fast Stream Development Programme, must not take part in national political activities, [and] must seek permission to take part in local political activities.

General standard of conduct

- Officials not in the 'Politically Free' category 'must not allow the expression of their personal political views to constitute so strong and so comprehensive a commitment to one political party as to inhibit loyal and effective service to Ministers of another party.
- They must take particular care to express comment with moderation, particularly about matters for which their own Ministers are responsible; to avoid comment altogether about matters of controversy affecting the responsibility of their own Ministers, and to avoid personal attacks.
- They must also take every care to avoid any embarrassment to Ministers or to their department or agency which could result, inadvertently or not, from bringing themselves prominently to public notice, as civil servants, in party political controversy ... (and they) must retain at all times a proper reticence in matters of political controversy so that their impartiality is beyond question.

Source: Extracted from *Civil Service Management Code* (Cabinet Office, 2006a, section 4).

of the merits of alternative policies where this is politically contentious. If official witnesses are pressed by the Committee to go beyond these limits, they should suggest that the questioning should be referred to Ministers. (Cabinet Office, 2005a, section 4A, para. 55)

Taken together, the *Civil Service Code*, the *Civil Service Management Code* and the Osmotherly Rules comprise the formal constitutional rules governing civil service impartiality.

Four risks of politicisation

Formal constitutional rules can only take us so far towards understanding these matters. As we saw when examining some of the historical themes above, the question of 'politicisation' is complex, and it arises in a variety of different contexts, including the power balance and working relationships between senior civil servants and government ministers. What are the principal risks associated with politicisation? Objectively, there would seem to be four forms of politicisation which could threaten the constitutional impartiality of the British civil service: the anti-government, 'reverse politicisation' that might occur if civil servants adopt covert oppositionalist stances towards official policies; partisan appointments within the civil service; a requirement or expectation that officials should carry out political work; and, finally, usurpation of civil service functions by external political appointees. We offer some brief comments on each of these risks.

Opposing government from within

The history of the civil service is punctuated by instances where officials have turned against their political masters, stepped beyond the confines of the *Civil Service Code*, and used leaked information as a means of undermining the government. Politically motivated leaks became a major cause for concern at times during the extended period of Conservative government between 1979 and 1997, with some officials reacting against specific policies or actions, or, more generally, against perceived negative treatment of the civil service as a whole.

A number of *causes célèbres*, particularly those featuring Sarah Tisdall and Clive Ponting, led to disciplinary and legal action being taken against civil servants. Charged under the Official Secrets Act, Tisdall served a prison sentence for leaking documents relating to the Greenham Common air base to the *Guardian* newspaper (see Pyper, 1985). Ponting was acquitted by the jury at his Old Bailey trial following his leak of documents that he alleged revealed ministerial intentions to mislead Parliament over the investigation of the sinking of the Argentine cruiser *General Belgrano* during the Falklands War (see Ponting, 1985). As a direct consequence of these cases, a statement was issued by the then Head of the Home Civil Service (the 'Armstrong Memorandum') which, while recognising the moral and ethical issues surrounding certain aspects of civil service work, restated the constitutional position of officials and reminded them of their fundamental loyalty to ministers. This statement was subsequently incorporated in the *Civil Service Code*. Ponting, Tisdall and others argued that their decisions to leak information were motivated by serious concerns about ethics and standards of ministerial conduct, rather than naked politics. There is a 'grey area' here, which the civil service has traditionally not managed particularly well. The Armstrong Memorandum's guidelines on how to report matters of 'conscience' failed notably during the Westland Affair mentioned earlier, when an official faced the type of ethical dilemma the Memorandum was supposed to cover (for details, see Linklater and Leigh, 1986). Since 1998, civil servants, in common with other employees, have enjoyed some limited rights under the terms of the Public Interest Disclosure Act, which protects those who disclose information concerning criminal offences, failures to meet legal obligations, miscarriages of justice, danger to health and safety, and damage to the environment. However, there is an expectation that normal lines of reporting such issues will be used, and the disclosures will take place in that context. The legislation does not legitimise leaks for political purposes.

Civil service leaks appear to be a feature of extended periods of single party government. In the period since 1997, the relationship between the Labour government and the civil service has been peppered with leaks stemming from particular grievances, and perhaps also from broader antipathy towards the government's management of civil service matters. Two brief examples will suffice for our present purposes. In 2004, the position of the Home Office minister, Beverley Hughes, was undermined – and her resignation precipitated – by leaks of official information on asylum seekers. In an even more sensitive case, it was argued in evidence to a House of Commons select committee (Public Administration Committee, 2004) that the Ministry of Defence official Dr David Kelly breached the terms of the *Civil Service Code* by moving beyond the facts and entering the realm of political conjecture when he briefed journalists about the government's presentation of evidence relating to Iraqi weapons of mass destruction.

Dr Kelly's subsequent suicide led to an official inquiry (Hutton, 2004) which in turn prompted the resignations of the BBC's Director General and Chairman of the Board of Governors.

The practice of civil servants opposing a government effectively from within by means of politically motivated leaks has not become widespread. Instead, such behaviour has tended to come from fairly isolated and individual acts of disenchantment. In this sense, the threat of outright politicisation of the civil service by means of a concerted oppositionalist stance is quite remote.

Partisan appointments in the Civil Service

The alleged use of overtly party-political criteria in the civil service appointments process became a serious issue for debate during the 1980s. For a time, it appeared that the Thatcher Government might be attempting to secure the politicisation of the senior ranks of the civil service by manipulating the system for making appointments to the top posts. As Hennessy (1989: 630–31) points out, some senior civil servants and observers, including the journalist Hugo Young, argued that the Thatcher appointments were designed to create a compliant Whitehall. However, closer analysis showed that there was little direct evidence of politicisation. As prime minister, Margaret Thatcher found herself in the fortunate position of being in Downing Street at precisely the time when an entire generation of senior civil servants was due to retire ('virtually a complete turnover' in Hennessy's (1989: 630) phrase). Unlike most of her predecessors, who took little notice of the body that oversaw the promotion of senior civil servants – the Senior Appointments Selection Committee (SASC), she monitored its work closely, and used her legitimate power to select from the short-lists produced by the SASC. These selections tended to be younger officials who were prepared to embrace new managerial ideas and challenge the traditional Whitehall orthodoxies. Although grumbles and discontent continued,

> an impressive group of the great and the good, convened by the Royal Institute of Public Administration under the chairmanship of Professor David Williams of Wolfson College, Cambridge, effectively cleared Mrs Thatcher of the charge of politicising the senior civil service, though the Williams Committee did detect an unprecedented level of interest in top appointments from the incumbent in No. 10 after 1979. (Hennessy, 1989: 634)

John Major and Tony Blair appeared to adopt a less proactive approach to the business of making appointments to the top ranks of the civil service. However, as Blair's premiership progressed, there were some indications of a growing impatience with certain aspects of Whitehall's operations, and hints were dropped that the government required a new breed of top mandarins. The Committee on Standards in Public Life (2003) expressed concerns that the government might be contemplating giving ministers the role of selecting those civil servants who were recruited by open competition. However, it soon became clear that the government's intentions were less radical, and the focus was to be on modernising the professional development of senior civil servants, rather than deploying political criteria to secure the appointment of the 'right' people. Blair's major speech on civil service reform in February 2004 (Prime Minister, 2004) argued for the development of more 'professional' and specialist skills in the civil service, and made it clear that faster promotion should be available to those who acquired the necessary skills. The underlying assumption was that the prime minister would take a closer interest in Senior Civil Service appointments than previously, although it seemed probable that this would be modelled on the Thatcher approach rather than being an attempt to politicise the Senior Civil Service by means of the appointments process.

Subsequently, the Professional Skills for Government agenda, launched in October 2004, set out the broad requirements for those working at senior and middle management positions in the civil service. One of the three career groupings created within the new agenda was 'policy delivery': encompassing staff dealing with the formulation, development and evaluation of policy. Those in or seeking to enter the ranks of the Senior Civil Service (where the policy delivery work is most concentrated) would require 'leadership skills' as well as additional skills in communications, marketing and strategy (for information on the content of the Professional Skills for Government Agenda, and comment on it, see Mottram, 2005; Talbot, 2005; Cabinet Office, 2006c).

Pressure to carry out political work

The third politicisation risk stems from the possibility that permanent, career civil servants will be required to carry out political work. This might include giving the governing party a potential advantage over its political opponents by presenting present facts and figures in a particular fashion, or, in other words, giving information a partisan 'spin'.

The Labour government under Tony Blair was frequently accused of resorting to this type of politicisation. The accusations largely stemmed from the way in which the Government Information and Communication Service was managed following the election of New Labour in

1997. As was noted above, Labour's slick and efficient 'Millbank machine' had served the party very well during the latter part of its time in opposition, and the party leadership was keen to see this professional approach to media liaison transplanted into Whitehall. However, as we note below, serious tensions arose between the incoming 'spin doctors' and the established civil service communications officers, with many of the latter feeling that they were being placed under pressure to carry out political, as opposed to governmental work. Sensitivities were heightened by the fact that the entire information and communication apparatus was under the control of a political adviser, Alistair Campbell, until his departure from government in 2003 (see Oborne, 1999; Jones, 2000, 2001; Oborne and Walters, 2004). The issue arose again, in dramatic form, during the months preceding the 2003 war in Iraq, when it was alleged that intelligence community officials were being pressurised into producing documentary evidence that would support the government's case for war. Suspicions remained concerning the conduct of ministers and special advisers, and the precise nature of their dealings with senior officials, despite the fact that the government was cleared of the key charges by the official report into the matter (Butler, 2004).

Takeover of civil service functions by political appointees

The final politicisation risk stems from the political appointment of external personnel to civil service posts, leading to usurpation of traditional civil service functions (as was alleged in the case of Campbell, who, though a political appointee, was given authority over career civil servants by means of an Order in Council). An associated risk comes from external appointees who do not necessarily occupy traditional civil service posts, but are none the less allowed to trespass on to civil service 'territory'. This latter risk can lead to debates about pressure being placed on civil servants to carry out political work (see page 78 above).

The political appointees whose work has raised this concern over recent years are the special policy advisers brought into government departments by ministers seeking to supplement certain elements of the policy work provided by the civil service. In principle, this procedure need not be particularly problematic. Prime ministers historically have sought additional advice from expert advisers of one kind or another, and, since 1964, ministers have been allowed to appoint limited numbers of special advisers, to varied effect (see Pyper, 2003). However, the experience of special advisers during the period of Labour government since 1997 has raised some important questions about the relationship between the work of political appointees and the civil service. As already mentioned, Labour's desire to transplant the successful Millbank media liaison operation into Whitehall was coupled with the lingering suspicion that the upper reaches of the civil service had been conditioned into adopting a particular 'mindset' by the extended period of Conservative government after 1979. The subsequent influx of unprecedented numbers of special advisers led to important questions being asked about the policy relations between ministers, civil servants and the temporary 'irregulars'.

Let us now look at these issues in more detail.

The impact of special advisers

The civil service has never had a complete monopoly in the business of providing policy advice to ministers. The political heads of government departments have always exercised their right to balance the advice proffered by their officials against that on offer from a range of other sources, including party research departments, academic experts, and external 'think tanks'. The latter have been particularly attractive to ministers. The Thatcher Governments had close working relationships with a number of independent research bodies broadly aligned on the 'New Right', including the Centre for Policy Studies, the Adam Smith Institute, and the Institute of Economic Affairs. New Labour has been associated particularly with a number of think tanks offering research based policy ideas from centre-left perspectives, including the Institute for Public Policy Research and Demos. Officials understand that their policy papers will often be considered within a broader comparative context, and that the work of external bodies will be taken seriously by ministers.

In the period since 1964, civil servants have also become accustomed to the presence of political advisers in ministerial offices (for a full account of the development and operation of the special adviser role, see Blick, 2004). While the British system of government has eschewed the continental European practice of appointing ministerial *cabinets* (small teams of policy advisers, drawn by convention from both the civil service and the minister's party), individual special advisers have been appointed by increasing numbers of ministers since the first experiment with this practice was authorised by Prime Minister Harold Wilson in 1964. After a decade, the total number of special advisers had risen to thirty-eight (partly as a result of the suspicions of Labour ministers such as Tony Benn and Barbara Castle (see page 66) that the senior civil service was determined to neutralise radical policy initiatives). Debates were already taking place about the relationships between these political appointees and the civil service (see Young, 1976; Blackstone, 1979). Most of the working relationships were relatively unproblematic, although there was marked tension in the Departments of Industry and Energy as Benn's advisers clashed with officials. Thatcher maintained a fairly tight control over the numbers and types of special advisers her ministers appointed, but her successor, Major, took a more relaxed view, and by the end of his premiership in 1997 it was estimated that thirty-five special advisers were in post around Whitehall.

The view in the civil service at this time was that special policy advisers offered ministers tailored, expert advice and support which were not available within the conventional civil service framework. They insulated the civil service from political matters by providing ministers with clearly designated sources of partisan advice; and, perhaps paradoxically, provided additional channels of communication to ministers which the civil service could use in a positive way to help persuade ministers of a course to follow. Robin Butler, as Cabinet Secretary and Head of the Home Civil Service during the transition from Conservative to Labour, seems to have taken a pragmatic view, as well he might, having had the experience of working amicably and effectively with Harold Wilson's policy advisers when he was private secretary to Wilson in the 1974–76 government (Donoughue, 1987: 19, 106). Butler told the Public Service Committee of the House of Lords (1998):

> The Prime Minister, who is always, as it were, in need of good advice, will draw it from the best people and that is a thoroughly good thing whether they are political or Civil Servants. . . (1998: Q2133)

> You have in opposition, Opposition spokesmen working with a very small group of advisers with whom they are intimately bound. They come into Government and that intimacy is not broken, it is maintained . . . so part of the transition will be the building up of the confidence that already exists between the Minister and the special advisers, between the Minister and the Civil Servants. You cannot do that overnight. It takes a little time to do so. That is perfectly understandable and natural. (1998: Q2140)

There was an immediate, marked increase in the numbers of special advisers appointed by Labour ministers following the 1997 election victory, with fifty-three entering Whitehall in the first few weeks, seventy-four by the end of 1999 (Richards, 2000) and later eighty-one (Jones and Weir, 2002). Butler's successor, Richard Wilson, does not seem to have been worried, and was quoted as saying that: 'I do not think the senior civil service of 3,700 people is in danger of being swamped by 70 special advisers' (Richards, 2000). The next Cabinet Secretary, Andrew Turnbull, pointed out that 'numbers' were not the important criterion. In evidence to the Public Administration Committee of the Commons (2004: 4 March 2004), he put the statistics in context:

> Is the civil service being politicised? I do not think you can judge this by simply looking at the number of special advisers ... There has been roughly a doubling of the number of special advisers from 36/7 to 70-something. Most of that increase [has] been in Numbers 10 and 11, Treasury and particularly Number 10. Out in the world of departments, the two per [minister] rule, two special advisers per secretary of state, pretty much rules ... by and large ... the number of special advisers is not significantly different and their impact on a department is not significantly different from what it was, say 15 years ago.

The New Labour special advisers were broadly of two types. The policy experts were assigned to work in ministers' offices or within the numerous task forces and cross-cutting policy units spawned by the new policy agendas. The media liaison experts or 'spin doctors' worked in communication roles. Regardless of category, however, there were debates about the extent to which some civil service posts had been politicised in all but name, and stories started to emerge about officials coming under pressure to mould their work around the political imperatives of the government.

Although they are not conventional civil servants, special advisers are paid under a special sub-section of the civil service pay scheme, and their work is now regulated by a *Code of Conduct*. Box 2.3 highlights some of the key elements of the *Code*, as they apply to the working relations between special advisers and civil servants.

From the early days of the Blair Government there was friction between some elements of the civil service and the special advisers, particularly the 'spin doctors' (see Draper, 1997). Within the first few weeks following the 1997 election, seven civil servants, including the Treasury's senior information officer, had left their posts; by the summer of 1998, a total of twenty-five Heads or Deputy Heads of Information had been replaced; and by August 1999 only two Directors of Communication who had been in position when Labour came to power were still in post (Public Administration Select Committee, 1998; Oborne, 1999). The friction extended beyond the world of the spin doctors. When the Treasury Permanent Secretary

---

***Box* 2.3 Special advisers and civil servants: rules of the game**

- The employment of Special Advisers adds a political dimension to the advice and support available to Ministers while reinforcing the political impartiality of the permanent civil service by distinguishing the source of political advice and support.
- Special Advisers are exempt from the requirement that civil servants should be appointed on merit and behave with political impartiality and objectivity. They are otherwise required to conduct themselves in accordance with the *Civil Service Code*.
- Special Advisers must not: ask civil servants to do anything inconsistent with the *Civil Service Code*; behave towards civil servants in a way inconsistent with the standards set by the employing department; have responsibility for budgets or external contracts; suppress or supplant the advice prepared for ministers by permanent civil servants (although they may comment on such advice); be involved in issues affecting a permanent civil servant's career such as recruitment, promotion, reward or discipline (with the exception of up to three posts in the Prime Minister's office).

Source: Extracted from *Code of Conduct for Special Advisers* (Cabinet Office, 2001a).

---

resigned in 1998, reports abounded that this was caused, at least in part, by the Chancellor's reliance on his team of special policy advisers, led by Ed Balls.

Debates continued around the question of the impact of special advisers on the civil service. At one point, the prime minister was asked by the Civil Service First Commissioner (who has oversight of the entire system of appointments) to limit the numbers of political appointments in Whitehall. An internal review in 1997 led by Robin Mountfield of the Cabinet Office examined the Government Information and Communication Service. Mountfield concluded that no damage had been done by the special advisers, and, in fact, the civil service should be prepared to learn lessons from the efficiency of the New Labour approach to media relations (Oborne, 1999). As a result, career civil servants and party appointees were brought together in Downing Street to work in a new Strategic Communications Unit.

A further investigation launched by the House of Commons Select Committee on Public Administration (1998) examined the role and responsibilities of the PM's official spokesman, Alistair Campbell. As noted above, at the start of the Blair administration a special Order in Council entitled up to three special advisers to give executive orders to career civil servants. In practice, only Campbell and the Downing Street Chief of Staff, Jonathan Powell, were so designated. This provision allowed them to breach the traditional division between 'politics' and 'administration' (Oborne, 1999). In the course of the Committee's inquiry, it became clear that Campbell had ordered social security ministers to seek advance clearance of their press communications with him (see Oborne, 1999: 156–57 for further details). Oborne saw the special advisers as a damaging influence, second-guessing and undermining the civil service from a constitutionally unorthodox position:

> The job of Cabinet ministers in Tony Blair's government is to do what they are told by Campbell, Miliband and one or two others at the heart of government . . . the fact that so much power is concentrated in the hands of a clique of unelected officials causes unease with many MPs and ministers. But that is one of the simple things which New Labour is all about: exercising power from the centre.

Indeed, in subsequent years, as Labour ministers started to publish their reflections on their time in government, it emerged that there had been a general requirement that media communications (even those emanating from Cabinet ministers) should be cleared by Campbell. Some ministers took this requirement more seriously than others – for the view of a sceptic, see David Blunkett's diaries (Blunkett, 2006). The Committee also looked into examples of negative briefings by some ministerial special advisers, particularly in the context of the political disputes between Gordon Brown and Tony Blair, which were often fought out through their respective spin doctors.

The Commons Public Administration Select Committee picked up these issues again in 2001, during its inquiry into the work of special advisers (Select Committee on Public Administration, 2001). The evidence submitted to the Committee during this inquiry revealed a variety of views about the impact of the special advisers on the civil service, ranging from those that expressed concerns about 'politicisation', to those arguing that political advisers served to insulate officials from political matters. The Committee concluded:

> All the available evidence suggests that special advisers can make a positive contribution to good government. In particular, they broaden the range of policy advice upon which ministers can draw. None of this need

be threatening to the traditional role of the civil service . . . However, we believe that it is time to put the position of special advisers on a firmer footing. This means recognising them as a distinct category; funding them in an appropriate way; appointing them on merit; and putting a proper framework of accountability around their activities. (Public Administration Committees, 2001: para. 81)

The saliency of this issue was illustrated when it was taken up for investigation by the Committee on Standards in Public Life (then chaired by Lord Neill). It offered a balanced view that sought to recognise the validity of the special adviser function while maintaining the traditional civil service role in policy advice, and curbing the activities of the more venomous spin doctors. Neill concluded that special advisers had not politicised the civil service, but recommended that some limits should be placed on their activities and their work should be governed by a *Code of Conduct* (Committee on Standards in Public Life, 2000). The *Code* was formalised shortly afterwards (see Cabinet Office, 2001a; and Box 2.3 above).

The content of the new *Code* was tested during the so-called Jo Moore affair in 2001–2 (see Jones and Weir, 2002; Public Administration Committee, 2002). This precipitated the resignations of a special adviser, a civil servant and a Cabinet minister. The series of events began on 11 September 2001, when Jo Moore, special adviser to Stephen Byers, the Secretary of State for Transport, Local Government and the Regions, advised colleagues to 'bury' some bad news by releasing media statements in the immediate aftermath of the terrorist attacks in the United States. When Moore's actions were revealed (via a leak from the Department), Byers resisted calls to sack his special adviser, although Moore was obliged to apologise publicly for her behaviour. This initial episode prompted further disclosures about the allegedly confrontational nature of Moore's dealings with civil servants, and, in February 2002 new allegations about the special adviser's conduct were leaked. This prompted an announcement that Moore and Martin Sixsmith, communications director at the Department (and, although a fairly recent recruit to the civil service, a 'permanent' official) would be resigning. Subsequently, Sixsmith denied that he had resigned, and raised questions about the Department's version of events. As a result, the Department's Permanent Secretary, Richard Mottram, released a public statement detailing the poor working relationships between Moore and the civil servants (see Ward, 2002). Mottram was damaged by the affair, but less so than his political boss Byers, who left the government in May 2002.

The Moore affair did not quite lance the boil, however, and debates continued about the behaviour of some special advisers, and the need for rules of a stronger legal character. The former Head of the Home Civil Service, Robert Armstrong (2002), summed up the new feeling even among traditionalists:

> Recent events have made it increasingly clear that the time has come to limit the number of special advisers, and to define with unmistakable clarity the duties and responsibilities that are proper to special advisers and those which are not, and their proper relationship with ministers and with civil servants. I have never been in favour of a Civil Service Act or of statute legislation to define and limit the responsibilities of special advisers . . . But I recognise that there are many people who think that codes of conduct are no longer sufficient.

The growing problem was illustrated during the period preceding the war in Iraq, as concerns were expressed about the management of the information on Saddam Hussein's weapons of mass destruction (as was noted on page 79 above). The Commons Public Administration Select Committee and the Committee on Standards in Public Life continued to monitor the issue (see Public Administration Committee, 2001, 2002, 2004a; Committee on Standards in Public Life, 2003) and the former tried to encourage the government to implement its pledge to introduce a Civil Service Act as a means of regularising managerial and ethical issues and preserving impartiality (Public Administration Committee, 2004b). Despite general statements of intent, the government has so far failed to introduce the legislation, partly because of mixed views within the senior civil service itself.

Conclusion

If this chapter had been written five or ten years ago it would probably have devoted a significant amount of space to the question of 'joined-up government' and its implications for the policy role of the civil service. However, the passage of time allows us to gain a certain perspective on one of the more modish concepts of the early period of the Blair administration. The concept figured significantly in the key *Modernising Government* White Paper (Cabinet Office, 1999a), and spawned a series of initiatives designed to ensure that officials worked in a coordinated fashion across the array of government departments, executive agencies and the myriad of cross-cutting units and offices that proliferated as the New Labour agendas spread across Whitehall (for some examples, see Chapter 4). However, as Page (2005: 139) points out, ' "Joined-up" has passed into the language of administrative change and reform as a good thing, but it is not the big thing that it was'. Page goes on to argue that joined-up government came to have less significance for the civil service than for the world of government beyond the centre. In part, the lack of relevance resulted from the fact that the policy work of the civil service largely takes place in a context of 'traditional conflicts, rivalries, and modes of behaviour' (Page, 2005: 148), stemming from the modus operandi of ministers and senior civil servants, and the organisational structure within which they function. In this context it would have taken a significant change in high political culture for an administratively-based initiative such as 'joined-up government' to have a major and lasting impact. In this respect, we can see how the perspective of those we described in Chapter 1 as gradualist modernisers, who place emphasis on the importance of organic, evolutionary change in the civil service, has a certain validity. The process, or processes, of modernisation bring in their wake multiple initiatives and reforms, not all of which have the lasting and complete significance that initially seemed probable. Put simply, some 'stick' to the fabric of government more firmly than others.

However, for adherents of the traditional Whitehall model of analysis, who perceive deep-rooted decline in the culture and fabric of the civil service, many of the themes of this chapter, particularly those that concern changes to the context of the policy work of officials, serve only to bring confirmation of their views. Campbell and Wilson (1995: 14–15) had seen three characteristics in combination as being unique to the Whitehall model: 'British bureaucrats at the most senior level constitute a *prestigious* profession expected to work with *equal enthusiasm* for any duly constituted government and enjoying a virtual *monopoly of advice* to it.' The last characteristic, at least, has disappeared. The impact of special advisers on the policy role of the civil service is seen by the 'civil service decline' theorists as evidence of fundamental change. O'Toole (2006: 45) argues that 'the civil service no longer exists in the sense that it existed only 25 years ago', and cites the impact of 'ethical decay' (as displayed in the Hutton and Butler reports), caused in no small measure by the work of special advisers, as a clear causal factor. He suggests that 'it should simply be publicly acknowledged that the policy advice role of the civil service has essentially been privatised, and that the really important ethical relationship at the centre of government is that between ministers and their special advisers' (2006: 45). Taking his argument on to its logical conclusion, O'Toole argues that the codes governing the work of civil servants should be reformulated to recognise that they have become 'managers' whose policy role effectively has gone.

This fairly apocalyptic view is countered by the evidence gathered by those who see Whitehall adjusting to new realities, absorbing changes, and retaining its essential purpose and function. The work of Page and Jenkins (2005: 117–21), for example, recognises the impact of the high-profile cases involving special advisers, and their research confirmed that special advisers in the Treasury had a particularly strong policy role when Brown was Chancellor. However, taking a broad view of Whitehall in the Blair era, they concluded that special advisers had a fairly limited impact 'as a direct source of instructions for policy bureaucrats' (2005: 121). The evidence uncovered by Page and Jenkins supports the view that civil servants were adapting to the challenge of working with, and sometimes through, special advisers, where this was appropriate, while recognising the distinctly political nature of the advisers' work in other contexts:

> Special advisers tended to have functions linked to the mobilisation and use of political authority – getting authorisation for a deal between departments, especially when there is a time pressure, 'beefing up' speeches or letters written for ministers by civil servants and high-profile contacts with the media. These overtly political roles were not necessarily in competition with civil service roles. Indeed it could be useful to have someone with political authority, albeit second hand, to be able to deal with issues when the minister was away or unavailable. (Page and Jenkins, 2005: 120)

In the next chapter we shall turn our attention to the impact of the increasingly complex structure of the UK polity on the work of the civil service.

3

Multilevel Mandarins and Complex Structures

The structure and organisation of the UK civil service has historically been interpreted in terms of the unitary principle. With the exception of the Northern Ireland Civil Service (NICS), which has a distinct organisational identity, officials employed by central government worked within a single structure, albeit one that contained sub-structural variations (including the executive agencies) with the potential for limited flexibilities in matters of pay and service conditions. The civil service was ultimately run from Whitehall, with the Permanent Head of the Home Civil Service as the clearly identifiable senior executive of the entire operation.

This structure matched the prevailing interpretation of the UK constitutional framework. The unitary state spawned a unified civil service. However, the impact of Britain's membership of the European Union (EU) and the consequences of devolution have transformed the traditional sovereign and unitary state. The purpose of this chapter is to explore the significance of these developments for the civil service. The broad meaning of the move from an apparently unitary state to a looser framework of multilevel governance will be examined before the challenges this move has posed to the unified civil service are assessed. Some of the specific developments that have flowed as consequences of devolution and membership of the EU will then be set out.

From the unitary state to multilevel governance

A key characteristic of a unitary state is the relative centralisation of the sources of governing power and authority. In the case of the United Kingdom, this can be illustrated clearly: the Westminster

Parliament produces the central executive, at the heart of which is located the Cabinet and the prime minister. The civil service, located within central government departments and their executive agencies, administers the policies produced at this level. In this form of unitary state the system of local government (staffed by officials who are not part of the civil service) exists effectively as the creature of the centre, and councils can be restructured, and in some cases merged or abolished, at the will of central government. Within this framework, allowance was made for some elements of sub-national and regional administration. In Scotland from 1885, in Wales from 1964, and in Northern Ireland from 1972, systems of devolved administration facilitated the implementation of central government policy with some distinctive features reflecting local traditions and requirements. Northern Ireland presented an anomaly in that this status followed fifty years of virtual autonomy (O'Neill, 2004: 43–4).

Devolved administration involved elements of decentralised policy-making and implementation, through the Scottish, Welsh and Northern Ireland Offices. These were departments of central government, staffed by civil servants who worked within the framework of the unified Home Civil Service. However, this arrangement did not allow for decentralised legislative power in Scotland and Wales; and in Northern Ireland, direct rule by the Westminster government was superimposed from 1972. Other types of regional administration could be seen in the sub-structures of certain central government departments (staffed by civil servants) and in the organisation of the National Health Service and the public utilities. None the less, taken as a whole, the system of government was based on the principle of the unitary state.

The traditional form of the unitary state in the UK was altered radically, within a relatively short period, to the point where it is now probably inappropriate, or at least misleading, to use the concept as a description of the system of government. In important respects it now makes more sense to discuss government, public administration and management in the UK in terms of multilevel governance. In simple terms, this refers to the existence of numerous locations of power and authority – various layers of decision-making and policy implementation. The relative simplicity, clarity and certainty associated with the unitary state have been replaced by complexity. In order to approach a full understanding of the modern civil service, we must now attempt to grasp the implications of additional levels of governmental power, including the EU and the devolved institutions in Scotland, Wales and Northern Ireland. Britain's accession to the European Economic

Community in 1973 heralded explicit recognition of the right of this supranational organisation to create law and policy affecting the citizens of the UK, and brought with it a series of consequences for the civil service. The first Blair Government's devolution programme saw the establishment of new governing institutions in Scotland, Wales and Northern Ireland in the late 1990s. These were granted powers that went far beyond existing arrangements for devolved administration, to encompass a much fuller form of devolved policy-making, and, in the case of Scotland, devolved legislative power. There were plans for bringing under the control of regional assemblies the Government Offices for the Regions set up by the Major Government, and Labour's Regional Development Agencies. Once again, there would be consequences for the civil service.

Multilevel governance implies complex policy-making, implementation and accountability relationships between these spheres of power and authority. Indeed, as we saw in Chapter 1, some analysts, such as Rhodes (1997) and Pierre and Stoker (2000) go further, to argue that multilevel governance involves a variety of state and societal actors at the levels of supra-national activity (including the EU and multinational business entities), central government, devolved government, local government and 'quasi-government'. Although it has been adopted by commentators and analysts as a useful concept that can aid our understanding of an increasingly complex political system, multilevel governance is in many respects a fairly loose idea. It carries a range of possible meanings. It is certainly clear that the complex interactions across institutions of government, and between these institutions and a plethora of non-governmental bodies, create special challenges for civil servants seeking to coordinate policy advice and implementation.

Pierre and Stoker (2000: 44–5) have identified some of the key political responses in the UK to what is now seen as a system of multilevel governance. For some, most typically the Liberal Democrats, multilevel governance is welcomed as a modern extension of federalism, to which the party has a traditional commitment. A federal UK (within a federal Europe) would have constitutionally-reserved areas of power and authority for the distinct levels of government and, presumably, a series of at least semi-autonomous civil services at each level, or a German-style system in which most administration (including that of national government) is carried out by regional authorities. In contrast, for many Conservatives, multilevel governance represents a threat to the cohesiveness and coherence of the UK. Hence their somewhat reluctant acceptance of devolution in Scotland, Wales and Northern Ireland, opposition to regional government for England and to any further extension of the powers of the European Union. Conservatives (and indeed some people from quite different political perspectives) identify potential problems with the steady drift of power away from the unitary state, including the emergence of overlapping and contradictory spheres of responsibility and the creation of new bureaucratic empires which would be even less susceptible to managerial reform than the traditional, Whitehall-based civil service. The spectre of another layer of local bureaucracy without even the merit of incorporating state regional bureaucracies was a factor in the failure of the 2004 referendum in north-east England. In London, on the other hand, public- and private-sector actors concurred in the need for a London-wide authority to pull together the organisations at all levels (borough, inter-borough, departmental, inter-departmental, voluntary sector, business sector) that had filled gaps left by the abolition of the Greater London Council (Travers *et al.*, 1991: 44–9, 90; Rao, 2006: 217).

A third approach, taken by the Labour government under Tony Blair, involves recognising the opportunities presented by multilevel governance, while seeking to manage or control some of its implications, partly through initiatives such as 'joined-up government', promoted in Blair's White Paper on the civil service, *Modernising Government* (Cabinet Office, 1999a). This strategy seeks to guide and coordinate the work of bodies and institutions involved in the creation and implementation of public policy, and has clear implications for modes of working in the civil service. Even in the case of the Greater London Authority, a mere local authority, its novel features meant that Whitehall found no precedents for conducting its central–local liaison (Greer and Sandford, 2006: 250). In the case of the more far-reaching devolution to Scotland and Wales, one of the dilemmas faced by those who adopt this type of approach towards multilevel governance concerns the extent to which they are prepared to surrender control over the broad strategic management of the civil service to the sub-elements of the new governing system (in Edinburgh, Cardiff and Belfast).

Let us now turn to a more specific examination of the challenge presented by multilevel governance to the tradition of the unified civil service.

The challenge to a unified civil service

As we saw in the Introduction, the historical development of the British civil service between the middle of the nineteenth century and the eve of the Second World War saw the gradual creation of a unified organisation based to a large extent on the blueprint of the Northcote–Trevelyan Report and moulded by Warren Fisher (see Hennessy, 1990: chs 1 and 2; Pyper, 1991: ch. 2; Theakston, 1999). The apogee of this unified structure was probably reached during the period between the 1940s and the 1970s. Thereafter, a number of developments challenged the organisational and structural integrity of the civil service, to the point where it was possible to discern a degree of fragmentation or Balkanisation. In particular, the process of agencification, initiated in a limited fashion by the Fulton Report, but then carried on to new levels by the Next Steps initiative, coupled with the introduction of a range of managerial 'flexibilities' in the realms of pay and recruitment, led some observers to question the very viability of the unitary civil service. Chapman (1997) took a highly critical view of the impact of these and other changes on the culture and ethos of the organisation, and wrote of 'the end' of the civil service. Other commentators were more sanguine, and followed the interpretation of the Head of the Civil Service, Richard Wilson (1999), who spoke of the effect of the structural and managerial changes of the 1980s and 1990s in terms of the creation of a more diverse, but still unified, civil service.

It might be argued that the fragmentation or diversification of state structures brought about by managerial reforms such as agencification was intensified by the creation of devolved administrations and the UK's accession to the EU. European negotiations increased the functional separation between departments as British civil servants in one department come to see their 'opposite numbers in other EU countries' (as Wilson called them in that same speech) as being closer to them than British colleagues in other departments. As shown in our discussion above, and in the sections of Chapter 1 on governance and hollowing-out, the British civil service has had to manage challenges coming from all directions to what was intended to be a relatively coherent and self-contained operating structure. The concept of centralised hierarchical control over policy conception and delivery (never really accurate in practice) has given way to an appreciation of the necessity of working within a much larger framework. On the one hand, government departments are now expected to deliver (or rather, ensure are delivered) their traditional responsibilities for public services but through a wide variety of agents, whether their own executive agencies and the private sector (as will be discussed in the following chapter), or through local government (see Leach and Percy-Smith,

2001, for a comprehensive treatment of 'local governance in Britain'). On the other hand, they have new or expanding policy-making relationships with other governmental bodies, both at 'lower' territorial levels (the devolved administrations) and at 'higher' territorial levels, namely with EU and international bodies.

Our concern for the remainder of this chapter is the specific impact of these latter elements of the emerging system of multilevel governance on the civil service.

The impact of devolution

The key documents setting out the Blair Government's programme for Scotland and Wales proposed plans for strengthened policy devolution and legislative devolution (primary legislative powers were to be conferred on the Scottish Parliament, secondary powers on the National Assembly for Wales), but they had relatively little to say about the civil service (Pyper, 1999). The White Papers (Scottish Office, 1997; Welsh Office, 1997) and the Acts of Parliament simply emphasised the point that officials working for the devolved bodies would continue to be employed within the Home Civil Service. Public and parliamentary debates during the period following the publication of the White Papers in the late summer of 1997, through the subsequent referendum campaigns, and the process of legislative scrutiny, shed little light on the implications of devolution for the civil service. Within government, some consideration was given to this issue. Officials working within the Scottish Office Constitution Group, the Welsh Office Devolution Unit and the Cabinet Office were concerned primarily with securing the production of the White Papers and bills, and the passage of the legislation. However, as time passed, consideration was given to the civil service dimension of devolution. Most attention was focused on the drafting of the 'concordats' that would set out the basic rules and structures for the new working arrangements between the departments of the Scottish Executive, the Welsh Administration and Whitehall departments. A Joint Ministerial Committee (JMC) was created to bring together officials, or ministers, for the same function (agriculture, health and so on) from the four governments to develop coordinated initiatives or resolve policy disagreements. However, the Lords' Constitution Committee (2002, para. 30) discovered that only the JMC on Europe met at all frequently, and that the JMC for Officials did not meet for three years.

Beyond this effort, a set of guidelines was developed on staff matters (Cabinet Office, 1998). In line with the prevailing tone of the other documentation, these guidelines placed great emphasis on continuity, and tried to reassure those civil servants who might have concerns about the career development implications of devolution. Officials working in Edinburgh and Cardiff would remain part of the unified Home Civil Service, and arrangements for appointments, pay and conditions of service would be fundamentally unchanged, albeit with some scope for appropriate minor variations to suit the requirements of the devolved administrations.

In brief, therefore, the broad underlying assumption was that devolution would have a limited impact on the civil service. While it was the dominant perspective in official and political circles during the formative phase of the devolution policy, the proposition that the creation of the new governing arrangements in Scotland and Wales would bring no changes of any significance for the civil service seemed distinctly improbable to analysts and observers. In practice, devolution affected the work of the civil service in four ways:

(1) *Organisational and structural changes.* The Scottish and Welsh Offices were reconfigured to facilitate the revised shape and structure of public policy that emerged from devolution and allow new working relationships to be forged with the new executive bodies, the elected Parliament and Assembly, and the institutions at Whitehall and Westminster. Parry and MacDougal (2005) contrasted the strategy of the Scottish Executive, which set out to maintain unity by appointing ministers for themes that crossed departments (Environment and Rural Development; Enterprise and Lifelong Learning, for example), with that of the Welsh Assembly Government, which adopted a structure of departments headed by ministers. Because the Welsh parliament and government were set up as one body, civil servants also supported Assembly members. The Assembly later agreed a de facto separation between the 'Welsh Assembly Government' and the 'Assembly Parliamentary Service', confirmed in the Government of Wales Act 2006. The Welsh Assembly Government reabsorbed the principal bodies of the Welsh 'quangocracy', such as the Welsh Development Agency, which had attracted animosity from the Welsh Labour Party because of its unaccountability to local people. In this as in other political strategies, Wales diverged from Scotland but also from Labour at Westminster.

(2) *Increased volume of work.* Devolution generated fresh demands for new policy initiatives from the public, organised interests of various kinds, and, of course, the elected representatives sitting in the Parliament and Assembly. It placed additional burdens on the civil servants working in Edinburgh and Cardiff, who had to provide their ministers with the policy advice necessary to enable them to respond to the rising expectations. Staff struggled with this task in addition to maintaining pre-devolution duties (Parry and MacDougal, 2005: 1). Units designed to support ministers who worked mainly in London now dealt with a larger number of ministers on site (Constitution Committee, 2002; para. 149). The Permanent Secretary of the Scottish Executive created what is in practice a prime minister's office. Its Strategy Unit, Delivery Unit and Performance and Innovation Unit mirror the set-up at No. 10. In Wales, policy-making capacity is weaker. Reasons for incorporating the quangos were said to include 'creating a critical mass' and providing career paths to retain civil servants in Wales, but, meanwhile, the new recruits had to be integrated. Civil servants were then faced with implementing the 2006 Act, which gave the Welsh Assembly greater powers.

(3) *Different nature and type of work.* For senior officials in Edinburgh and Cardiff, devolution brought a new set of challenges. Having previously worked as fairly conventional departmental civil servants (albeit within the framework of territorial ministries) for a Secretary of State and a small ministerial team, they now had to function as an effective 'Prime Ministerial and Cabinet Office', to support a First Minister and a Cabinet. A new set of strategic and coordination skills were required in order to give life to these new roles, made extra-challenging by the novelty of coalition governments. In Scotland, the top priority was to place the Executive 'at the centre of Scottish life', whereas in Wales the main problem seemed to be that of improving officials' programme management and leadership skills. There was a greater emphasis in Wales on collaborating with service users, partly reflecting a greater commitment to broader societal aims (Parry and MacDougal, 2005: 1–4), and partly because of the need to overcome weak administrative capacity by making use of local government resources and expertise (Jeffery, 2006: 141)

(4) *Increased scrutiny and volume of accountability.* Before devolution, it could be argued that the demands of parliamentary accountability for civil servants in the Scottish and Welsh Offices

were fairly remote. The need to prepare their ministers for oral questions in the House of Commons came round only once a month, their territorial departments were subject to relatively few investigations by the Public Accounts Committee, and the Parliamentary Commissioner for Administration was called upon only rarely to investigate cases of alleged maladministration in Edinburgh and Cardiff. Furthermore, while the Scottish Office and the Welsh Office each faced scrutiny by a dedicated House of Commons select committee, these committees faced a daunting task. The multifunctional, territorial nature of these departments of state meant that specific policy spheres attracted relatively less scrutiny than was the case in the typical, single-function Whitehall departments. Devolution brought a significant change and increased the sheer volume of scrutiny imposed on the civil service (Kirkpatrick and Pyper, 2001). More regular ministerial questioning (which in turn brought the need for more background preparatory work by officials), increased the number of debates, and, crucially, in the Scottish case an array of committees that combined the functions of standing and select committees as agents of legislative and policy scrutiny. In the case of Wales, there was a growth in scrutiny and accountability through informal mechanisms, including a large role for voluntary sector and smaller interest groups (McMillan and Massey, 2004: 242)

If Scotland and Wales are providing evidence for the 'differentiated polity model' (Rhodes, 1997: 7; and see Chapter 1 of this volume), the civil service in Northern Ireland shows signs of becoming less differentiated from the other British civil service(s). The NICS is the 'lineal descendant' of the Irish Civil Service and has remained separate from the Home Civil Service since partition in 1921, though its Civil Service Commission is a reserve power of the Crown (Constitution Committee, 2002; para. 150), and its grading structures and organisational reforms 'have tended to replicate those obtaining in Great Britain' (Carmichael, 2002: 26; and see Hyndman and Eden, 2001). NICS deserves more than the 'footnote' status it is sometimes given, as Carmichael argues (2002: 23), yet to deal correctly with NICS would require another book (see Loughlin, 1992; McConnell, 2000; Carmichael, 2002). However, a brief analysis under the same headings as above shows something of the way in which Direct Rule in 1972 brought NICS closer to the Home Civil Service in its administrative roles and procedures, before 'devolution-plus' in 1999 brought changes to its dealings with elected politicians.

(1) *Organisational and structural changes.* Before 1972, the NICS staffed the Northern Ireland Departments (NIDs), administering devolved matters and supporting the Northern Ireland prime minister. 'Reserved' matters were (and are) dealt with by the Home Civil Service under UK ministers, including in tax and other offices in Northern Ireland (over 6,000 people in 2005).

At the start of Direct Rule, the UK government set up the Northern Ireland Office (NIO) in Belfast and London. Although the principal posts were staffed by 'Whitehall' civil servants and diplomats, other posts in Belfast were staffed by NICS officials on secondment (Hennessy, 1990: 470; Constitution Committee 2002, para. 153). Many local government services were transferred to the NIDs. The Head of NICS was made Second Permanent Secretary under the NIO's Permanent Secretary, but even those concerned were divided over whether this title was merely a courtesy, and whether the NIDs thereby became part of central government (Carmichael, 2002: 28, 44). 'Administrative modernisation' reforms like those in Great Britain were adopted (see Chapter 4), such as the Financial Management Initiative and executive agencies.

Devolution-plus in 1999 divided the six NIDs into ten, added the Office of the First Minister and Deputy First Minister, and new N–S and E–W coordinating committees, which altogether 'owe little to administrative efficiency and much to political expediency' (Carmichael, 2002: 46). The NICS provided the administration under Assembly ministers. The head of NICS left NIO: the two bodies were now working for different governments. It was thought that ministers would reabsorb quangos and executive agencies (Carmichael, 2002: 44–5), but there was little opportunity to test that thesis. In 2002, the Assembly was suspended and the ten NIDS came under the direction of UK ministers.

(2) *Increased volume of work.* Under Direct Rule the NIO took over the briefing of the political executive. NICS staff were given additional 'local government' responsibilities, but they were joined by 2,500 former local government officials (Carmichael, 2002: 36), and executive work was delegated to area boards.

In contrast, devolution-plus led to a large expansion of business for the NICS, including support for twelve ministers in complex coalition arrangements. The Office of the First Minister and Deputy First Minister had 400 officials by 2002, for reasons that remained unclear (Constitution Unit, 2002: 5). The NICS had learnt new techniques from NIO officials during Direct Rule, such as how to present a coordinated Northern Ireland position to Whitehall or the EU (Hennessy, 1990: 472). Partition in 1921 meant that NICS did not participate in the unifying process led by the Treasury from 1919 (described in the Introduction). Post-suspension, the legislative initiative was again driven by UK ministers, and therefore the NIO.

(3) *Different nature and type of work.* During Direct Rule, the NIDs received little input from UK ministers concerned with the conflict. NICS officials had more overt power on policy decisions than under the earlier regime; they lost anonymity (Carmichael, 2002: 3). NICS had a high capacity for making and implementing policy but did not have 'to develop skills in dealing with politicians' (Osborne, 2002: 297). The NIDs and Whitehall departments gradually overcame initial tensions – some more than others. The Head of the NICS set up a Policy Coordinating Committee to advise ministers on adapting UK legislation in Northern Ireland; in 1997, it became a 'Civil Service Management Board', like its Whitehall equivalent (Carmichael, 2002: 31–3).

With devolution, the NICS expected to support the four political parties and revert to anonymity, but in 2002 they were again working under UK ministers.

(4) *Increased scrutiny and volume of accountability.* Under Direct Rule, legislation on Northern Ireland took the form of Orders in Council: policies were locally-differentiated, but without local input (O'Neill, 2004: 44). The NICS tended to present policies as being technical, outside the political domain, to remove ideological conflict, producing what some term a 'technocracising of politics' (Carmichael, 2002: 33).

In the devolution-plus arrangements, NICS staff came under pressure, because the assembly committees not only shadowed departments, but could also ask for help on policy development and legislation (Carmichael, 2002: 43). Senior officials were criticised by the Assembly when they seemed to be trying to introduce Westminster conventions, limiting the issues that could be discussed (Osborne, 2002: 297). However, the few critical committee reports were undermined by members voting on party lines (Wilford, 2004: 150–1). After suspension, the NIO again used Orders to introduce public sector reforms similar to those in Great Britain.

In Northern Ireland, therefore, Direct Rule seems to have led to some harmonisation of the NICS with the Home Civil Service in working methods and internal organisational structures. The NICS did not demand integration into the Home Civil Service; rather, it was preparing to service a devolved government in a context of party conflict of which Whitehall had little experience. Suspension then brought NICS staff more closely under the control of UK ministers, which may give rise to further harmonisation, but 'the NICS functions as it does because the way government works in Northern Ireland is different from that obtaining in other parts of the UK' (Constitution Committee, 2002: para. 167).

In Scotland and Wales too, the established principles of the UK civil service have not so far been called into question, if only because they have not imposed constraints on 'what the administrations have been trying to do' (Parry and MacDougal, 2005: 1). Ministers in devolved administrations are able to appoint political special advisers and have their say on senior appointments and secondments. However, in both Scotland and Wales, but more intensively in Wales, there have been discussions on whether the civil service should be allied more closely with other public services, at least through a freedom of movement between the sectors that falls short of creating a unitary public service, as exists in some smaller European countries. This concept seems have to found greater resistance in Scotland, with civil service trade unions raising the problem of pay and grading differentials, and others worrying about a separation from the rest of the civil service in 'Whitehall' and indeed from civil servants in Scotland dealing with 'non-devolved' domains (Parry and MacDougal, 2005: 7). The Welsh Assembly is more overtly engaged in a form of governance, implementing policy through a wider range of public and voluntary sector actors, perhaps because the Welsh Office lacked operational capacity. However, if, as Jeffery implies (2006: 141), the Assembly is influenced by 'old Labour' and public-sector union interests, the outcome will not be sufficiently pluralist to count as 'governance'.

The tasks of the 'civil services' working for the devolved governments seem to have diverged gently since devolution, whether we consider the organisational and structural changes they have had to implement, the increased volume of demands placed on them, and potentially in the different roles they may play in relation to service users and other public-sector workers. These signs of divergence raise some doubts about how 'unified' across departments the civil service of Great Britain ever was. Top officials stressed to the House of Lords the value of the unified service for enabling officials to move between departments to widen their expertise; but only twenty-two officials from the devolved administrations were working in a central department other than the Scotland or Wales Offices; and even fewer from UK departments have worked in the devolved administrations (Constitution Committee, 2002; para. 159). The Richard Commission (2004; Summary Report: 6) found that the Welsh Assembly Government felt itself to be 'the junior partner in the relationship' with Whitehall departments. Parry and MacDougal gained the impression that Whitehall was uninterested in the experience of devolution: 'Scotland and Wales with their local politics are mentally marginalised as long as they do not cause trouble' (2005: 8).

As with Northern Ireland, the impact of devolution in Scotland and Wales is conditioned by the past. McMillan and Massey (2004: 238–9) argue that devolution changed very little for the civil service in Scotland; it 'formalised a situation in territorial politics that was already well developed'. The bureaucracy in the Scottish Office had long been a powerful professional group in the Scottish polity, with its roots, education and experience in Scotland, even if postings to Whitehall were useful stages in a high-flyer's career. McMillan and Massey suggest that the desire of senior officials in the Scottish Office to preserve their power base brought cooperation with ministers because the transition had to be seen to go smoothly, but this successful transition might in future be succeeded by politicisation once the authoritative position of officials is challenged by the growing expertise of ministers.

In contrast, in Wales, the earlier and closer integration with England had led to the civil service in Wales being the part of the Home Civil Service that served Wales, with no strong identity as a distinct Welsh service (McMillan and Massey, 2004: 240–2). Then, because the Welsh Assembly was a single corporate body, Welsh Office staff became the advisers of the Assembly (rather than exclusively of the executive authority). A civil service that was not seen as the service of Wales had to work for Assembly members keen to achieve the degree of devolution Scotland had been given, and in the context of highly complex interpretations of the Assembly's legal powers. The Labour–Liberal Democrat coalition in the Welsh Assembly's first term said it would 'seek to move towards an increasingly independent and Welsh-based civil service' (McMillan and Massey, 2004: 242). The Welsh Assembly Government seems readier to 'distance itself from Whitehall, leading to more fundamental departures in terms of civil service roles and processes' (Parry and MacDougal, 2005: 1). For the moment, however, devolution to Scotland and Wales, intermittent devolution to Northern Ireland, and the wide reluctance to introduce English regions, seem to have revealed existing differentials within a more or less unified British civil service, but not to have brought noteworthy changes to the management and accountability of officials.

The European and international dimension

Devolution to Britain's sub-nations was a radical break from the unitary state even if there was already distinctiveness between these areas in their public administration. In the same way, Britain's entry into the European Union (EU) in 1973 was undoubtedly a turning point, yet it continued a long history of interaction at international level.

Intergovernmental cooperation: an international civil service

The growth of intergovernmental bodies seems to parallel that of the British civil service. A few were created at about the same time as the 'Northcote–Trevelyan' report, including the still very active International Telecommunications Union (ITU), set up in Geneva in 1865, and which Britain joined in 1871. Peace negotiations after the First World War led to the creation of more international organisations, notably the League of Nations. The league proved inadequate for promoting peace, and was replaced by the United Nations (UN) after the Second World War. Other new bodies were created. The International Maritime Organisation (IMO), established in London in 1948, consolidated an earlier arrangement in which the British and Belgian governments acted as hosts for intergovernmental conferences. Negotiations in Brussels between five European nations, including Britain, were sealed in 1949 in the North Atlantic Treaty Organisation (NATO). The Organisation for Economic Co-operation and Development (OECD), based in Paris, is a more global version of the Organization for European Economic Cooperation, which had coordinated the spending of American aid to European states. It has specialist bodies that involve ministers and officials from member countries, such as the Working Group that developed and monitors the OECD Anti-Bribery Convention of 1997. A final example is the European Free Trade Area (EFTA), created in 1960 at Britain's instigation, which linked countries who wanted the benefits of a trading zone but not the 'European project' that underpinned the European Economic Community (EEC) formed in 1957.

Intergovernmental organisations turn British civil servants into 'multilevel mandarins', whether at home or abroad. Each organisation has its 'sponsor' UK department, coordinating British policy inputs and resources: the ITU has the Office of Telecommunications; the IMO the maritime section of the Department for Transport (DfT); and the UN the Foreign and Commonwealth Office (FCO). Officials bring other policy actors into this activity when preparing the British case. For example, when an IMO panel examined the safety of 'roll-on, roll-off' ferries in the mid-1990s, DfT panel members were advised by a 'shadow panel' from the Chamber of Shipping, ferry operators, the Consumers' Association and trade unions.

Civil servants are also sent abroad to staff the organisations. States compete for the higher posts in agencies for their nationals. Montin (2000: 300) argues that governments like a return on their 'investment', and that because the benefits (policy change, information and so on) are hard to measure, they focus instead on the distribution of posts (see Page, 1997: 40–68, on 'The nationality problem in the EU'). For example, the MoD nominates Whitehall officials for the directorships of NATO agencies and seconds staff as 'detached national experts' or 'national contributions' to other posts. The FCO organises the second-ment of civil servants to the UN; it paid for the MoD's Dr David Kelly to work as a UN weapons inspector; the expertise he gained on Iraq was then used by the FCO and MoD (Hutton, 2004; para. 17). In the UN, there is 'a "sort of osmosis" between national diplomatic services and the UN Secretariat' (Montin, 2000: 302).

The Whitehall official 'parachuted' into an agency becomes part of an 'international civil service' in that the larger organisations have similar rules on recruitment and pay (Montin, 2000: 308–9). Organisa-tions tend to adopt the characteristics of the civil services of the dom-inant founding members (Montin, 2000: 301); thus the administrative techniques of the League of Nations were French and British: its first Secretary-General, Eric Drummond, came from being principal pri-vate secretary to the British foreign minister; his deputy was Jean Monnet, a French civil servant working in London, and later the founder of the EC institutions (see Page, 1997: 4, 18). Long-serving officials may identify with the multicultural approach of their employer, yet they still 'tend to try to convince colleagues that their outlook is more efficient or more acceptable than others' (Montin, 2000: 299–300).

These relationships between states are conventionally referred to as 'intergovernmental', in which 'nation states, in situations and conditions that they can control, cooperate with one another on matters of com-mon interest. The existence of control, which allows all participating states to decide the extent and nature of this cooperation, means that national sovereignty is not undermined' (Nugent, 2003: 475). This definition is used to draw contrasts with 'supranational' arrangements, in which individual states can be over-ruled: 'That is, states may be obliged to do things against their preferences and their will because they do not have the power to stop decisions. Supranationalism thus takes inter-state relations beyond cooperation into integration, and involves some loss of national sovereignty' (Nugent, 2003: 475). These concepts are used in interpreting the development and impact of the EU (see Nugent, 2003: 463–93; George and Bache, 2001; or Nelson and Stubb, 2003). There is some overlap between the categories; notably, in NATO assigned national forces come under the command of the Supreme Allied Commander in Europe in time of war. Wallace and Wallace (2000: 33–4) use the term 'transgovernmental' for such 'strong' and lasting relationships that operate without a powerful set of central organisations.

Intergovernmental relationships do not conflict with the 'Whitehall–Westminster' model. The principles describing the role of civil servants ('officials advise, ministers decide'), and the sovereignty of Parliament (ministers accountable for their decisions, which Parliament can reject or replace) are unharmed. If agreements are made 'at the level of officials', the civil servant acts within a framework of instructions from higher officials and the minister, and the agreement can still be rejected at the political level. For example, an 'official-level' meeting of NATO agreed to embark on an uncontroversial research project through a 'memorandum of understanding', which was approved by the UK Parliament as a 'negative procedure Order' (a decision by one of the Houses to vote against would have annulled it), but the Netherlands' Cabinet reduced its budget. For the same reason, intergovernmental organisations are weak. The OECD *Convention on Combating Bribery of Foreign Officials* was signed in 1997 by the UK, though the government did not enact appropriate legislation until 2001 (OECD, 2006; para. 10). The UN *Convention on Corruption* of 2003 was ratified by the UK in February 2006. Yet there was little the OECD or UN could do but complain when Tony Blair and his Attorney-General announced on 14 December 2006 that the Serious Fraud Office would discontinue its investigations of allegations that a British company had bribed foreign officials (*Economist*, 2006).

For these reasons, the intergovernmental character of the League of Nations was thought to have been its crucial handicap (George and

Bache, 2001: 6, 46–7). On the other hand, many technical intergovernmental bodies, such as the ITU, have made headway. This contrast led 'functionalist' theorists such as Mitrany, and practical planners such as Monnet, to argue that the way to overcome national rivalries was not to devise ambitious federal schemes but to set up intergovernmental agencies for technical 'functions'. As their activities expanded and overlapped, enmeshing them in a multilevel network, not only would governments not be able to take independent aggressive action, but also the interactions would socialise politicians, civil servants and other actors into a less nationalist outlook (Mitrany, 1943 and 1966, reprinted in Nelson and Stubbs, 2003: 99–119). After the early post-war failure of European federalist ideas, six states in 1951 were willing to adopt Monnet's 'functional' scheme for the European Coal and Steel Community (ECSC), which led eventually to the EU.

Negotiating membership of a supranational Europe

The ECSC brought the coal and steel industries of six states under a quasi-autonomous bureaucracy (the 'High Authority'), with a Council of Ministers (one minister from each state) and a parliamentary Assembly to provide some political control, and a Court of Justice to rule on disputes. These four institutions set the pattern for the current EU arrangements (see Figure 3.1). In 1957, two more Communities were launched: the EEC and the European Atomic Energy Community (Euratom). They had their own bureaucracies (Commissions) and Councils of Ministers, but the Assembly (which became the European Parliament) and the Court of Justice integrated the new functions. In 1965, the six states merged the three European Communities (EC), creating a single European Commission, and one Council of Ministers (although different ministers attend meetings, depending on the sector under discussion). The Treaty on European Union signed at Maastricht in 1992 added further functions (the single currency, foreign and security policy, immigration and asylum). However, whereas decision-making on 'EC' functions is now mainly supranational in character (member states can be outvoted), the newer functions have procedures that are intergovernmental (every state has a veto), or even 'transgovernmental', because the states have not given much (or any) power to the Commission on these issues.

Britain did not join the ECSC in 1951. Its governments had recently nationalised British coal, were optimistic about Britain's position in the world, and preferred intergovernmental solutions and traditional partners. They accepted the 'three-circle theory' promoted

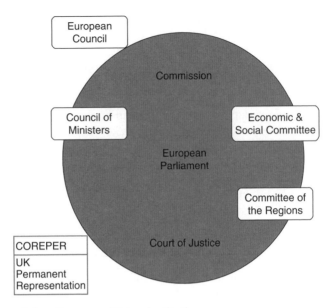

Figure 3.1   European Union institutions

Note: The Commission, Parliament and Court of Justice are *supranational-level* institutions, whose role is to develop policies from an EU-wide perspective. The UK Permanent Representation of civil servants (UK Perm Rep or UKRep), and its counterparts from other EU states, who meet in the Committee of Permanent Representatives (COREPER), are *national-level institutions*, helping national ministers adjust EU-level proposals to national goals. The 'half-in, half-out' bodies (Council of Ministers, Economic and Social Committee, Committee of the Regions) *mediate between supranational and national levels*: they amend the EU level's proposals in the name of national government, business, trade union, social or local interests, although only the Council of Ministers has decision-making power. The European Council (the 'summit meetings' of president or prime minister of each member state) decides the most politically important issues, in each country's *national* interest.

by the Foreign Office (FO) that Britain maximised its power through maintaining equal relationships with Europe, the Commonwealth and the USA. Civil servants from the Board of Trade participated briefly in the preparations for the EEC but left when it became clear that it would be more than a free trade area. However, UK departments maintained contact. It is typical of the current ways of working with the EU (see below) that the same official who dealt with iron and steel in the Ministry of Power was sent to meetings on iron and steel at the ECSC in Luxembourg, the OECD in Paris and the EEC in Brussels, where Britain had 'observer' status (Le Cheminant, 2001: 65, 69).

The limited intervention of the FO in the 1950s seems surprising by comparison with its modern role in Brussels. However, the 'diplomatic service' is both separate from the Home Civil Service and historically reluctant to engage in 'trade' (Hennessy, 1990: 79). The separateness dates back to 1782, when the prime minister split what was then a double-headed Office of the Principal Secretary of State into home and foreign divisions because two ministers could not work together (Hennessy, 1990: 28). FO officials were (and are) recruited separately from other civil servants; and are selected traditionally for social background and personality as much as intellectual skills. Even in 2006 only 16 per cent of the Foreign Office's senior civil servants (see Chapter 6), were women, compared with 30 per cent for the Home Civil Service. The diplomats resisted efforts by 'modernisers', such as Trevelyan, Gladstone or Warren Fisher, Head of the Civil Service 1919–39, to control FO appointments (Hennessy, 1990: 48, 78–80). Officials were divided into classes: the Foreign and Diplomatic Services were not amalgamated until 1919; and the overseas commercial and consular services integrated into the FO only in the 1940s. Though a number of official reports have proposed mergers with the Home Civil Service (which provides the diplomats' administrative officers and assistants), the Diplomatic Service remains separate, in part because its conditions of service (frequent postings abroad, sometimes in difficult physical conditions), and tasks (working with administrators from other cultures and developing a wide range of personal contacts) are different.

In 1960, Prime Minister Harold Macmillan decided to seek membership of the EEC, despite a pessimistic prognosis from the FO (Heath, 1998: 204). Edward Heath, as junior foreign minister, was placed in charge, and asked the Cabinet Secretary to choose a multilingual negotiating team (Heath, 1998: 212). The team included the ambassador to Paris, officials from the Treasury, Board of Trade, and Foreign and Commonwealth Office officials. Of the four diplomats, two were economists, one was heading the Ministry of Agriculture, and another had been deputy to Monnet in the Anglo-French Coordination Committee of the wartime Cabinet Office. The Cabinet Secretary was, unusually, also Treasury Permanent Secretary, and Treasury committees coordinated the EEC application, probably because the Treasury was Whitehall's coordinator of economic issues (Bulmer and Burch, 1998: 608). The ECSC team was led by Ministry of Power officials in London and Luxembourg (Le Cheminant, 2001: 73). The FO led the negotiations in Brussels, though (correctly) sceptical about the outcome: discussions were terminated by the French president in 1963.

Harold Wilson's Government announced in 1966 that it would make a new application. This time central coordination was supplied by a European unit in the Cabinet Office which still has this role. A junior foreign minister led officials from the FO, Treasury, Ministry of Agriculture, Board of Trade and Customs & Excise (Bulmer and Burch, 1998: 609–10). After another veto by the French president, some ministries continued to keep in contact; the same official from the Ministry of Power (DTI from 1970) represented the UK on oil policy at the EC and the OECD (Le Cheminant, 2001: 120).

When Heath became prime minister in 1970 he restarted the application process. He rejected the strategy proposed by some FCO officials of working with the other states to isolate the French government (Heath, 1998: 364). A Cabinet Office minister coordinated the UK effort 'in an attempt to prevent Whitehall rivalries and tensions scuppering the application' (the diplomat Stephen Wall, quoted in Geddes, 2004: 71). By 1970, the potential impact of EC policies had increased considerably. The DTI 'oil' official was now in its 'regional development' division, and worked with the Cabinet Office and his EC 'counterparts' to institute a European Regional Development Fund to balance the losses some UK regions would incur from the EC's agriculture and fishing policies; the FCO complained about his efforts (Le Cheminant, 2001: 124, 131–2).

Britain has now been a member of the EU for decades. What part are British civil servants currently playing in this multilevel policy-making? What impact has membership of the EU had on departmental organisation, civil servants and the civil service as a whole?

Policy-making between national and supranational levels

Although many British newspapers give the impression that the EU is run by 'Brussels bureaucrats', EU legislation is negotiated by national civil servants and ministers, and implemented by national ministries with very little oversight from Brussels (see Burnham and Maor, 1995). The Commission formally proposes draft legislation but uses hundreds of committees to determine its details and monitor implementation (see Figure 3.2). Committee members are nearly all national officials, nominated by their governments. Though not officially representing their states, they give the Commission some idea of likely objections if modifications are not made, thereby pushing the proposal towards incorporating national points of view (Nugent, 2003: 131–40).

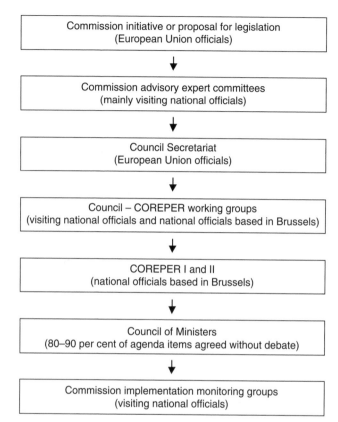

Figure 3.2   The role of national officials in EC policy-making
Note: COREPER is the Committee of Permanent Representatives (see text).
The policy processes of the European Union (EU) vary, depending on which
Treaty governs the particular policy area. This diagram represents the basic
'Community' policy-making process. It does not apply to foreign policy or
monetary policy (the euro).

The amended proposal then goes to the Council Secretariat, which
administers the meetings of the Council of Ministers (the General
Affairs Council, Council of Agriculture and Fisheries Ministers and
so on). Its standing committees of national officials prepare the grand
themes (international trade, economy and finance, foreign policy),
while specific proposals for decision are discussed in working groups,
of which there were about 250 in 2006. Each group has two or three
officials from each state. The UK team will have one or two from the
Whitehall department or devolved administrations responsible for

that policy sector, and one from the UK's Permanent Representation in Brussels. 'UKRep' has about 40 officials from the FCO, other departments and the devolved administrations, and its Permanent Representative is always a senior diplomat, experienced in European affairs. UKRep officials serve in Brussels for about three years. Thus EU legislation is thoroughly examined by British civil servants, working within a framework of instructions from ministers.

Once the working party has agreed a text (noting any conflicts that have still to be resolved), the document is discussed by the Committee of Permanent Representatives (COREPER). COREPER meets either as COREPER II the Permanent Representatives of each state) to deal with politically-sensitive issues, or COREPER I (Deputy Permanent Representatives) for uncontroversial or technical subjects. Agriculture, which has more business than other subjects, has a special committee of officials from the capitals and from the Permanent Representations. The decision-preparing process operates on 'efficient' principles similar to the UK Cabinet committee system. If the working party agrees a text acceptable to all home governments, it will be approved without debate by COREPER, and then by the Council of Ministers. If there are outstanding issues, COREPER will try to resolve them. When the Council of Ministers meets, it can use its limited time for dossiers with unresolved conflicts (Nugent, 2003: 165). Dossiers of high political importance (such as fish quotas), or on issues ministers have personally debated in international negotiations (such as climate change) are always dealt with by the politicians (Bostock, 2002: 231).

British officials follow Whitehall norms in briefing ministers to defend the UK position and be aware of problems that might arise from accepting another state's suggestions. The European Secretariat in the Cabinet Office is formally responsible for coordinating the UK position on topics that cross departments and devolved governments. It tries to influence Commission proposals even before they are issued by agreeing an early inter-departmental negotiating line which it pursues through its contacts in the Commission (Lee *et al.*, 1998: 176–80). The Joint Ministerial Committee bringing together the UK and devolved government ministers on Europe meets to decide 'the UK line' before important meetings; agricultural business was routinely coordinated in this way even before devolution (Constitution Committee, 2002, paras 30–7; Jeffery, 2006: 156). Bulmer and Burch (2000: 56) sum up the British approach as having adapted to the EU process within the Whitehall logic by preparing a coordinated presentation of the UK position. Yet in legislation linked to the Single

Market (the EEC), decisions are made by majority vote, putting Britain at a disadvantage if it has remained outside the very difficult alliance-building logic of the EU.

Other actors are involved, such as the interest groups consulted by the Commission, and especially the European Parliament (EP). The Maastricht and Amsterdam Treaties gave the EP equal legislative powers ('co-decision') with the Council of Ministers in many policy areas. David Bostock, a highly-regarded Deputy Permanent Representative from the Treasury (Ludlow, 1998: 575), describes how co-decision-making can put to the test the principle that ministers decide (2002: 218–25). In the co-decision procedure, COREPER officials may not have time to consult home governments. If either the Council of Ministers or the EP will accept a proposed bill only if it contains their own amendments, a Conciliation Committee of equal numbers from the EP and COREPER (representing the Council) has just six weeks to prepare a text mutually acceptable to EP parties and a Council representing twenty-seven countries (by a special majority vote), or the legislation fails. COREPER officials would still be operating within national instructions. Nevertheless, they are making last-minute, complex bargains, balancing the interests of each country with what they think the EP will accept, if all the previous work is not to be lost. 'If all EU negotiation is a dark mystery, legislative co-decision is a blacker shade of black' (Bostock 2002: 221). COREPER is at such times practising the 'Community method' associated with the federalist ideal (Lewis, 1998: 486–7), even if from a functionalist perspective it is an 'intergovernmental bargaining table', like the Councils of Ministers it advises.

Organising for EU policy-making

Heath's view was that departments should 'think and act European', integrating the European factor into their work, and organising themselves appropriately. Cross-departmental coordination would be a relatively limited affair in the Cabinet Office (Bulmer and Burch, 2000: 52).

Until the mid-1980s, the core 'European' ministries were Agriculture, the DTI and the FCO and, at the centre, the European Secretariat, the Treasury Solicitor's Office (for legal advice), and the Prime Minister's Office. Other departments were drawn in as the Single Market developed (see Stevens, 2004, on transport). In the mid-1990s, the Minister for Agriculture observed that '80 per cent of what [he] spent was decided round the table in Brussels', while the 'trade' side of the DTI and half the 'environment' side of the Department for the Environment were negotiating or implementing EU legislation (Burnham and Maor, 1995: 187). The Ministry of Agriculture had no special EU unit, 'since all parts of the department have to take European considerations into account in formulating policy' (Maor and Stevens, 1997: 539). The DfT was more typical in having a European unit for specifically EU topics, such as Trans-European Networks, but left to policy divisions, such as shipping, the EU aspects of those areas. The Department of Health (DH), put 'Europe' in its international division.

The Scottish Office (SO) was reorganised for Europe by its Secretary of State in 1991. A Unit in the SO's Industry Department coordinated European issues within the SO and with the European Secretariat's network and UKRep (Bulmer and Burch, 1998: 616). Scottish ministers have sometimes represented the UK in Councils of Ministers both before and after devolution, especially where Scotland's interests are paramount (such as Fisheries Councils). In 2004–05, Ministers from the Scottish Executive attended seven Agricultural and Fisheries Councils and four other Councils in other devolved matters (education, justice, transport). Yet, as James Smith (2001: 149) points out, Scottish ministers attend Councils by permission of the UK minister and must adhere to the UK line (paradoxically, Scottish ministers at the Fisheries and Transport Councils were Liberal Democrats). Officials from the devolved administrations participate in Council working parties and in preparing the 'UK line' but may not reveal any 'intra-UK' disagreements, even to their own Parliaments (Constitution Committee, 2002, para. 172). In Brussels, Scotland's EU Office is dependent on UKRep for diplomatic status and thereby access to EU papers, an important instrument when 'the Scottish Executive estimate that 80% of their business "has a strong EU dimension" ' (Constitution Committee, 2002, para. 170). Most sub-national authorities try to influence the Commission, but Scotland's legislative powers give it more credibility than most when it discusses with EU officials the practicalities of multilevel governance (regulation, subsidiarity, implementation).

The UK government's Welsh and Northern Ireland Offices were 'less purposeful' than the Scottish Office in their responses to the EU (Bulmer and Burch, 1998: 616). The Welsh Assembly and the Northern Ireland Executive are now following Scotland's example with offices in Brussels and seconding civil servants to UKRep, but they have a more limited Brussels presence. To complete the 'territorial picture': the Government Offices for the [English] Regions were created in part to improve the programming of European development aid – though they were also an 'anticipated reaction' to Labour and Liberal Democrat electoral manifestos in 1992 and 1997.

'Organisationally, the Treasury itself has embraced European integration less than have other key departments' and takes less notice of European than international institutions, such as the City and the IMF (Bulmer and Burch, 2005: 881; and see Dyson, 2000). The Treasury treats core EU work in a 'European' unit of its 'overseas' division (where it undoubtedly takes second place to the international institutions); and 'farms out' other EU issues to the relevant policy division; for example, the Common Agricultural Policy goes to the division dealing with the UK agriculture budget (Pickering, 2002: 587–90). While Pickering provides substantial evidence to show that the Treasury is interested in (if not positive about) Europe, he concedes that the Treasury could do more to 'pull together' its various European interests (budgetary issues, tax and financial services) and see them in the wider context of the UK's European relations (2002: 584, 598).

Strong central coordination plus departmental responsibility remain the formal strategy for organising Whitehall for Europe. The European Secretariat coordinates within Whitehall; and the FCO with Brussels. Bulmer and Burch (1998: 620) showed that the norms of Cabinet government and of a unified civil service encourage the earliest possible delineation of a 'collective line', which for difficult cross-departmental policies is hammered out in weekly meetings in the Cabinet Office. There is a sharing of information within Whitehall: departments copy information to the FCO and the European Secretariat, which 'brokers differences' between them, where necessary. However, different practices can be observed. First, those departments whose policies are the most 'Europeanised' (Agriculture, DTI, Environment) conduct their own negotiations with the relevant section of the Commission and equivalent ministries in other member states. A British agriculture minister in 1993 said he did not need the European Secretariat to broker the package of measures decided at Agriculture Councils; the decisions were merely copied to the Cabinet Office and the FCO (Burnham and Maor, 1995: 194). Second, the European Secretariat's capacity to coordinate disappears when ministers disagree, as was the case in the Major Government. When it was Britain's turn to preside over Councils of Ministers in 1992 and 1998, the Cabinet Office found it difficult to run the presidency effectively; and the FCO was handicapped by its lack of power over the Home Civil Service. These presidencies demonstrated the general inexperience and 'rudimentary knowledge' of EU processes and institutions in Whitehall and Westminster (Ludlow, 1993: 252–4; 1998: 580).

The 1997 Labour manifesto had proposed changing Britain's strategy on Europe; this intention was 'reinforced as a result of a policy review that was conducted in the aftermath of the 1998 UK presidency of the EU' (Bulmer and Burch, 2005: 886). The Secretariat was enlarged, and put under a top FCO official with the rank of Permanent Secretary and the title of the 'Prime Minister's adviser on Europe'. *Modernising Government* (Cabinet Office, 1999a: 55) exhorted staff in all departments to integrate the EU dimension into policy thinking. However, policy thinking on Europe cannot be effective without a better understanding of the EU policy process.

The civil service adapts to Europe

The UK government has tried since the late 1980s to improve EU expertise, having realised how 'underrepresented' Britain was in the EU administration (Bulmer and Burch, 1998: 619). There are no national 'quotas', and Commission staff should serve European, not national, interests. None the less it is useful to have British perspectives and contacts present in the Commission. Yet figures for 1993–94 showed that there were sixty-one fewer Britons in senior Commission and Council grades than would be expected by Britain's relative size in the EU population (Page, 1997: 44–6).

In response to such findings, the Cabinet Office set up a European Staffing Unit, and introduced a special European Fast Stream alongside the General Fast Stream recruitment scheme described in Chapter 6. These civil servants are given posts related to Europe, and coached for the EU examinations, which require specialised expertise (economics, law, international relations or European public administration), and knowledge of Europe. They are offered placements in European institutions (about two dozen were going to Brussels or Luxembourg by the mid-1990s; one Fast Streamer in 2006 was serving in the 'international public services' division of the French prime minister's office). Despite these efforts, there were still too few British officials in 2006 in the Commission, and the Cabinet Office started offering advice to any British national who thought of applying, with or without civil service experience (see www.eu-careers-gateway.gov.uk).

British civil servants continue to be reluctant to take up posts in Brussels. Maor and Stevens (1997: 540) cite evidence showing that service in Brussels was less advantageous to officials' careers than experience in a minister's private office, the Treasury or the Cabinet

Office, and noted that 'staff returning from Brussels are still liable to find they have been not only out of sight but out of mind while they were away'. Their own surveys (1997: 541–3) found that, while the Ministry of Agriculture gave knowledge or experience of European institutions more weight than other criteria when recruiting and promoting civil servants, the Transport and Health departments gave it only about the same amount of importance as other criteria, even in selecting staff for posts with significant EU responsibilities. When seconded officials return to Whitehall, little effort is made to learn from the expertise acquired. Pickering (2002: 588) observed that the Treasury's European Unit served to further ministers' ambitions for 'propagating UK ideas in the EU ... [it] has not traditionally played the role of harvesting good ideas from elsewhere in the Union'. Departments may offer (or have to offer in periods of cutbacks) a home posting unrelated to the European experience. The management reforms of the 1980s and 1990s were strong disincentives for officials to absent themselves from their department.

A few ministers in the Major Government (Chris Patten and John Gummer at the DoE; Ian Lang at the Scottish Office), tried to add 'European professionalism' to civil servants. They encouraged their officials to be seconded to UKRep and to contact 'colleagues' in similar policy areas in other EU countries; and they provided information on 'how to negotiate in Europe' (Bulmer and Burch, 2005: 874–5). The 1996 White Paper, *Development and Training for Civil Servants,* recognised the need for departments 'to become more professional in their dealings with Europe' (Cabinet Office, 1996: 32). Maor and Stevens (1997: 541–2) found that the Ministries of Agriculture, Transport and Health only really pushed staff to learn about the EU after they had taken up an EU-related post. The National School of Government (and its predecessor, the Civil Service College) has a well-established programme of courses on the EU, focusing on how decisions are made. Yet Europe has never had a large place in its prospectus because the pressure for officials is on acquiring management skills.

Bulmer and Burch (2005: 884) concluded that adaptation by UK officials to the different policy-making styles of the EU or other European civil services was 'confined principally to those who had served in Brussels', which meant essentially the staff in the European Secretariat, the FCO, the DTI and Agriculture. Elsewhere in Whitehall or the devolved administrations, such experience was distributed in a rather haphazard way. However, Bulmer and Burch are here discussing that important group of senior officials who have served in the core bodies that form 'the European policy-making network in Whitehall', and who understand the elements of the policy-making process from early lobbying of the Commission to the finer points of Council of Ministers' bargaining (2000: 58).

Many more British civil servants, however, play an intermittent part in multinational policy-making, as they have always done, as illustrated above by the Ministry of Power/DTI official who represented UK fuel interests in inter-governmental organisations, or by officials from the Scottish Office's Department for Agriculture and Fisheries (even before devolution) who were directly involved in the annual fixing of quotas in Brussels (Lequesne, 2000: 353). The numbers of such officials are hard to estimate, but the evidence on working parties and committees in the Commission and Council Secretariat suggests that some hundreds of UK officials take part each year in a working party or committee in Brussels. Like the less 'Europeanised' ministries, 'their participation in the EU policy-making machinery is very much on an "as needed" basis' (Bulmer and Burch, 2005: 869).

For decades now, officials across the EU have worked together to develop and implement common legislation. They negotiate with 'their counterparts' from other national ministries the details of a policy instrument that best satisfies their professional criteria and the interests of their member states, as expressed by their ministers and national policy communities. The same official is likely to prepare the government's initial position, pursue it through negotiations in working parties and committees at EU level, and finally (if still in the same post), oversee its incorporation into national legislation. Moreover, the civil servant is likely to have visited ministries in other states for 'pre-meetings' to build potential alliances on crucial points before formal discussions commenced (Siedentopf and Ziller, 1988: 29). The Treasury and the Office of Science and Technology 'built alliances, mainly through other finance and science ministries, aimed at keeping Fourth Framework Programme spending down to a manageable level' (Pickering, 2002: 593). As an Environment official told Richards and Smith (2002: 156): 'There is a continuous process of consultation and communication on a bilateral basis ... We also have a lot of bilateral contact with our opposite numbers in the Environment Ministries in other member states.'

Across the spectrum of policy domains, some general themes emerge:

- *A dominant role for national civil servants in EU policy-making*, although one that does not leave out political interests: civil servants put forward the views of the interest groups powerful in their sector at home. 'This is illustrated by the statement of a British civil servant in the Ministry of Agriculture: "We exist to protect the UK industry"' (Siedentopf and Ziller, 1988: 40).

- *The fragmentation of policy-making into a series of sectors*, in which officials responsible for that sector in different states work to negotiate policy instruments and look for alliances, and press their views on the relevant Commission directorate. As the Environment official said: 'We also have a lot of direct bilateral contact with officials in DG 11 in the Commission who are dealing with the areas that we are concerned with' (Richards and Smith, 2002: 156).
- *The 'technocracising of politics'*, which is in part real (regulations and directives are technical and negotiated by the specialists), but is also a product of officials deliberately categorising the instrument as 'non-political' to keep out the central coordinating bodies (the Cabinet Office; the FCO) and thereby preserve the self-interests of the department and its favoured interest groups (Siedentopf and Ziller, 1988: 78).
- A *decline in the role of the coordinating institutions* relative to the 'technical' divisions. By the mid-1980s there was already a question about the role of the Cabinet Office and the FCO as EU business expanded. In the UK, 'the domestic departments feel … that the secretariat lacks the expertise for more technical policies: "The European Secretariat and the Foreign Office must be asked to comment but are unlikely to be of much help"' (Siedentopf and Ziller, 1988: 33; and see Richards and Smith, 2002: 155–6).

Putting these points together, they seem to show, first, the continued development of transgovernmental or transnational administrative coalitions. Civil servants are dealing with their 'opposite numbers' or 'counterparts' in other countries and identifying them as colleagues, linked by a similar professional interest. A Permanent Secretary remarked that officials in his department who had been visiting Brussels weekly for a year to prepare a directive had spent more time there than with departmental colleagues; he wondered whether they might start to think in terms of coordination with their professional European colleagues rather than with colleagues in other ministries across Whitehall (Burnham and Maor, 1995: 194–5). Second, there is a differentiation between the departments of Whitehall, each focused on particular sectors, and each with its own network of particular types of societal actors and economic or political contexts. They too risk losing sight of each other: the classic case is agriculture, which is not covered by COREPER, the only 'generalist horizontal committee' in the EU system of vertical structures (Bostock, 2002: 225), but has its own special committee which 'helped to preserve the pre-eminence of national interests in the policy process on agricultural matters, with its characteristic segmentation' (Rieger, 2000: 188). Each food crisis in the UK (salmonella, BSE, foot-and-mouth) seems to demonstrate again that ministry officials have lost touch with their ministerial colleagues in other sectors (health, tourism, army), outside England (Scottish, Welsh and Northern Ireland Offices) and on the ground (local authorities, police) (Maor and Stevens, 1997: 544; Richards and Smith, 2002: 9, 204; Smith, 2004; 321–3; Constitution Committee, 2002, box 1). While the model of 'multilevel governance' is becoming increasingly apt as a way of understanding the negotiations linking the EU, the UK and the devolved governments, the details of the model are highly differentiated according to the policy area being observed.

Conclusion: a network of civil services?

A chapter that examines the impact on the civil service of a more diversified state risks emphasising unduly the signs that the civil service itself is diversified. It is therefore important to recall that civil servants in the devolved administrations have vigorously defended the unified 'Whitehall' model. The Welsh Assembly even seemed to regard its civil servants as being *too* unified. Members of the UK civil service still work for UK ministers in every part of the United Kingdom, and for the Welsh and Scottish executives. They can transfer within the constituent countries with no greater difficulty than between departments. The fact that the NICS under Direct Rule discovered (and adopted) some 'Whitehall' norms confirms that the post-1919 reforms had constructed a civil service with a special, unified culture. The participation of the devolved administrations (even before devolution) in preparing a UK negotiating line in Europe demonstrates the in-built norm of 'one administration': the accommodation of regional diversity is a re-affirmation of the unitary state.

Yet, other evidence showed that the unification of the British civil service was always incomplete. A unitary state spawned a unitary civil service only by disregarding Northern Ireland and its devolved administration. Since 1972, the legal or constitutional position of the NICS within the UK's administrative system has been ambiguous (to define it would define Northern Ireland). Even so, a British civil service is at work in a territory also administered (for national functions) by another British civil service. The Diplomatic Service too has not been integrated with the rest of the service, and remains a 'special-purpose' civil service for foreign affairs. However, both civil services are losing their distinctiveness: the NICS has adopted some Whitehall working patterns and undergone 'administrative modernisation'; and the Diplomatic Service works closely with the Cabinet Office on EU issues, and is 'modernising' its personnel policies.

A more informal differentiation within the UK civil service was created or revealed by devolution. The Scottish Office possessed a cadre of self-confident bureaucrats who could be distinguished from the rest of the civil service; but the Welsh Office had a weaker presence. Before devolution there was already a de facto differentiation of personnel, experience, culture and policy communities between mainstream departments and the Scottish/Welsh Office. The more active promotion at EU level of distinctive Scottish and Welsh interests adds to the pressure on the unifying norms and procedures of the UK civil service as departments become pulled by the EU's policy-making processes into their sector's policy-making community.

The fragmentation and diversity support the view of Rhodes and others (see Chapter 1) that Britain had not fully developed into the unitary state presupposed by the 'Westminster–Whitehall' model but was a 'differentiated polity ... characterised by functional and institutional specialisation and the fragmentation of policies and politics' (Rhodes, 1997: 7). Unification and a standardised administration were incomplete. Rather than devolution creating a variety of systems that will fragment a unified civil service, devolution has expressed more openly the diversity that already existed within the unified civil service and derived from the local context.

The new political powers may eventually produce more distinct changes to the civil service, though Mitchell (2003: 178) warns that territorial diversity should not now be overstated where it was previously understated. However, for those who, with Rhodes, argue that differentiation and 'complexification' of the polity has weakened government, devolution has the capacity to free UK ministers and their civil service advisers of those responsibilities that do not need to be decided at national or supra-national level (subsidiarity). Looking to the future, there is scope for civil servants in Scotland and Wales inventing a 'public service' that integrates health and other services organised or organisable at regional level, a model that could be transferred to English regions. Senior civil servants in national and devolved governments will then need to deploy more broadly across the sectors their negotiating skills as 'multilevel mandarins' that many officials in departments and devolved administrations currently exercise in relation to inter-governmental organisations and the EU. Such an expansion in policy-making across tiers of government (local, regional, national, international), together with the cross-cutting linkages between the levels created by private and voluntary interests, would amount to the 'multilevel governance' model we described earlier.

4

Restructuring for Efficiency, Control and Delivery

For many academics, party politicians and civil servants, the structural changes that the Thatcher and Major Governments made to the civil service were assaults on the Whitehall model that would have disastrous consequences. However, the worst fears were not realised and there was much cross-party consensus on the reforms by the time Tony Blair became leader of the Labour Party. Yet there *were* problems, to which New Labour responded with its *Modernising Government* agenda.

This chapter examines more closely the restructuring of the civil service and the distinctively different motivations that appeared to drive the changes:

- An effort to *economise and increase the efficiency* of the civil service, chiefly associated with the Thatcher and Major Governments, particularly where it was based on cutbacks, contracting-out, and the privatisation of service delivery. Although the Labour Party in opposition had opposed these policies, the Blair Government embraced the private sector, more especially for capital investment than in the civil service itself, where recruitment increased sharply before a new efficiency drive was announced in 2003;
- A concern to give ministers *more control* of their departments to ensure that resources were spent effectively: that is, achieving policy objectives. Greater delegation, especially through the restructuring of departments into executive agencies, working to government aims, was intended to give ministers more time for policy development. These Conservative reforms were adapted by Labour to its own needs, with budgetary negotiations being used to give strong direction to civil servants;

- A desire to *deliver a better service*, which the Conservatives sought to achieve by fragmentation or differentiation, adapting working conditions within departments according to the tasks performed, and by publishing performance standards in service charters. The incoming Labour government responded to the problems that cut across traditional policy domains by promoting 'joined-up government' *across departments* and *across delivery organisations* (public, private and voluntary bodies), to provide citizens 'with a seamless delivery of services'. From the 'governance' perspective, this formula recognised the contribution of other actors and networks that governments relied on to deliver services.

These driving forces have been presented in the chronological order in which they came to political leaders' attention, but more analysis is required below before determining whether they constitute 'modernisation'; whether they have damaged the 'Whitehall model' fundamentally, or whether they match more closely some other view of civil service 'decline'.

Restructuring for economy and efficiency in government

The slimming-down of the civil service from its peak of 751,000 in 1976 was initiated by Labour. The Labour Party of the 1970s wanted services delivered by public servants, but in government it met severe economic difficulty and had to cut budgets to obtain a loan from the International Monetary Fund. The Callaghan Government cut 15,000 jobs and instituted a pay policy that ended in strikes which helped to determine the fate of the civil service. The Conservative Party's 1979 manifesto included a promise to attack waste, bureaucracy and 'over-government' (Drewry and Butcher, 1991: 198).

Margaret Thatcher was persuaded of the need for change by the practical examples of inefficiency cited by a retired civil servant, Leslie Chapman (1978), and by the theories of 'public choice' academics such as W.A. Niskanen (Bevir and Rhodes, 2003: 150; Campbell and Wilson, 1995: 304). According to Niskanen (1971: 21–2, 38), public bureaucracies are inevitably inefficient because officials 'build empires' to maximise their budgets and pay grades. They 'oversupply' a service by expanding it to cover everyone (whether or not people want it), without paying great attention to the cost, because it is a monopoly service whose value cannot be challenged easily. In contrast, private companies are constrained to work efficiently because, to survive and make a profit, they must make or stock only those goods they are certain to sell at prices that undercut those of their competitors. In the words of Michael Heseltine, Conservative minister and business leader, 'private sector management is always likely to be more efficient than public sector management, not because the people are different but because of the twin stimuli of the profit-and-loss account and the workings of competition' (Heseltine, 1990: 71).

Cutbacks and transfers in the Thatcher Government

On winning power in 1979, the Conservative government demanded a 2.5 per cent reduction in staff expenditure, and set targets for reducing the number of officials from 732,000 to 630,000 by 1984, followed by new cuts each year until 1988. In 1990, the year Thatcher left office, there were 580,000 civil servants; and the numbers fell further under Major, reaching 495,000 in 1997. (All staffing figures in this chapter are 'full-time equivalents', unless otherwise stated, and are drawn from the annual series of *Civil Service Statistics* issued by the Cabinet Office.)

In the first half of Thatcher's premiership there were significant reductions in both industrial ('blue collar') and non-industrial ('white collar') posts (see Figure 4.1). The largest cuts affected staff in technical services, including the Property Services Agency, whose work of maintaining government buildings was contracted-out. Some tasks were transferred to other public organisations, such as dealing with housing benefit to local councils. Others were abandoned: in 1979–80 the Inland Revenue cut 6,000 posts by simplifying the income tax regime and cancelling rating revaluation. The 'Rayner Review' of Government Statistical Services cut data collection: 'With many ministers indifferent to statistics, research and analysis, and eager for costs savings, many professional sources of advice in Whitehall were run down' (Foster, 2001: 729).

As was seen in Chapter 1, Mrs Thatcher appointed Derek Rayner, a managing director of Marks & Spencer who had also worked in Whitehall, as her Efficiency Adviser. Rayner's Efficiency Unit, based in the Cabinet Office, led 'scrutinies' of departmental work and made recommendations for change. The Unit claimed savings of £1.5 billion by 1993 (Theakston, 1995: 127). Although Rayner hoped the lessons

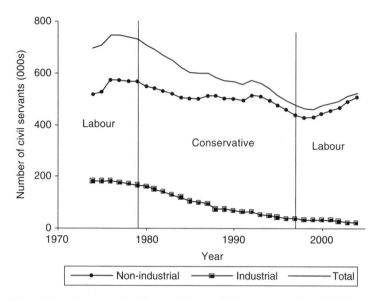

Figure 4.1   Changes in the number of civil servants since 1974
Source: Please see Table I.2.

would spread throughout Whitehall (Hennessy, 1990: 594–6), Parliament's National Audit Office (NAO, 1986), concluded that only about half the economies would be achieved. Ministers put up objections: for example, they rejected the idea of paying pensions and benefits monthly into bank accounts rather than by weekly order at post offices, because pensioners objected and the viability of village shops was threatened: 'There is some evidence that productivity in the big clerical operations that employed the bulk of civil servants stayed constant in the 70s and early 80s, and may indeed even have declined' (Mountfield, 2000: 3).

During the second half of the Thatcher premiership the reduction in civil service posts continued, mainly through privatisation of blue-collar jobs: 19,000 at the Royal Ordnance Factories; and 16,000 in the Naval Dockyards. More than 3,000 were removed from civil service statistics when staff in the Department of Health's Special Hospitals were reclassified as Health Authority officials. The reduction in numbers achieved by these transfers made good headlines, but if the government still required housing benefit administration, defence equipment or special hospitals, which it largely did, they still had to

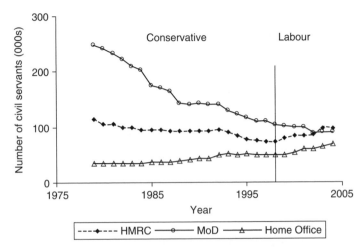

Figure 4.2   Changes in the size of departments since 1979
Note: The figures include industrial and non-industrial officials.
Source: Data from *Civil Service Statistics* issued by HM Treasury or the Cabinet Office in 1983, 1987, 1991, 1996, 1999 and 2004 (HMSO or The Stationery Office).

be paid from public funds. However there were savings in the Dockyards, where Heseltine found 'there was no budget of cost, only a record of what had been spent' (1990: 73).

The civil service was reshaped as some ministries – for example, the Ministry of Defence (MoD) – cut back more than others. Figure 4.2 shows there were also reductions at the Inland Revenue (now part of HM Revenue & Customs), because of computerisation and then privatisation of IT services. However, there was expansion at the Home Office and in its Prison Service, because ministers created new prisons and therefore jobs for prison officers. Ministers also came under external pressures, such as periods of high unemployment that required more staff for Job Centres and Benefit Offices.

Restructuring for ministerial control of policy and delivery

A more radical reshaping was introduced in 1988 with the Next Steps programme, which restructured individual ministries into core departments (mainly concerned with policy advice) and executive agencies (mainly engaged in implementation). The Efficiency Unit was now led by Rayner's successor, Robin Ibbs, an ICI manager who had once headed the Central Policy Review Staff, Whitehall's in-house 'think tank'.

Improving management in government

The report, *Improving Management in Government: The Next Steps* (Efficiency Unit, 1988) responded to the obstacles to efficient manage-ment it had found in Whitehall. At Heseltine's request, from 1980 the Efficiency Unit developed a 'management information system for min-isters' (MINIS), that set out the activities of each 'unit of accountability' in the Department of Environment (DoE), its staffing, costs, objectives, past performance and targets. Though MINIS was used to weigh up options for staff reductions, it also helped ministers and senior officials to manage the department more effectively by showing which activ-ities were performed less well and needed more or better-trained staff.

With Thatcher's backing, this system was promoted throughout Whitehall from 1982 within the broader framework of the Financial Management Initiative (FMI). However, few ministers were enthusi-astic or capable managers. Most were in post too briefly or did not see that management systems would help them control policy imple-mentation. Even Heseltine found it more difficult to apply his system to the MoD, 'the perpetually jostling scene of infighting bureaucrats, boffins and politicians-in-uniform' (Hennessy, 1990: 414), defending the prerogatives of the Navy, Army or Air Force.

The Public Accounts Committee of the House of Commons (1987, paras 20–43) found that 'progress was very slow' on FMI. Many top civil servants were more interested in being ministers' policy advisers. Younger officials felt constrained by central controls on personnel management, and saw no sign that management skills would help them rise up the career ladder. Heseltine (1990: 27) was frustrated that offi-cials benefited little from the efficiency savings they achieved, because of the 'centralisation, standardisation and rigidity' of pay determination.

Trying to separate policy and delivery: Next Steps *agencies*

The *Next Steps* report proposed an answer to these problems. It said that the civil service was too large and had too many diverse func-tions to be managed effectively within the unitary 'Whitehall model'. It recognised that most ministers were unable to be both politicians and skilled managers. *Next Steps* suggested ministers should delegate the operational work to middle-ranking officials, giving themselves more time to focus on policy-making with their top advisers. There should be an organisational divide within the ministry between the strategic functions (policy development, budget negotiations), dealt with by a small number of officials in the 'core' department, and the day-to-day administrative or delivery functions, which, it was argued, rarely needed to come to ministers' attention.

Most departments had several different delivery functions. Effective management of each function was inhibited by the uniform grading and pay structures, which made it difficult to vary employment conditions according to the demands of the task. *Next Steps* proposed that each function should be allocated to a semi-autonomous 'executive agency', run by a chief executive with freedom to adapt recruitment, organisation and pay to the needs of the work and the local labour market. Autonomy would be controlled by a framework document that set out the responsibilities of department ministers, permanent secretary and chief executive, and the government's objectives for the agency, to be supplemented with annual performance targets: however, within these constraints, the chief executive would have substantial freedom.

The report was the subject of one of Margaret Thatcher's rare statements to the Commons, which demonstrated to doubters that it would be implemented. Quasi-autonomous public bodies were not new to British government, either Labour or Conservative. British Rail, for example, was one of the 'public corporations' promoted by the Labour Minister Herbert Morrison (1933), combining ministerial responsibility for funding, appointments and objectives; parliamentary accountability for spending and outcomes; and the managerial autonomy of a private business. The 'non-departmental public body' ('quango'), such as the Environment Agency or the Teacher Training Agency, was another familiar model. While each is linked to a minister who is accountable to Parliament for their continuing utility, efficiency and public funding, they have independent legal identities and their staff are not civil servants.

The Heath Government's 1970 White Paper, *The Reorganisation of Central Government* (Cmnd 4506), supported the suggestion of the Fulton Report (1968) that executive work should be 'hived-off' to accountable agencies, yet Heath set up only a few agencies, including the Defence Procurement Executive (whose first 'chief executive' was

Derek Rayner), and the Property Services Agency. Like the Next Steps Agencies, they had no separate legal identity from their department and their officials remained civil servants (Pyper, 1995a: 53–4). Unlike the corporations and quangos, the government did not need parliamentary approval to create them (or, as it turned out, to privatise them).

The most radical features of *Next Steps* were: first, constitutional change to 'quash the fiction that ministers can be genuinely responsible' for everything done by officials in their name; second, devolution to agency chief executives of personnel management power for the 95 per cent of civil servants estimated by the Efficiency Unit to be executing rather than developing policy (Hennessy, 1990: 620).

Some of these controversial features are considered in other chapters; here it suffices to note that the logic of the reform was for ministers to delegate political responsibility to managers along with the operational responsibilities. However, some MPs were unwilling to challenge the 'fiction', even if in practice officials were already accounting for their actions to parliamentary committees and administrative tribunals, and through judicial review. The government therefore continued to state that ministerial accountability was unchanged, while encouraging MPs to refer constituency cases to chief executives. The 'fudged' arrangements reflected rather than resolved the overlap between policy and administration (see Jones *et al.*, 1995; Pyper, 1995b; and Giddings, 1995b, more generally).

In practice, the less controversial agencies seem to be those where the respective functions of department and agency could be divided in a way that avoided ministerial intervention in the agency (which did not preclude the chief executive giving advice to department officials and ministers). The Department for Transport (DfT) used this principle in selecting divisions for the Highways Agency. The Agency was given responsibility for the technical and operational aspects of road-building and maintenance, but the politically sensitive decisions on which projects should go ahead remained in the core department, with ministers (Glaister *et al.*, 2006: 48).

The Treasury would not at first countenance a loss of central control over staff numbers and wage bills, yet it soon agreed to allow agencies to recruit junior staff, and introduce performance bonus systems (Hennessy, 1990: 620–1, 626). Following another report by the Efficiency Unit (1991) urging more delegation, the Civil Service (Management Functions) Act 1992 enabled ministers to delegate personnel management responsibilities; however, the freedom of chief executives on this, as on other issues, was limited by agency framework documents. For example, the framework document for the Defence Science and Technology Laboratory (Dstl), summarised in Box 4.1, bars the chief executive from interfering in the careers of those staff who are members of the centrally managed Senior Civil Service group and requires all other decisions to fit the MoD's organisation, management and staffing needs as determined by the MoD's Permanent Secretary. These constraints helped to assuage the fears for the Whitehall unified model.

These continuities and safeguards do not diminish the radical nature of the project. First, the unitary core (the Senior Civil Service), ultimately included fewer than 1 per cent of civil servants. Second, the speed and extent of agency creation were surprising to observers of earlier reforms: within three years, forty-eight agencies, employing 35 per cent of civil servants, were in place; and the proportion would reach 78 per cent in 2000, before starting to decline once more. The overall case for agencies was soon accepted by opposition parties. John Smith, then shadow Labour Chancellor, said his party would not reverse the changes (speech to Royal Institute of Public Administration, reported in the *Guardian*, 9 May 1991).

So, at the time that Margaret Thatcher left office, it seemed that Niskanen's theory was wrong: either civil servants did not seek to maximise their budgets and build empires (since so many posts had gone), and/or political leaders controlled the outcome. But Dunleavy put forward another proposition that better fitted the changes he had observed. His 'bureau-shaping' model assumed that bureaucrats *did* maximise their interests, but that what officials wanted was to 'work in small, elite, collegial bureaux close to political power centres' (1991: 202). Senior officials would expand entities dealing with innovative policy work close to ministers, but would shunt routine functions off to peripheral units (private companies under contract, local government, executive agencies), and retain overall control of budgets without the problems of maintaining large offices (1991: 202–9). In short, according to Dunleavy, the Thatcher reforms reflected the interests of senior officials.

In support of this theory, the greatest impact of the Thatcher restructuring fell on industrial workers and administrative assistants (down by 14 per cent between 1979 and 1983). However, the lower levels of the Senior Civil Service were affected almost as much (grades 4 and 5 down by 10 per cent over the same period). Even the most senior grades (1 to 3) lost 20 per cent of posts between 1980 and

---

***Box* 4.1 Summary of an Agency Framework Document**

Agency	**Defence Science and Technology** December 2001 **Laboratory (Dstl)**
Aim	To provide independent, high quality scientific and technological services to the UK armed forces and government, in areas inappropriate for the private sector.
Output goals	• Excellent scientific research important for defence and government • High quality coherent analysis • Integrated technology advice and solutions

Accountability and responsibility

Secretary of State for Defence	• Responsible for Dstl • Accountable to Parliament for policy and operations • Determines policy and resources framework • Sets Dstl's objectives and performance targets
Chief Executive (CE)	• Appointed by Secretary of State for fixed term after open competition • Accountable to Secretary of State for Dstl's performance in accordance with Framework Document, Corporate Plan and financial targets • Responsible for propriety and regularity with which resources are used, and for prudent and economical administration
Chief Scientific Adviser	• The focal point within MoD for Dstl matters

Finance, planning and control

Planning	• CE to prepare and agree with MoD Junior Minister each year a Corporate Plan stating

---

1986. From 1986 to 1991 the numbers in grades 1 to 3 remained stable but many traditional posts transmuted into agency chief executive roles, running large offices, in competition with outside candidates for five-year contracts. Thus, while senior civil servants may as a collective body have gained from the Thatcher reforms, few as individuals could have been certain to remain, let alone benefit from the restructuring.

	strategic objectives for five years and how they are to be achieved
Performance targets	• To be agreed annually with Secretary of State
Annual Report	• CE to sign each year a statement of accounts and an Annual Report that sets out aims, objectives, this year's performance, next year's targets
People	• Civilian staff in Dstl are MoD civil servants
	• The CE will exercise an agreed level of authority, within the authority delegated to Secretary of State by the Cabinet Office and Treasury
	• All staff to be recruited on the basis of fair and open competition
	• CE has no authority to recruit or manage Senior Civil Service staff in Dstl: they will be managed centrally, in consultation with CE
Review	• After 5 years the Minister will evaluate Dstl performance and review its future options; staff and trade union representatives will be consulted
	• The Minister or the CE can propose amendments to this Framework Document at any time.

Annex: Letter of authority from MoD Permanent Secretary to Chief Executive

• The Permanent Secretary retains overall responsibility for the Department's organisation, management and staffing; and the Department's financial system
• CE must consider the parliamentary, political, policy and presentational aspects of all proposals; the interests of Departments; the need to consult policy staffs and Ministers

Source: Compiled from information in Ministry of Defence (2001).

Customer service and privatisation in the Major government

Some thought restructuring would stop when Thatcher went, especially when the official in charge of the Next Steps project, Peter Kemp, was dismissed. Yet in Major's first year, not only were more agencies created but also two new policies introduced: the Citizen's Charter to improve public service quality; and the 'market testing' programme to increase value for money. Then after the 1992 election a rolling review of departments began, under the direction of new personnel: Peter Levene as John Major's Efficiency Adviser, William Waldegrave as Cabinet Minister for Public Service, and Stephen Dorrell as junior Treasury Minister, encouraged by a new set of Thatcherite MPs (Theakston, 1995: 149). Waldegrave promised a 'smaller ... public service ... of a comparatively small core, and a series of devolved delivery organizations' (Waldegrave, 1993: 23).

The Citizen's Charter

Before the 1992 election, John Major launched *The Citizen's Charter: Raising the Standard* (Cabinet Office, 1991). Its principles had been enunciated in a Cabinet Office report, *Service to the Public* (1988), but it had not attracted Thatcher's interest. 'Charterism' was chosen by Major's advisers as a theme that would differentiate him from 'Thatcherism', but it also translated fairly Major's views about 'anonymous bureaucrats', and the need to help 'ordinary people' gain access to services, which he had held since his days as a Lambeth councillor (Seldon, 1997: 33–5, 182–95). Major defended the Citizen's Charter even when others derided it as trivial in comparison with the benefits of privatisation, or trivial in comparison with a *real* Citizen's Charter (a Bill of Rights).

Major claimed, rather implausibly, that the Citizen's Charter was the 'big idea' that encompassed agencies, contracting-out and market testing – and the Chancellor, Norman Lamont, let his junior minister organise charters on the equally improbable grounds that it would drive privatisation (Seldon, 1997: 191). Charterism nevertheless reorientated public services away from concerns with inputs and due process towards outputs determined by user preferences. For that very reason, some ministers and officials objected to it, since demands would drive up public expenditure (Seldon, 1997: 190–4).

The Citizen's Charter Unit exhorted departments from the Cabinet Office, advised by a panel chaired by James Blyth, the chief executive of Boots and a former Head of Defence Sales in the MoD. It pressed agencies and other public services to come up with Charters including certain principles such as audited performance standards; choice where possible; and a possibility of redress (see Table 4.1 comparing the principles and two Charters). Departments and agencies whose main 'business' was with individual citizens, such as the Inland Revenue, the Employment Service and the Benefits Agency, had

Table 4.1 Charter principles and Charters

Traveller's Charter 'Improving Our Services to You' (HM Customs & Excise, 1997)	*The Road Users' Charter 2000 'Making Roads Work' (Highways Agency, 2000)*
Set performance standards and publish outcomes	
Will treat fairly and respect rights; explain delays of more than ten minutes; surveys and publishes user opinions	Has targets on improving safety; and reducing noise, nuisance to non-road users and congestion; gives results in Annual Report
Information and openness in provision of service	
Wear identity badges when in uniform; offer to explain how duty and tax are worked out; give a receipt; give reasons for personal search; have a 'Guide for Travellers'	Will improve information through more advance warning, more roadside displays, more explanation of coned-off lanes, cleaning road signs; provide written replies in three weeks
Choice where possible and consultation of users	
Payment accepted in five ways; right of appeal to JP before search, and before or after payment by a free independent tribunal	Is working with road users (Roads Users Committee), public transport operators and local authorities to give more choice
Courtesy and helpfulness	
Will cause as little delay as possible; offer to repack bags; simple claims for damage will be compensated within two weeks, others within a month	Aims to schedule road works for less busy times, give advance warning; and give information on work and delays by phone, website, with links to bus and rail services
Provide redress and easy-to-use complaints system	
Suggests ask for senior officer, then to complain to Head of Customs; gives postal, telephone, fax contact details	Gives telephone, web, e-mail, postal address. Aims to reply to letters in three weeks; Charter includes comment postcard (SAE)
Independent adjudication	
Says how to refer to Parliamentary Ombudsman through MP and to Independent Adjudicator (postal, telephone, fax contact details given for both)	Says can refer to Parliamentary Ombudsman through MP, and to independent mediator via Agency, but no contact details given

Sources: Compiled from information in HM Customs & Excise (1997) and Highways Agency (2000).

already adopted similar principles and reworked existing documents (Butcher, 1997); the many agencies set up in the early 1990s incorporated Charter principles within their framework objectives. However, gaps remained several years later, as Table 4.1 shows.

Citizen's Charters did not offer the full rights of a citizen (accountability, freedom of information, legal redress), but the new consideration they gave to service users was often badly needed. Both Labour and Liberal Democrats supported the concepts, were often practising them at a local level, and said they would not abolish the Charter. However, it was hard for many observers to take charterism at face value after a decade of cutbacks and 'the disdain of many Ministers, although not all, in the 1980s' for the civil service (Peter Hennessy to Public Service Committee, 1998: para. 285).

Market testing and contracting-out

Chief executives of Next Steps agencies had been given freedom to manage, but were now told to develop and fulfil Charter objectives. Then, within six months of the publication of *The Citizen's Charter*, the Treasury issued *Competing for Quality* (1991) requiring 'market testing' and contracting-out to be established across the public sector. Waldegrave described it as 'a revolution in the organisation and delivery of our public services' (Jones and Burnham, 1995: 335). Market testing was a procedure in which departments compared the cost of a task 'in-house' with that of similar services provided by companies. Levene set departments and agencies targets for market testing. If the private option cost less, the service would probably be contracted-out. Yet agencies had been set up on the basis that administration would be more efficient if managers were free to manage, contracting-out or not as they thought best. There was opposition to market testing even from ministers who favoured privatisation: Heseltine at the Department of Trade and Industry, and Peter Lilley at the Department of Social Security were noticeably slow to implement the programme (Pyper, 1995a: 68). Agency chief executives, permanent secretaries and trade union leaders described it as having 'socked [staff] in the solar plexus', having 'serious costs in terms of staff morale', and a 'stupid thing' to have after the Charter (Butcher, 1997: 67). The decision to market test was quietly delegated to departments (Cabinet Office, 1994a).

Some functions that 'market tests' showed cost less within the public service were transferred to the private sector in a procedure Waldegrave called 'strategic contracting-out'. Theakston gives the example of personalised car number plates, for which the contract went to a private company, although that cost £2 million more than leaving it with the Driver and Vehicle Licensing Agency (DVLA). By 1995, work performed by 54,000 civil servants had been market tested, and the work of 26,000 civil servants awarded to the private sector, some without letting the officials bid for the work. About half the officials became employees of the private contractors, a quarter went to vacant posts in the civil service, about 3,000 were made redundant, and others left through 'natural wastage' (Theakston, 1995: 150–1).

By 1997, according to the Cabinet Office, there had been average savings of 20 per cent of the pre-test costs, whether the outcome was to retain in-house or to contract out (Minogue, 1998: 27). This implied that officials, if required to examine a task carefully, could find cheaper ways to do it.

From the start of the Next Steps programme, departments had been required to 'review options' and consider five possibilities: abolition of a function, privatisation, contracting, agencification, or leaving it within the core department. The government in 1992 formalised the procedure as the 'Prior Options test', which gave preference to a private-sector solution even before the performance of the department had been considered. Stephen Dorrell asked departments to list their 'core functions', defined as 'essential to meet the department's objectives and cannot be discharged other than by the department' (Jones and Burnham, 1995: 337). In a speech to the Centre for Policy Studies in November 1992 he announced that 'support functions will be subcontracted. Non-core activities will be privatised', and that the government would transfer to the private sector all those activities not part of 'the inescapable core' of government (Jones and Burnham, 1995: 328). He explained to the public-sector accountancy association (CIPFA) in September 1993 that 'When once Government asked: "What shall we sell?", we now ask: "What must we keep?"' (Lee *et al.*, 1998: 245).

Privatisation of agencies

The agencies, with their own financial accounts, 'product lines' and a virtually guaranteed customer (the government), were tempting targets for privatisation; this aspect had earlier persuaded Nigel Lawson as Chancellor of the Exchequer to support agencification (Theakston, 1995: 140). Opposition politicians were opposed to privatisation, as summed up by Harriet Harman MP (later to become a Labour minister), when she told the Commons on 26 April 1993 that Lamont's financial crisis was giving 'the Tory right wing ... a chance to take the axe to services in which it has never believed' (*Hansard, HC Debates*, 223: 744).

In the Lords, the Public Service Committee recommended the government not to sell the Recruitment and Assessment Services Agency (which recruited civil servants; see Chapter 6), and the former Labour Transport Minister, Barbara Castle, vigorously opposed the sale of the Transport Research Laboratory (TRL), but to no avail in either case. Waldegrave admitted that the TRL had been set up as an agency because it was unsuitable for privatisation, yet it was up for sale. TRL exemplified the arguments made for and against privatising specialised services: if the new company did not prove to be viable without guaranteed state funding, expertise would not be available to ministers in future years; on the other hand, the main department and TRL had already developed a customer–contractor relationship, and with a privatised agency the government pays only for the research that matches its current priorities (Glaister *et al.*, 2006: 48). By 1997, a dozen agencies and 7,000 staff had been transferred to the private sector.

Politicians in the 1980s had given the restructuring policies logical justification in terms of the state ceasing to carry out functions that (it believed) were no longer needed, and importing private-sector management techniques for those that remained. In the 1990s, with 'strategic contracting-out' the idea of a level playing field between the public services and the private sector was lost (Kemp, 1993: 40), and the game sometimes made little sense.

Privatisation of public investment: the PFI

The Private Finance Initiative (PFI) was announced in 1992 by Norman Lamont as Chancellor, and the details published by his successor, Kenneth Clarke, in *Breaking New Ground: The Private Finance Initiative* (HM Treasury, 1993). Departments (and the bodies they supervise) were accustomed to awarding contracts to supply equipment such as hospitals, roads and weapons. They specified what was to be done, and paid the contractors when the project was delivered. The Treasury also allowed private investment in physical infrastructure provided it fitted within the Treasury's planned public expenditure, and the private company took the risk without public-sector involvement. Examples from transport – the biggest public user of private investment – include the Channel Tunnel and the Channel Tunnel Rail Link, the M6 Toll Road north of Birmingham, and toll bridges across the Severn and Thames and to Skye, all signed and sealed though not necessarily delivered before the advent of PFI (Glaister *et al.*, 1998: 209–17).

Private constructors proved unwilling to undertake other projects that the government proposed in 1990, and the economic downturn encouraged the Treasury to change its rules. With PFI, the government could bring in public investment sooner (and without the cost of borrowing immediately appearing on the public balance sheet), by letting the private sector design, finance, build and (usually) operate the new equipment. The public authority or consumer would pay for its use over twenty or thirty years ('buy now; pay later'). At the end of the period the equipment would remain with the private contractor or enter/return to the public sector, depending on the contract.

The PFI applied to public investment the market ideas that the Thatcher Government applied to public services. Traditional procurement had a reputation for delays and cost overruns, for reasons (familiar to anyone with a project) of over-optimistic initial assessment, technical problems emerging, and labour difficulties. The profit motive should encourage private companies to manage staff and technical problems efficiently; and to design in higher quality to reduce long-term maintenance costs and attract users. The early PFI projects are likely to cost on average about 10 per cent less than similar public projects (Allen, 2003: 30). The first prison PFIs, which were to be operated by private-sector staff, were strongly opposed by the Prison Officers' Association (Public Service Committee, 1998: para. VIII). The National Audit Office (NAO) estimated that Bridgend and Fazakerley Prisons would cost about 10 per cent less than prisons operated by the private sector but built with public finance (NAO, 1997). The Director General of the Prison Service Agency said the private prisons performed as well as the better public-sector prisons, but wages and other contractual conditions were poorer, enabling private operation to be '11 to 17 per cent' cheaper than in public-sector prisons (Public Service Committee, 1998: 275).

The Major legacy

The post-1992 reforms renewed the fall in the number of non-industrial civil servants. According to the official heading civil service management at the time, Robin Mountfield, it declined between 1993 and 1999 by nearly 4 per cent a year: 'approaching 1% a year was due to privatisation or similar "boundary" changes, and the rest, nearly 3% a year, was due to increased productivity' (2000: 5). Senior officials were not spared, because the White Paper *The Civil Service: Continuity and Change*

(Cabinet Office, 1994a), announced an intention to 'de-layer' the civil service, removing a third of senior officials. There was a real impact on individual senior officials, with large numbers retiring early; however, the size of the SCS scarcely changed. 'The greatest reductions in staff over the period 1994 to 1997 have occurred at AA and HEO levels, while the smallest reduction has occurred at SCS level' (Cabinet Office, *Civil Service Statistics 1997*: 11). Posts of administrative assistant (AA) and higher executive officer (HEO) were cut by 17 per cent, but only 2 per cent of SCS posts disappeared. Table 4.2 suggests that some SCS staff, especially men, retired early, while others, especially women, were promoted or recruited into the SCS: it included 450 women in 1994, and 540 in 1997. That is, in the final years of Conservative cutbacks, the senior civil service was rejuvenated, but not much reduced. As many other writers have remarked, the Thatcherite goal to 'de-privilege the civil service' (Hoskyns, 2000: 141), had the greatest impact on the officials with the fewest privileges.

A comprehensive review of the changes to the civil service in the Conservative years was conducted by the Public Service Committee of the House of Lords (1998). It criticised the government's organisational strategy: 'there has been little or no coherent rationale underlying the changes made in the civil service in recent years' (paras 423–4). However, the Committee had seen evidence from a variety of sources that 'the executive agencies have performed well and have led to greater efficiency' and, in some cases at least, were 'giving better service to the public' (1998: para. XVI). It believed that the

Table 4.2   Men and women in the Senior Civil Service

1 April	Men	Women	Total
1994	3,300	450	3,780
1995	3,250	430	3,680
1996	3,200	480	3,690
1997	3,160	540	3,700
1998	3,120	590	3,720

Note: Number given is that of full-time equivalent staff 'at SCS level', including permanent secretaries and diplomatic staff. Totals do not sum exactly because of rounding.
Source: Compiled from data in Cabinet Office, *Civil Service Statistics*, 1995 and 1998.

Recruitment and Assessment Services Agency should not have been privatised, but did not think that the privatisation of any other agency needed to be reversed (1998: para. VI). It accepted that contracting out could make 'good sense' in respect of goods and services that were readily available commercially, though it would be worried if it extended to state prisons (1998: para. VII). C. D. Foster and F. J. Plowden, consultants with extensive Whitehall experience, also found that most agencies achieved more efficient management and customer satisfaction (Foster and Plowden, 1996: 147–67), even if these authors had concerns about other consequences for the civil service as they had known it (see Foster, 2001).

Despite its generally positive opinion, the Public Service Committee had warnings for the Labour government. The multiplicity and speed of the structural changes, together with substantial cutbacks in staffing, had 'had a very unsettling effect' (para. XX). The Committee recommended that the civil service be given 'a period in which to assimilate' the organisational changes (para. XXII). The possibility of damaging 'fragmentation of the public service' would also need to be considered before any further structural change took place (para. XVII).

New Labour: coordination and consolidation

The new government addressed the fragmentation issues and consolidated the Conservatives' reforms rather than introduce new ones, yet there was much modification and amendment that might have been equally unsettling had it not been accompanied by expansion of the civil service. Labour did not intend to revert to its traditional 'command' model, nor to pursue the Conservatives' line that the market was intrinsically better. A 'third way' was sought. With a need to demonstrate to voters that Labour could practice 'sound financial management', the government found competition and privatised investment useful for keeping down public expenditure. Labour would not reject the agencies and Charters that gave politicians more say in deciding public service objectives, and/or responded to the demands of consumer-voters, and which it had approved in opposition.

The New Labour agenda for the civil service

The White Paper *Modern Public Services for Britain* was the first major document to signal the new government's attitude to civil service structures; and it came from the Treasury. It started with populist assumptions about bureaucracy, portraying 'back office' functions as wasteful, although they are the basis of 'front line' work and/or raise the money that enables public services to be provided:

> This White Paper, *Modern Public Services for Britain: Investing in Reform*, sets out how public expenditure has been reallocated to match the Government's priorities and root out waste and inefficiency ...
>
> The Government will deliver these objectives by:
> Investing in reform to modernise public services by, for example, cutting bureaucracy to improve front line services. (HM Treasury, 1998: Summary)

Modern Public Services treated the public, private and voluntary sectors on equal terms: 'Services should be provided through the sector best placed to provide those services most effectively' (HM Treasury, 1998, para. 4). The 'Prior Options Test' would continue (but called 'Challenge'), with five-yearly reviews of departments and agencies, although in a format that no longer automatically favoured the private sector (para. 4.13). At the same time there were hard messages. The spending plans included more money for public services, but not for civil servants: 'Civil service running costs will broadly be held flat in real terms' (para. 4.11). A new instrument, the Public Service Agreement (PSA), would tighten government control over departments' delivery. During budget negotiations, each department had to commit to the objectives and targets it would achieve, in the knowledge that under-performance would affect subsequent years' allocations. Table 4.3 shows the PSA for the DfT, an example of a department which, to achieve the targets, would have to work with privatised service deliverers over whom it had few formal controls.

The prime minister and the minister for the Cabinet Office, Jack Cunningham, issued their own White Paper, *Modernising Government*, the following year (Cabinet Office, 1999a). It emphasised coordination of policy-making across departments and with those who delivered the policies (Cabinet Office, 1999a: 15). In contrast to the earlier fragmentation, Labour would pursue 'joined-up government'. For complex social problems there would be new cross-departmental units: indeed, the prime minister had already set up a Social Exclusion Unit and a (short-lived) Anti-Drugs Co-ordination Unit. The Performance and Innovation Unit, and the Office of the e-Envoy (promoting e-business in the UK and the use of IT to provide public services) developed other inter-departmental themes.

Table 4.3 Public Service Agreement targets in the Department for Transport (DfT)

Targets set in 2002	Performance indicators	Progress in 2003
Roads		
Reduce congestion below 2000 levels by 2010	Average time lost per vehicle kilometre compared with uncongested conditions (new indicator being developed)	Road building is creating extra capacity. More information from National Traffic Control Centre Traffic officers recruited to manage incidents
Rail		
Improve punctuality, reliability	Public Performance Measure (PPM) combines figures for punctuality and reliability	PPM of 80.5% in 2003, up from 79.1% in 2000–01
Increase use by 50% from 2000 to 2010	Passenger kilometres travelled	Passenger kilometres 5.8% up in 2003 on 2000–01
Buses and light rail		
Improve accessibility, punctuality and reliability Increase use by more than 12% from 2000 to 2010	Passenger journeys per year Vehicles with low-floor wheelchair access (%) Bus reliability (%) Punctuality indicators being developed	12% increase in journeys 2000 to 2003 (all growth is in London) 29.3% of buses wheelchair accessible in 2002–03 compared with 28.8% in 2001–02 Bus reliability 98.2% in 2003; no change from 2000–01

(Continued)

Table 4.3   (Continued)

Targets set in 2002	Performance indicators	Progress in 2003
Road safety		
Reduce the number killed or seriously injured in accidents by 40% (children by 50%) from 1996 to 2010	Number of people killed or seriously injured in accidents	17% fewer killed or seriously injured in 2002 than in 1996
	Number of children killed or seriously injured in accidents	33% fewer children killed or seriously injured in 2002 than in 1996
Tackle the higher incidence in disadvantaged communities	Reduction in road deaths and injuries in 88 poorest councils, compared with England	Bigger percentage drop in casualties in poor districts than in England
Air quality		
Meet National Air Quality Strategy objectives for 7 chemicals (Joint target with DEFRA)	Assessed annually with data from the national air-quality monitoring network (England only)	5 of 7 indicators on course
		Targets for NO_2 and PM_{10} may not be met in all urban areas

Notes: DEFRA is the Department for the Environment, Food and Rural Affairs; NO_2 (nitrogen dioxyde) and PM_{10} (carbon particles) from vehicle engines are harmful to humans and bio-diversity.
Source: Summarised from DfT, *Annual Report 2004* (The Stationery Office, 2004), Appendix D: 125–40.

Improving coordination was one reason for Blair's restructuring of departments. The creation in 1997 of the Department for the Environment, Transport and the Regions (DETR), was supposed to integrate environmental and social concerns with transport. In 2001 the Department of Work and Pensions (DWP) brought together policies on benefits and employment. The fusion in 2005 of the Inland Revenue and HM Customs & Excise into HM Revenue & Customs was the outcome of a review (HM Treasury, 2004) by Gus O'Donnell, then Treasury permanent secretary. It would enable a million businesses to deal with one 'joined-up' department, and pool information on 'those who make a business out of cheating the tax system' (according to the minister), as well as saving 3,000 posts and bringing the two institutions under closer control (Seely, 2004: 3–4, 13–17). However, some 'joining-up' was undermined when ministers proved to be unable to lead departments without political controversy (the components of DETR were re-organised in 2001, 2002 and 2006).

Like Thatcher and Major, Blair had units working within the Cabinet Office to promote civil service reform, but the structures changed more frequently. In 1997, a new Public Service Delivery division housed the Efficiency and Effectiveness Unit formerly under Levene (still working on agencies, market testing and performance standards); the Citizen's Charter Unit, rebranded as the Service First Unit and supporting other Blair initiatives, such as the People's Panel; and the Better Government team preparing the White Paper. The Constitutional Secretariat, established in 1997 to prepare for devolution to Scotland and Wales, paid only limited attention to the inferences of devolution for the civil service (see Chapter 3).

In 1999, with *Modernising Government* published, Efficiency and Effectiveness, and Service First merged to form a Modernising Public Services Group, whose Effective Performance Division continued the tasks of the two Units. The Better Government team became a secretariat following up implementation of the White Paper. It produced the first *Citizen's First Modernising Government Annual Report* in which the Cabinet Office minister, Ian McCartney, promised to report on progress the following year (Cabinet Office, 2000: 3), but by 'next year' the ministers and structures had changed again. A new Office of Government Commerce (OGC), run by Peter Gershon (former commercial director of Marconi), was set up as a semi-autonomous body to give departments advice on procurement, including through PFI. When the agenda moved towards efficiency, the OGC monitored departments' efforts to deliver 'efficiency gains'.

Following the election of 2001, Blair set up his 'Prime Minister's Delivery Unit', directed by Michael Barber, to work on public service reform. The Cabinet Office continued its own work on delivering public-sector reform, both within its existing civil service management division, temporarily renamed Civil Service Corporate Management and Reform, and in a new Office of Public Services Reform (OPSR) for the wider public sector. In 2002, the new Cabinet Secretary, Andrew Turnbull, encouraged closer working relationships between Civil Service Corporate Management, OPSR, the Prime Minister's Strategy and Delivery Units, and the Unit of the e-Envoy (Winstone, 2003: 25), yet the arrangements remained confusing.

The post of e-Envoy ceased to exist in 2004, and the e-government unit became a conventional, if sizeable, IT department, bringing back into Whitehall some of the skills that had been lost by privatising or outsourcing departments' IT units. After the 2005 election, the OPSR's responsibilities were dispersed among older Cabinet Office bodies (www.archive.cabinetoffice.gov.uk is a useful repository of past initiatives). The Prime Minister's Delivery Unit coordinated the departmental 'Capability Reviews', introduced by the new Cabinet Secretary, Gus O'Donnell, which examined whether civil servants had 'the required set of capabilities to lead and deliver public services' (Cabinet Office, 2006d: 7).

If the central units promoting reform were so subject to the frequent, multiple changes that the House of Lords had deplored in the civil service, how consistent were the reforms they were supposed to be promoting: agencies, public procurement, and responsiveness to users?

Evolution of the executive agencies

On the tenth anniversary of the first *Next Steps* report, the Labour government said the main agency programme was complete and it would turn its attention to improving their performance (Cabinet Office, 1998b: 1). At that time there were 116 Next Steps agencies in the Home Civil Service, employing 77 per cent of civil servants. By April 2004 there were ten fewer agencies, and 73 per cent of civil servants were in agencies. Notwithstanding the minister's picture of a 'finished' reform, the agency landscape continues to evolve. Table 4.4 shows that in just one department, some part is always in process of being agencified, privatised, or merged into an agency.

A similar pattern can be seen across government. Between 1997 and 2004, at least ten new agencies were created for England or Great Britain, and three by the Scottish Executive. Seven had been announced for the Northern Ireland Civil Service; and seven other agencies were reconstituted by mergers. The largest and most significant in terms of 'joined-up government' was the merger between the Benefits Agency and the Employment Service to form Jobcentre Plus. Two agencies were transferred to different departments, one became a quango and another (the Radiocommunications Agency) part of the new OFCOM regulator. Departments brought three agencies back within the main organisation when it was decided they could not function autonomously. If some changes, such as Jobcentre Plus, are stimulated by new ideas for delivering policy, others, like the successive mergers of MoD agencies (see below), or the creation of Transport Scotland to handle the considerable powers devolved to Scottish ministers in the Railways Act 2005, are responses to changes in the external (albeit governmental) environment.

The five-yearly agency reviews gave ministers and senior officials the chance to update policy objectives as well as to reconsider whether functions are still essential or value-for-public-money. On the other hand, they could damage staff morale without commensurate benefits, according to the OPSR. The OPSR recommended that the reviews considered, not just the agency's performance, but the whole policy chain from its development (by the core) to the delivery outcomes achieved by the agency. Whereas in the mid-1990s official reports complained of too much departmental intervention, by 2000 it seemed departments risked becoming too divorced from their agencies (OPSR, 2002: 10–11), perhaps a response to earlier political conflicts in which some ministers and chief executives (Derek Lewis of the Prison Agency; Ros Hepplewhite of the Child Benefit Agency) were unable to maintain a distinction between policy and management (Pyper, 2004: 524–5).

Privatisation of agencies

Half a dozen agencies, mainly in the MoD, were privatised by the Blair Government. The largest concerned 8,000 officials in the Defence Evaluation and Research Agency (DERA). The restructuring of MoD research establishments was accelerated by the end of the Cold War in Europe; from 1991, Conservative ministers 'rationalised' the various MoD research agencies and properties into one agency, DERA. The Blair Government's first defence minister, George Robertson, initiated a DERA review in 1997 that led to the MoD seeking private funding to support research that could not be justified in value-for-money terms. In 2001, DERA was divided into a small agency, Dstl (see Box 4.1 on page 130), continuing the research too sensitive to be

Table 4.4 Executive agencies in the Department for Transport (DfT)

	Date set up	Number of staff	Tasks
Core department		1,940	Advice on strategy and financial, human and legal resources; on air, sea, road, rail transport; logistics, local transport, major projects, security, statistics
Vehicles Inspectorate	1988	–	In 2003 combined with Traffic Commissioners to become Vehicle and Operator Services Agency
Driving Standards Agency	1990	2,450	Tests drivers, motorcyclists; approves driving instructors
Driver and Vehicle Licensing Agency (DVLA)	1990	6,290	Registers and licenses drivers and vehicles; collects vehicle excise duty
Vehicle Certification Agency	1990	110	Tests and certificates new models of vehicles and components against European and international standards; publishes data on emissions, fuel consumption and noise
Driver Vehicle and Operator Information Technology	1992	–	Created from DVLA; 371 staff in 1993; sold to EDS for £5.5 million in 1993; EDS awarded £70 million for a 5-year contract
Transport Research Laboratory	1992	–	423 staff in 1995; privatised in 1996
Highways Agency	1994	2,100	Responsible for maintaining, improving and managing the use of the strategic road network
Maritime and Coastguard Agency	(1994) 1998	1,160	Combined Marine Safety Agency and Coastguard Agency, both set up in 1994; inspects UK ships and checks ships in UK ports, including for pollution; provides maritime search and rescue services

(*Continued*)

Table 4.4   (Continued)

	Date set up	Number of staff	Tasks
Vehicle and Operator Services Agency	2003	2,580	Trains and monitors operators of the MOT scheme; tests lorries, buses and coaches; and licenses operators
Total number of DfT civil servants		**16,630**	

Note: The 'number of staff' refers to industrial and non-industrial FTEs, in post on 1 April 2005, as given in *Civil Service Statistics 2005*.
Sources: Compiled from Cabinet Office, *Civil Service Statistics*, various years (The Stationery Office), and websites of agencies.

privatised, and Qinetiq, a government-owned company, 'privatisable' with certain restrictive conditions – but the private sector was not interested. In 2002, the MoD sold a third of DERA to Carlyle Group for £42 million; employees were given shares and could buy others. When 80 per cent of Qinetiq was sold in 2006, Carlyle made £160 million, the Exchequer £300 million and DERA's former chief executive £27 million. Carlyle's advice was said to have radically altered Qinetiq's value as a company, and it seemed unlikely that the NAO would consider the sale to have been badly handled (*Financial Times*, 13, 21–2, 26 January 2006; *The Independent*, 11 February 2006). The government had learnt lessons from earlier privatisations and in 2004 created the Shareholder Executive, to 'improve the value of State investments in the interest of the taxpayer'. This official body advises and represents the government on part-privatised and privatisable public bodies. Criticism of Qinetiq's privatisation was about the apparent undervaluing of DERA in 2002, not privatisation as a principle, which now seemed to be accepted.

Better Quality Services: public–private partnerships

The White Paper *Modern Public Services*, followed by *Modernising Government*, introduced the 'Better Quality Services Initiative' on public purchasing. Though the New Labour government had declared that it would be 'open-minded' about public, private or public-private partnership solutions, it insisted that competition would be the norm and that departments would have to ask both the Cabinet Office and the Treasury if they envisaged an internal solution without competition (Cabinet Office, 1999a: 41).

With its experience of running city councils under severe financial constraints, by 1997 Labour had realised the advantages of leasing arrangements; and it adopted PFI enthusiastically as the most common form of public–private partnership. From the hundred or so PFI projects signed before 1997, the list of PFI agreements on the Treasury's database grew to 750 by 2006. It seems that education, transport and health officials were convinced that the Treasury would approve capital expenditure only if it was in the form of a PFI (Glaister *et al.*, 2006: 229). The civil servants in the Prison Service Agency and the Highways Agency, whose early projects were the most likely to show savings, have since become more cautious about entering new PFI agreements, while schools, hospitals and local authorities, which departments supervise 'at a distance', are still turning to PFI, though the resulting savings tend to be minimal (Allen, 2003: 26, 33).

By 2003, there were serious issues about the PFI programme: its burden on future budgets (the capital value of the signed deals was then about £36 million, but committed the Exchequer to paying contractors £110 billion in the period 2003–28); and the difficulty of tracking debts in public-sector accounts. The responsibility for PFI policy was transferred in April 2003 from Peter Gershon at the OGC to Gus O'Donnell in the Treasury, along with the PFI database, in an effort to improve transparency on PFI debts (Allen, 2003: 11, 16). HM Treasury (2003) was still proposing new areas for PFI: social housing, urban regeneration and running existing prisons; though it did acknowledge that PFI had not proved to be good value for small projects and IT systems.

After the 2005 election, departmental ministers drew back from new privatisation projects. Charles Clarke at the Home Office decided to postpone the proposed contracting-out of the management of three older prisons after the prison officers' union agreed to help improve standards across all prisons (*Financial Times*, 30 May, 30 June 2005). Patricia Hewitt suggested that fewer hospitals would be built using PFI techniques, soon confirmed by the NHS confederation of health authorities and trusts, which had decided, following warnings from departmental officials, that 30-year contracts were too inflexible to follow changing patterns of patient choice and health care. The private sector too was increasingly wary of the costs involved in competing for new PFI projects (*Financial Times*, 16 June, 29–30 July 2005). The PFI programme was slowing down, if not coming to an end.

Citizen's Charter and Service First

By 2005 there were questions too about the value of 'Charterism'. The Cabinet Office minister, John Hutton, asked Bernard Herdan, former chief executive of the Driving Standards Agency, to report on whether the Charter Mark 'could be amended, updated and revitalised' (Herdan, 2006: 12). The Service First Initiative was supposed to give more say on service standards to users. Opinions of public services and particular providers were sought from a People's Panel of 5,000 citizens between 1998 and 2002. However, Service First standardised the criteria for Charter Marks on New Labour's objectives: accessibility and choice; innovation and partnerships that improve delivery; and consultation of frontline staff as well as users. (Research by MORI showed that what was most likely to satisfy public service customers was simpler: delivery of the promised service at the promised time; Herdan, 2006: 19–20.) The capacity for local users to affect criteria was further reduced by the Treasury's introduction of PSA targets (see the discussion earlier in this chapter). On the other hand, Service First's quality control meant that really poor service providers, such as the Passport Agency in 1999, lost their Charter Mark or did not renew it.

The Charter Mark Scheme received so many applications that the Cabinet Office found it expensive to run, and in 2002 the scheme was reviewed (Herdan, 2006: 39). Though the Charter Mark helped to motivate staff, there has never been 'robust evidence' of 'a causal link between Charter Mark and the quality of public services or the level of customer satisfaction' (Herdan, 2006: 14). Yet evidence was a particular concern of the new Cabinet Secretary, Andrew Turnbull: 'We need urgent change if we are to respond effectively to new problems and the expectations of service users. This may mean facing some uncomfortable issues, such as whether we are sufficiently customer-focused, and whether we are sufficiently insistent on evidence-based policy' (March 2003, quoted by Winstone, 2003: 1). From 2003 the Cabinet Office reshaped the scheme as a lower-profile benchmark, on which candidates could be assessed, at their own expense, by one of four certification bodies.

In 1991, the Citizen's Charter was an innovation that was much-copied in other countries (the Foreign Office promoted it heavily as *Raising the Standards: Britain's Citizen's Charter and Public Service Reforms*; Varin, 1997: 204–8). By 1998, other governments, such as Canada's federal and provincial administrations, were more advanced, with schemes for improving service performance that closely matched customers' expressed demands, as the Public Administration Committee of the House of Commons told ministers (2005a: 68). Labour government rhetoric over-emphasised 'choice' (something people did not usually select as a high priority), and had failed to pay attention to 'voice' as a way of improving the responsiveness of public services (2005a: 45, 66, 68). The Committee recommended that the government should develop a standard 'public satisfaction index', similar to Canada's Common Management Tool (CMT), that facilitates comparison across provinces yet can also be adapted to individual services.

The OPSR's reply to the Committee greeted favourably the idea of a public satisfaction index (OPSR, 2005: 17), and Hutton announced that work would start on an index that would be applied to all public-service providers (*Financial Times*, 25 August 2005). A MORI survey in Britain found that a very large part of customer satisfaction with a public service depended, as in Canada, on five factors, listed in order of their importance to interviewees: delivery; timeliness; information; professionalism; and staff attitude (Herdan, 2006: 19–20). In his report to the government, Herdan was therefore able to state with some confidence that the Charter Mark should be reorientated as a tool that would help public services demonstrate that their performance was improving, as measured by customer satisfaction, and that the criteria for the Charter Mark should be 'totally aligned with the key drivers of customer satisfaction' (Herdan, 2006: 5).

Restructuring for efficiency and service delivery

As part of the drive for efficiency within Whitehall, the Blair Government developed and expanded the system of analysing public spending. 'Fundamental expenditure reviews' of key spending programmes had been initiated by the Major Government in 1993, in order to supplement the politically driven examinations of the normal annual public expenditure round with longer-term and more strategic analyses of the public finances. Under Blair, Gordon Brown's Treasury adopted a series of rolling Comprehensive Spending Reviews (CSRs) to assess all departments and expenditure programmes on an item by item basis and produce fixed total expenditure plans, over three-year cycles. One consequence of this more strategic approach to public expenditure analysis was the adoption of new forms of accounting and budgeting within government departments. The private sector system of resource accounting and budgeting was steadily adopted in piecemeal fashion by executive agencies from the 1990s onwards, and was then formally introduced as a core principle underpinning the CSRs across the entire central government system under a Treasury implementation programme (Likierman, 1998). Resource accounting and budgeting combined the traditional system of accounting for financial resources with a broader-based approach that accounted for non-financial assets, tested for 'value for money' and measured the outputs of spending. In simple terms, the new approach sought to establish close links between the full range of 'inputs' (including money), the aims and objectives of public spending, and the measurable 'outputs', in order to allow judgements to be reached about each department's deployment of resources in pursuit of its policy targets.

A natural consequence of these developments would be the search for efficiency savings. Under Blair, two major reviews led by Lyons and Gershon were used in pursuit of this goal. When interviewing Gershon for its study of 'Choice and Voice', the Public Administration Committee (2005a: 35) identified a contradiction between the government's policy on choice (and therefore spare capacity, or a lower value-for-money option), and its focus on efficiency savings from economies of scale, on which Gershon had recently reported (see below). The Thatcher Governments had made a virtue of economy. The Blair Government adopted new policies that led to increased civil service recruitment. The Home Office had continued to expand its immigration and prison divisions. The drive for more joined-up government through the strengthening of the Cabinet Office, and the Chancellor of the Exchequer's new family tax credit and changes to stamp duty, brought further growth. By 2003, the number of civil servants was once again over 500,000, an increase of 25,000 since 1997. Moreover, the first attempt by the Office for National Statistics to measure public-sector productivity seemed to show it had fallen sharply since Labour took office (*Independent*, 5 June 2003).

Brown's Budget speech of 2003 announced a drive to produce 'efficiency savings and so release resources for front line public service delivery' (Gershon, 2004: 5). The prime minister and Chancellor of the Exchequer jointly commissioned two inquiries into ways to save staff costs. Michael Lyons, retired chief executive of Birmingham City Council, examined how many civil servants could be moved from Whitehall to areas where costs were lower. Gershon conducted an efficiency review of the public sector to find ways in which 'back office' administration could make savings that could be transferred to front line services.

The Lyons review (2004) identified 20,000 posts that could be relocated, to save £2 billion by 2010. As in the *Next Steps* report, Lyons worked on the principle that the department's headquarters should contain only the core staff the minister needed: other staff should be at a distance. By 2006, only 7,000 posts had migrated, because of staff resistance and the cost of breaking office lease agreements, but Lyons expected the programme would be completed on time, and followed by a second phase to 2015 (*Financial Times*, 24 July 2006).

The Gershon review (2004: 3) identified changes to departmental structures, processes and equipment that would produce 'efficiency gains' amounting to £20 billion a year by 2008. Two-thirds would be 'cashable gains', producing similar services with fewer resources, freeing money for front-line services. The rest would be 'non-cashable gains' in which a higher-quality output would be produced from the same budget. Civil service and defence support posts would be reduced by 84,000 (a net 71,000 posts since 13,000 staff would be transferred elsewhere). The Department of Work and Pensions (DWP) would close 40,000 'back office' posts but 10,000 officials would move to 'front-line' activities. About 4,000 DWP officials would be relocated out of London as part of the Lyons review. Some other examples of staff reductions and relocations are shown in Table 4.5, but for most departments the Gershon report does not clarify how these reductions would transfer into front-line delivery.

Taken together, the Lyons programme, the Gershon programme and the merger of HM Revenue & Customs was seen as 'the most significant restructuring of public services for a generation' (The Work Foundation, 2004: 4). If the Lyons and O'Donnell reviews largely found political consensus, the same was not true of 'Gershon'. It met serious criticism for its impact on civil servants, the evaluation of its outcomes, and, most seriously, its practical results for service-users. The Treasury's assertion that normal staff turnover could be used to manage the huge reduction in numbers did not seem realistic, and there were forecasts of substantial industrial relations problems (The Work Foundation, 2004: 8; and see Chapter 6 of this volume). The NAO questioned the validity of figures given by departments and the Chancellor in budget statements. 'Progress has been made but the reported efficiencies of £4.7 billion should be regarded as provisional and subject to further verification.' Some departments had reported gross savings without counting the cost of the investment that produced them; 68 of the 300 projects had no baseline data from which

Table 4.5   Recommendations from the Gershon and Lyons reviews

Department	Reduction in staff numbers by 2008	Number of staff to be relocated by 2010	Examples of front line investment
Education & Skills	1,460	800	Retraining of administrative staff as classroom assistants
Work & Pensions	40,000	4,000	10,000 staff to front line, e.g. work-focused interviews
Communities & Local Government	400	240	More social housing
Home Office	2,700	2,200	Police to have more time for front-line activities
International Development	170	85	Increased support for the International Development Association funding round

Source: Compiled from data in Gershon (2004), Appendix C.

to measure the gains (NAO, 2006a: 5). 'Non-cashable gains' were particularly difficult to check. In a subsequent report, the NAO found that 'reported efficiency gains still carry a significant risk of inaccuracy' (NAO, 2007: 5). Observers were sceptical, especially as the OGC was made responsible for monitoring progress, rather than the Office for National Statistics, which is relatively independent of government ministers (*Financial Times*, 8 April 2006; see also Treasury Sub-Committee, 2006, for a good discussion of the problem of organising trusted official statistics for the UK).

The consequences of 'Gershon' for DWP clients were examined by the Commons Select Committee on Work and Pensions after the 'catastrophic failure' in summer 2005 of Jobcentre Plus services to people claiming benefits. The Committee found that Jobcentre managers were 'struggling' with problems caused by 'the myriad of IT, staffing, process, telephony and financial programmes' as the efficiency projects overlapped the substantial organisational changes already under way in Jobcentres. 'One of the tests of the Gershon programme is that service quality should not deteriorate as a result of the efficiency programme. As far as Jobcentre Plus is concerned, particularly in the summer of 2005, it failed that test, and failed its customers and staff' (Work and Pensions Committee, 2006: 3, 4, 39).

Yet within a month of the Committee report the Chancellor made clear in the 2006 Budget Statement that he would pursue the programme. Having required departments to cut back on spending by 2.5 per cent a year in efficiency savings, 2004–07, he announced that budgets for the DWP, Revenue & Customs, the Cabinet Office and the Treasury would be cut by 15 per cent over the period 2008–11. The Home Office's budget would be frozen. In July 2006, other departments were told they must make administrative efficiency savings of 2.5 per cent a year until 2011. The government would also seek to sell or turn into public–private partnerships more of those parts of the civil service that had products that could be marketed (Ordnance Survey and the QEII Conference Centre opposite Parliament, for example); or where the 'private sector can generate operational efficiencies'. The government wanted 'to retain only those assets that are required to meet its public service objectives' (HM Treasury, 2006b: 33–4).

The programme announced by Brown in 2006 bore a remarkable resemblance to that promoted by the Conservative government a decade earlier. The Work Foundation pointed out that the emphasis for civil servants during the Conservative period of government had been on reducing costs, while under the Blair Government their resources had increased significantly. 'But at no point in recent history have managers been confronted with an absolute imperative to control costs *and* deliver service improvement', as they had with the introduction of the efficiency gains programme (Work Foundation, 2004: 8, our emphasis). While perhaps underestimating the pressures on earlier civil servants of 'the unholy trinity: agencies, contracts and charters' (Rhodes, 1997: 97), the statement sums up admirably the spirit of the times, as government sought to respond to citizens' demands for both higher-quality services and lower taxes.

Conclusion

A chapter showing how the civil service was broken up into a plethora of diverse units would seem to provide a central piece of evidence for 'the end of Whitehall' (Campbell and Wilson, 1995). Chapman (1992) even identified the agencification process as the crucial element that accelerated the changes he saw in other components of the Whitehall model (see Box 1.1 on page 38). Blair's retention of the

Conservative's agency system would support a 'death of Whitehall' interpretation, even without Labour's additional effort to break out of departmental structures to 'join-up government' across multiple service providers. On the other hand, some restructuring reforms are reminders that the civil service never matched the Whitehall model accurately. For example, the industrial officials present since the Second World War did not fit the generalist administrator mould; and their presence is now greatly reduced. Agencification and contracting-out have left the core department nearer the size of older departments, in which ministers and senior officials had time to debate policy (see Table 4.3 on page 146). Finally, the careful elaboration of framework documents, and objectives and targets, have enabled ministers to control work delegated to officials more effectively than they could through their formal direct responsibility in the recent past. In contrast, the traditional model was silent about the quality of policy delivery as experienced by the customer, which has been the object of much attention since 1991, as shown in this chapter. Thus, although agencification called into question some parts of the Whitehall model (especially its unitary aspects), it also reinforced other elements of the model (policy advice), while yet other changes to the civil service (loss of industrial workers, focus on delivery) exposed characteristics of the civil service that the Whitehall model never purported to describe.

Agencification, alongside privatisation and contracting-out, also provides strong empirical support for the 'governance' narrative, and in part for the related idea that the state has been 'hollowed-out' (Weller *et al.*, 1997; and see Chapter 1 of this volume). Senior officials, on behalf of their ministers, now have to negotiate at arm's length with a much more fragmented and complex network of providers than in the 1960s and 1970s, when they used their hierarchical powers to deliver services with their own clerical and industrial staff. The civil service itself was 'hollowed out' during the 1980s and 1990s as functions were abolished and staff made redundant or transferred to the private sector. Senior civil servants may have lost the capacity to advise ministers on specialised or technical issues as a result of the outsourcing of functions – though the willingness of ministers to listen has also changed (Foster, 2001: 741). Yet they have a more significant role in advising ministers on the more strategic decisions, such as on whether, and to which company, to contract out, and what objectives to set agencies and other delivery bodies. There is still a significant 'steering' role in the top layers of departments, even if the 'rowers' are now in executive agencies or private companies.

The narrative that replacing 'government' with 'governance' has weakened the state has its limits. Poor performances, such as those of the Child Support Agency and of some PFIs occurred in hierarchical Whitehall too (the Vehicle and General collapse that left a million vehicle-owners without insurance; the Vehicle and Driver Licensing Office at Swansea that cost more than double its estimate; and the poor value-for-money of the Navy's torpedo project, to take just the illustrative examples from one book (Drewry and Butcher, 1991: 81, 207–8)). The fact that execution is carried out within the main department rather than a semi-autonomous agency is not a guarantee of good outcomes, as in the contemporary case of the working family tax credit, administered by the Inland Revenue under the Chancellor's command.

As the tribunal examining the Vehicle and General case found, by the 1970s the growth of departmental business was such that the traditional administrative system did not enable a minister to live up to the theoretical principle of knowing all that went on in his or her department. Without the new financial management systems of the 1980s, even a management-minded minister, such as Michael Heseltine, could not have a strategic overview of the department's functions, budgets and performance. Even with these systems, most ministers prefer to give time to political rather than managerial tasks. The Thatcher and Major Governments did not 'lose' functions and thereby become weaker, but they deliberately shed those they thought should not be the state's concern, to make their control stronger over those functions that were important to them. Contracting out what could be contracted out left ministers and senior officials with more time to steer rather than to row. The agencification process, with its framework documents, and annual budget and target-setting, enabled ministers to gain a more effective idea of the work and outputs of parts of their department that in former times scarcely came to their attention, while giving those who wanted to intervene at will in certain areas the capacity to do so. Yet, and for the same reason, ministers and top civil servants may have become too divorced from executive agencies that do not draw attention to themselves.

Furthermore, 'hollowing-out' does not seem to be a general trend or principle. There are periods when governments create new bodies that are later 'lost', such as the nationalised industries of the Wilson and Heath eras in the 1960s and 1970s or, further back, the boom in government agencies when Harold Macmillan set up economic planning councils and restructured the Treasury: 'Between 1958 and 1964 ... there was anything but a "hollowing out" of the state' (Lowe and

Rollings, 2000: 112). After the Thatcher–Major cutbacks, the Blair Government increased its intervention in some areas (family and social policies, immigration control), supported by larger departments. Michael Saward's alternative diagnosis, that 'the state is being redefined or reshaped, not hollowed out, at least on the internal dimension' seems more apposite (Saward, 1997: 26).

Macmillan's economic policy-making reforms formed part of 'the attempted modernisation of Britain', a historical break-point, when the government made a great effort to adjust to the economic, social and political realities of the post-war world (Lowe and Rollings, 2000: 100). The reforms described in this chapter seem to be evidence of a similar break-point, in which Britain's civil service was, or is, being modernised to meet the challenges of a post-industrial, better-educated, more individualised and less deferential society. Thatcher and Major, unlike New Labour later, did not make grand claims to be modernising the civil service; and the evidence in this chapter seems to show that one efficiency project led to another in piecemeal fashion. However, many other European governments (Austria, Belgium, Denmark, France, Greece, the Netherlands and Portugal) pursued 'administrative modernisation' programmes in the late 1980s that had similar themes of reducing the size of the public sector; improving financial and performance management; increasing administrative deconcentration to smaller units; privatisation; contracting-out; and improving customer relationships (OECD, 1990, 1995). Academics described the cumulative effect of these initiatives as 'New Public Management' (see Chapter 1 of this volume). In relation to these themes, Britain's civil service could be said to have been modernised early (having learnt much from Sweden, Australia and New Zealand). On the other hand, the modernisation programmes of several countries (Sweden, Denmark, France, Spain, Italy), reduced the load on central government by including strong or further decentralisation of powers to sub-national governments, and that element was missing from the Thatcher and Major reforms. As Richards and Smith observed, the Conservatives had 'reconfigured' or 'transformed' the state with their public sector reforms but 'the constitution had remained static' (Richards and Smith, 2002: 233–4). In Britain, that part of the 'New Public Management' agenda had to wait for the Labour government, as we showed in Chapter 3.

5

Accountability, Freedom of Information and Open Government

The fundamental argument put forward in this chapter is that the processes of civil service modernisation have extended into the realm of accountability, freedom of information and open government, with the mixed outcomes and consequences that earlier chapters have led us to expect. The traditional 'chain of accountability' that linked civil servants, ministers and Parliament, as encapsulated by the Westminster–Whitehall model, has been subject to waves of change, as the complex realities of the world of network governance and the differentiated polity – not to mention the different expectations of an 'Information Age' electorate – have encroached upon the apparent simplicities and certainties of 'tradition'. The result, as with so many other aspects of modernisation, has been slow adaptation by the civil service to the new challenges (in line with its capacity to assimilate change, as seen in each of the three previous chapters), and an accommodation (not always complete, nor completely successful) with the messy realities of modernised governance.

Beyond the Whitehall model

As we noted in Chapter 1, a key feature of the traditional Whitehall model of the civil service was the framing of accountability requirements around the constitutional doctrine of ministerial responsibility, within which lines of accountability ran clearly, and apparently straightforwardly, from the junior ranks of the civil service upwards to senior officials, and then beyond, to ministers. Ministers were, in their turn, accountable to Parliament, leaving the accountability of Civil Servants, from start to finish, as an internal matter within departments, with the sole exception of the financial responsibility before Parliament of a department's Accounting Officer (usually its Permanent Secretary). The first paragraph of the 2006 version of the *Civil Service Code* states the position succinctly: 'Civil servants are accountable to Ministers, who in turn are accountable to Parliament.'

This Whitehall model was enunciated clearly in 1985, in *The Duties and Responsibilities of Civil Servants in Relation to Ministers*, by the then Head of the Home Civil Service, Robert Armstrong, after the officials Sarah Tisdall, Ian Willmore and Clive Ponting and others leaked documents, in effect 'taking it upon themselves' to account to the public or MPs (see Chapter 2). Tisdall, a clerk in the Foreign and Commonwealth Office (FCO), had sent a document about the arrival of missiles at the Greenham Common air base to the *Guardian*, and Willmore, a Department of Employment 'fast-streamer', sent to *Time Out* records of a discussion between his incoming Permanent Secretary and a top judge about possible anti-trade-union legislation (Willmore believed the judge had compromised his independence from the executive at a time when he was about to decide a controversial case involving trade unions; see Pyper, 1985). Ponting, a grade 5 official in the naval department of the Ministry of Defence (MoD), sent documents to an MP because he thought Parliament was being misled about the sinking of the Argentine cruiser *General Belgrano* in the Falklands War (Ponting, 1985). The Armstrong (1985) rules instructed civil servants with 'a fundamental issue of conscience' to appeal up the hierarchy, in the last resort to their Permanent Secretary, who in turn could consult the Head of the Home Civil Service (yet, for Ponting and Willmore, departmental superiors were part of the problem, as well as determining their careers).

As we noted in Chapter 2, the Armstrong guidelines failed during 'the Westland Affair' of the following year, when Colette Bowe, a press officer in the Department of Trade and Industry (DTI), was instructed by her minister, Leon Brittan, and encouraged by civil servants in the Prime Minister's Office, to leak to the Press Association a confidential document intended to discredit the former defence minister, Michael Heseltine; she was unable to contact the DTI personnel director or Permanent Secretary (Pyper, 1987b). Furthermore, the principle that officials are accountable only to ministers was used by the government to stop the Commons Defence Committee questioning the officials concerned. The Treasury and Civil Service Committee examined Armstrong's guidelines and said that 'a mechanism must be provided to make officials, in cases in which Ministers deny responsibility for their actions, accountable to Parliament' (Treasury and Civil Service Committee, 1986, i: para. 3.19). Armstrong told the Committee he saw no need for revision: 'These matters are well understood' (*ibid.* 1986, ii: 230). Nevertheless, he revised them in 1987 ('The Armstrong Memorandum'), giving officials the right of direct appeal to the Head of the Home Civil Service.

The most recent version of *The Duties and Responsibilities of Civil Servants in Relation to Ministers* (1996), was issued by Armstrong's successor, Robin Butler, in conjunction with the new Code of Conduct (see Chapter 2) published after more inquests on 'affairs', such as the Treasury and Civil Service Committee Report (1994); the Nolan Report on *Standards in Public Life* (1995); and the ongoing 'Arms to Iraq' inquiry (Scott, 1996). The *Code* offered officials the possibility of appeal to the Civil Service Commissioners (though only after raising the matter within the department, an obstacle that was not removed until 2006). The 'traditional' doctrine remains in force:

> The basic principles of accountability of Ministers and civil servants are as set out in the Government's response (Cmnd 9916) to the Defence Committee's Fourth Report of 1985–86 [which examined the Westland Affair]:
>
> - Each Minister is responsible to Parliament for the conduct of his [*sic*] Department, and for the actions carried out by his Department in pursuit of Government policies or in the discharge of responsibilities laid upon him as a Minister.
> - A Minister is accountable to Parliament, in the sense that he has a duty to explain in Parliament the exercise of his powers and duties and to give an account to Parliament of what is done by him in his capacity as a Minister or by his Department.
> - Civil servants are responsible to their Ministers for their actions and conduct. (Butler, 1996: para. 4)

This doctrine created an expectation that ministers would shoulder the blame for mistakes made within the department, as well as claiming the credit for successes. Civil servants would remain 'faceless' or 'anonymous', and would be shielded from the glare of publicity. Civil servants share a common written (and to a large extent unspoken) code of conduct, and a requirement to account for the efficient, effective and economical discharge of their responsibilities. The nature of that accountability is necessarily diverse, dependent on whether the accounting concerns policy advice, management functions or service delivery. However, only in limited and strictly-regulated circumstances are officials 'constitutionally' or 'traditionally' accountable to Parliament, still less to the general public. Ministerial responsibility to the sovereign Parliament and the corollary of civil service anonymity were, and are, the twin concepts that together assured the accountability of departmental activities, according to the Westminster–Whitehall model.

Yet it is doubtful if the doctrines of ministerial responsibility and civil service anonymity ever operated consistently in the way supporters of the model imagined. Barberis (1997b: 132–7) and Pyper (1987a) show how the 'traditional' ideas about the accountability of ministers and civil servants that developed during the mid-nineteenth century were in large part the artificial constructs of academics specialising in constitutional law, especially A.V. Dicey (1835–1922) and Ivor Jennings (1903–65). These scholars were writing less about what they saw happening than deducing logically what ought to be required of ministers and officials in a constitutional monarchy when parliamentary sovereignty and the rule of law were the fundamental elements of the Constitution.

According to Dicey, in a text first published in 1885, 'ministerial responsibility' meant, first, that ministers had the legal responsibility for the acts of the Crown in which they participated, specifically in this case the actions of the departments of which they were the Crown's Secretary of State. Officials were therefore operating not in their own name but in the name of the minister. Second, ministers were responsible for these actions to Parliament, meaning that they were liable to lose their posts if they did not retain the confidence of the House of Commons – that is, if MPs were sufficiently dissatisfied with the policies or individual actions of the department to want to see the minister resign. Finally, if officials were operating in the minister's name, it was for the minister to accept responsibility, and the official should remain anonymous (Dicey, 1959; see also Barberis, 1997b: 132).

Jennings developed these ideas further in *The British Constitution* (first published 1941), arguing that if a minister chose to delegate decisions to officials, he or she had to take the political consequences of any subsequent administrative error (Jennings, 1966; see also Barberis, 1997b: 133). The minister would resign for having made a poor decision not to get involved (Jordan, 1994: 216). It would also be unfair to blame officials without giving them the chance to blame the minister, and that was impossible given the primacy of the doctrine that civil servants should be non-partisan and anonymous in order to stay as a pool of expertise for any future government. Civil servants would be held to account for mistakes they made, but within the department. This principle, as a principle, is still ingrained in the modern civil service, as shown in the MoD's treatment of Dr David Kelly (see Chapter 2), who breached the terms of the *Civil Service Code* and MoD rules when he moved unwisely into political comment on the 'Iraq dossier' with BBC reporters. The initial response of MoD's Permanent Secretary, personnel director and line manager was to settle it as an internal disciplinary matter, with Kelly's name (but not the basic facts) withheld from the Defence Secretary (Hutton, 2004: paras 48, 51). The convention of anonymity was even supported in a paradoxical way by the considerable trouble that MoD press officials took to devise 'Question and Answer' material enabling reporters to 'guess' Kelly's name rather than just give it to them (paras 295–7).

In any case, the general conclusions reached by Dicey, Jennings and others seemed to Marshall (1989a: 7) to be 'just' doctrines about the minister's legal responsibilities for officials' actions – not conventions about how these actions were to be treated as if they were in fact the actions of the minister, who would therefore resign in their place. It was always difficult to find examples of ministers resigning 'vicariously'; that is, on behalf of other people. In 1864, at the beginning of the Westminster-style party democracy, Robert Lowe resigned as the equivalent of an Education Minister, after MPs voted to sanction his office's tampering with a school inspector's report. Yet a select committee later absolved Lowe and agreed his resignation had been unnecessary (Barberis, 1997b: 135). More recently, Diana Woodhouse (1994: 35) found that Lowe resigned because of the slur on his honour, not because he accepted responsibility for his officials' conduct. S. E. Finer (1956) demonstrated that during the previous century only a handful of resignations could be attributed to MPs demanding as a principle that the minister should take responsibility for departmental errors. Finer found that whether a minister resigned depended principally on the minister, the prime minister and the party. In modern times, because the Commons is tightly controlled along party lines, whether a minister resigns depends less on the error itself than on the political damage being suffered by the government and the party.

There is no consistent interpretation, let alone application by ministers, of the principle of ministerial responsibility for departmental failings. When the Foreign Secretary, Lord Carrington, resigned in 1982 following the invasion of the Falkland Islands, we argued (in Pyper, 1983), that it was not the straightforward case that it seemed of a minister exercising responsibility for his department's acts; because the failures in policies, intelligence assessments and military preparedness concerned a number of departments, including the Prime Minister's Office (Franks Report, 1983: 79, 93; Campbell and Wilson, 1995: 270). Rather, it was a case of minimising the damage to the credibility of the government and the prime minister. Similarly, when Brittan resigned following the Westland helicopter dispute, it was to save the prime minister, not to acknowledge any fault of his own (Lawson, 1992: 679).

Even the Crichel Down affair of 1954, which was widely held to be the last time that a minister resigned 'vicariously', turned out on examination of the records (Nicolson, 1986) to have been driven by the government's desire to limit political damage. A flawed public inquiry (Nicolson, 1986: 162–74), had accused officials of not giving the minister 'a proper brief', 'highly improper' behaviour and 'grave errors of judgement' (Nicolson, 1986: appendix 2; paras 8, 13, 14). However the inquiry was wrong to support allegations by the descendants of the landowner that the Agriculture Ministry was obstinately refusing to sell back, as promised by the pre-war government, good farmland compulsorily acquired for bombing practice. Nicolson (1986: 10–17, 32–4, 49–61, 70–8) found that the owner had voluntarily sold some poor land, without expectation of return; that the difficulties were mainly caused by the complainant; that the minister was legally obliged by the Agriculture Act 1947 to ensure full production; and that the minister, Thomas Dugdale, and his junior minister, Lord Carrington, had personally decided that the land would be farmed more productively as a larger unit.

However, Conservative backbenchers were annoyed because the minister had not reverted to traditional Conservative farm policy, nor taken 'disciplinary steps' against his civil servants. After a meeting with the prime minister, Dugdale resigned. Under-secretaries (Grade 3) were moved to less interesting posts; and two junior officials resigned in protest at their treatment by the inquiry. Although the inquiry also criticised the Permanent Secretary and Deputy Permanent Secretary, they were not similarly disciplined (Nicolson, 1986: 189–93, 201). The Crichel Down case, which was supposed to exemplify the Whitehall model of ministerial responsibility, followed the 'real world' formula that political factors determine whether ministers take the blame when things go seriously wrong in their departments; in addition, the careers of officials with executive responsibilities were seriously damaged, but not those of their most senior colleagues.

Ministers rarely resign on behalf of officials in circumstances in which the Whitehall doctrine suggests they should have done. Among examples that could be cited are the Home Secretaries James Prior, Kenneth Baker and Michael Howard, who failed to resign after escapes from high-security gaols: the Maze prison in 1983, Brixton in 1991 (see Pyper, 1992), and Whitemoor and Parkhurst in 1995. Baker said he 'accepted his responsibility', but made clear it belonged to officials and a junior minister (Jordan, 1994: 235). In all these cases, prison governors resigned, and in 1995 the chief executive of the Prison Service Agency, Derek Lewis, was wrongfully dismissed by Michael Howard – the Home Office later agreed to pay Lewis £220,000 not to take the case to court (John Rentoul, *Independent*, 23 May 1996). Nor did Baker resign in 1991 when he became the first minister to be found in contempt of court after Home Office officials rejected an application for political asylum and deported the asylum seeker despite a judge having requested a delay (Jordan, 1994: 235).

The Scott Report, on the granting of export licences of weapons to Iraq despite an official embargo, found that statements made to Parliament by ministers 'failed to discharge the obligation imposed by the constitutional principle of ministerial accountability' (1996: D4.63). Three junior ministers made the decision to withhold information from Parliament (D4.42). Other ministers signed Public Interest Immunity Certificates to withhold documents from the court that would have helped the exporters' defence. No minister resigned. Yet several officials were named and criticised by Scott for drafting misleading parliamentary answers, not reading intelligence reports, and not paying attention to export licence applications. Some paid the price in career terms: a DTI official was sent to a regional outpost (*Independent*, 1 March 1996); a more junior diplomat, whose duty it was to draft letters sent by the minister, William Waldegrave, which were 'untrue' (Scott, 1996: D4.13), told Scott that not telling the truth was one reason for him resigning from the FCO in 1990, and that he was now unemployed (Bogdanor, 1996: 32).

The Child Support Agency (CSA) 'can claim to be the biggest administrative fiasco in the history of the welfare state'; in its first year, 86 per cent of its assessments were incorrect. Ten years later, it was still collecting only two-thirds of the amounts owed by parents (Nicholas Timmins, *Financial Times*, 18 November 2004), and in 2006 ministers announced that neither the policy nor the agency was 'fit for purpose' (Ben Hall, *Independent*, 10 February 2006). Two of its four chief executives in ten years have resigned, but no Social Security minister.

The Whitehall mantra of ministerial responsibility continues to be asserted because Parliament will not abandon the idea that ministers are democratically accountable to them for departmental affairs (Barberis, 1997b: 149). Yet these examples show that the 'sanctions' element of the doctrine (including the expectation that ministers would resign in cases of serious error) has long functioned erratically, and that officials are liable to be named and blamed when things go wrong, if this suits ministerial convenience.

Modernising ministerial responsibility

In the parliamentary debate on Crichel Down, the Conservative Home Secretary, David Maxwell Fyfe (1954), and his Labour counterpart, Herbert Morrison, agreed that, while ministers still bore responsibility for every paperclip, and that Parliament could demand that they resign, it was nevertheless permissible in some circumstances to blame officials publicly (Marshall, 1989a: 9–10). Maxwell Fyfe in effect abandoned the doctrine that could have been implemented in a small nineteenth-century ministry but was no longer credible. As the Cabinet Secretary, John Hunt, told the Commons Expenditure Committee in 1977 when it investigated the civil service: 'The concept that because somebody whom the minister has never heard of has made a mistake means that the minister should resign is out of date and rightly so' (quoted in Marshall, 1989a: 11–12). Maxwell Fyfe rather struggled, as many have done since, to distinguish the circumstances in which officials would be held publicly responsible, but thought that they would be cases that did not involve important issues of policy or individual rights, or where the official undertook actions of which the minister would not have approved, or were details that the minister could not be expected to know about (Pyper, 1995a: 14). This formulation, which has not changed since in any important respects, left ambiguous the manner in which the minister should exercise his or her responsibility, especially on important policy issues, but it is currently exhibited in several forms (see Pyper, 1996).

Answerability, or *explanatory accountability* is the basic method of accountability for departmental policies or activities, which means that there is a duty on office holders to provide accurate factual information in response to queries about matters of policy or management. Untruthful answers to Parliament are particularly criticised, as the following frequently cited quotations from the Scott Report show:

> Mr Gore-Booth [a senior diplomat] agreed that answers should be accurate but said that 'half a picture can be accurate' . . . Sir Robin Butler . . . like

Mr Gore-Booth, regarded it as acceptable in some circumstances for a statement to disclose only part of the full picture. The problem with the 'half a picture' approach is that those to whom the incomplete statement is addressed do not know . . . that an undisclosed half is being withheld from them. (Scott, 1996: D.4.54–55)

The Report concluded:

It ought . . . to be recognised that the obligation of Ministers to give information about the activities of their departments and to give information and explanations for actions and omissions of their civil servants lies at the heart of Ministerial accountability and that every decision by a Minister to withhold information from Parliament and from the public constitutes an avoidance, and sometimes an evasion, *pro tanto*, of Ministerial accountability. (Scott, 1996: D.4.56)

This form of accountability requires ministers to give an account of departmental actions even if they had not approved of them or Parliament would not expect them to be involved. An illustration of this came when Nick Brown, Labour's agriculture minister, answered questions about the Phillips Report (2000) on the BSE epidemic ('mad cow disease') during years of Conservative responsibility. The report exposed excessive secrecy and complacency among civil servants in his department, and 'buck-passing' between agriculture and health officials. Brown stalled criticism by explaining that he had already transferred the defence of consumer interests to a new Food Standards Agency (Michela Wrong, *Financial Times*, 2 October 2000, 27 October 2000). In contrast, when Home Secretary Charles Clarke explained that over a thousand foreign prisoners whom the judge had recommended for deportation 'walked free' because of poor communications between the Immigration and Nationality Directorate (IND) and the Prison Service Agency, and because of the priority IND was giving to asylum issues, the explanation failed to satisfy MPs, the media or the Prison Service (*Independent*, 23 and 27 May 2006). The 'Prime Minister judged that [Clarke's] continued occupation of the post [was] likely to stand in the way of the continued reforms which remain necessary' (Clarke, 2006).

Amendatory or remedial actions are those where a minister acknowledges that serious mistakes have been made because of failings in the department's procedures or organisation, and then proposes how they will be put right. Dugdale had annoyed MPs by not offering to change the decision or the officials. When John Reid succeeded Charles Clarke, he soon gave evidence to the Home Affairs Committee, and offered it 'a fundamental overhaul of our whole Immigration and Nationality Directorate' and a structural review of the Home Office; and promised that 'if there are people culpable they will have to bear responsibility' (2006: Q.866–79). Associated with this formula is the concept of redress of grievances, which can involve compensating those who have suffered as a consequence of government failings, and is the special province of the ombudsman system (see page 180).

Sacrificial responsibility refers to ministerial resignations or other sanctions where important policy errors have been made in which the minister was involved or should have been. Spontaneous resignations related to departmental failures are rare; but sacrifices may be imposed by others. Charles Clarke paid the price for operational failures. Such incidents, whether ministers resign or not, may put 'black marks' against their future careers (Woodhouse, 1994: 174); yet there are also examples to the contrary; for example, Lord Carrington became Foreign Secretary and Michael Howard went on to lead the Conservative Party.

There are two further points to note. First, the accounts given by ministers nearly always implicate officials as individuals or relatively anonymous 'directorates', but civil servants are not permitted to 'go public' to defend themselves (and if they do they often have the government's media machine against them).

Second, the Maxwell Fyfe convention that officials may be named in relation to lesser decisions, but that ministers must shoulder the blame for important policy issues means that middle and junior managers are more likely to be named and blamed than top officials. The Tribunal of Inquiry into the Vehicle and General affair of 1971 (in which an insurance company collapsed, leaving a million drivers without compulsory third party insurance) concluded that little administrative work came to the attention of DTI ministers, and therefore ministers could not be expected to take responsibility – though it seemed unlikely they did not know of the company's problems (Pyper, 1995a: 14). An Under-secretary (grade 3) and Assistant Secretaries (grade 5) were named and blamed, while the minister was left unscathed (Drewry and Butcher, 1991: 82, 154). Because of the multiple recent inquiries into 'scandals', including Scott (1996 – arms to Iraq); Legg (1999 – arms to Sierra Leone); Phillips (2000 – BSE); Anderson (2002 – foot and mouth disease outbreak); Hutton (2004 – death of David Kelly), civil servants of all ranks are much less protected from parliamentary and public scrutiny than the historical myths in the Whitehall model have led us to believe.

A culture of official secrecy

The civil service was always less 'enclosed' in some senses than the doctrines allowed; for example, senior mandarins of the mid-twentieth century, such as Warren Fisher and Edward Bridges, had rather high public profiles (Theakston, 1999; Fry, 2000); and from the late 1960s parliamentary select committees started to question civil servants in full public view – albeit only with the minister's permission. There was none the less an important corollary to the model of collective cabinet government and individual ministerial responsibility which tended not to be formally acknowledged; and that was the prevailing culture of secrecy at the heart of British government (Vincent, 1998). The culture was established in legislative form around numerous key statutes that in effect criminalised the unauthorised disclosure of information, even after the civil servant retired from public service. The foundation stones were the Official Secrets Acts of 1911, amended in 1920 and 1939, and rewritten in 1989 – on this last occasion to prevent further use of the 'public interest defence' that Ponting deployed at his trial in 1985.

The laws on secrecy are buttressed by a set of rules, codes and conventions designed to govern the behaviour of those working within government, and to place clear limits on the types of information they might disclose, even to parliamentary committees of investigation. In Chapter 2 we saw that the 'Osmotherly Rules' restrict the evidence given by civil servants to select committees, especially about advice to ministers on their policy options. Ponting (1990: 1) asserted that 'Britain has one of the most extensive systems to control the flow of official information of any Western democracy'. The culture of secrecy stems from a variety of factors – constitutional, historical and political.

Constitutional factors

The 'unwritten' or uncodified nature of the British constitution makes it easier for governments and officials to mould it to enhance the retention rather than the disclosure of information, and hamper public access to certain categories of government information. Further, the convention of collective responsibility places a duty on ministers to support all the policies and deeds of the government and refrain from exposing the content (and conflicts) of policy debates taking place within the closed worlds of the Whitehall departments, the Cabinet and its committees.

Historical factors

In particular, extended periods of war (including the Cold War), and international crises have had an impact on modes of behaviour within government; and above all in the abhorence of the unnecessary or premature release of information. Article 2 of the 1911 Official Secrets Act was renowned for the comprehensiveness of its secrecy provisions; it applied to all Crown servants and to all categories of information whose disclosure had not been positively authorised. Introduced amid panic about German espionage and presented as a defence against foreign enemies, it now seems its real purpose was to control the flow of official information from the growing ranks of junior officials – who could not be relied on to combine the competence, trust and confidentiality expected of 'gentlemen' (Vincent, 1998).

The 1989 reform of the Official Secrets Act 1911 and its Article 2 was presented by the government as a liberalising measure (Drewry and Butcher, 1991: 192), because it reduced the domains covered by Article 2 to defence, security and intelligence, international relations and law enforcement. For example, David Kelly's discussion with the BBC reporter Andrew Gilligan, about the 'Iraq dossier' having claimed that weapons could be ready for use in 45 minutes, was not seen by the MoD as breaching the Official Secrets Act (Hutton, 2004: paras 49, 60). Yet the new Act denied the possibility for a civil servant to plead that the information released was 'in the public interest' (as Ponting did) or was already in the public domain (as accepted by an Australian court in 1987 when it refused to grant the UK government's application to ban *Spycatcher*, written by a former MI5 official, Peter Wright, since similar material had already been published by two non-officials). Furthermore, the areas of information that were no longer protected by criminal law under the Act were added to the *Civil Service Management Code* (see Chapter 2), meaning that civil servants could still be disciplined for disclosing information, including by being dismissed from the civil service.

Political factors

The adversarial, 'two-party' political system contributes to the culture of secrecy, because it reinforces the importance of governments keeping to themselves information that might be used by the opposition to undermine the credibility of the government's case, or to crack its façade of collective Cabinet government. The Welsh Assembly Government's decision to share a set of expert policy advisers, even when in a coalition, shows that other modes of behaviour are possible in the UK. Meanwhile, civil servants in Whitehall are the guardians of the files belonging to a previous government, enhancing their own access to information but limiting the lessons that could be available to current ministers.

For the civil service, the cumulative effect of these different factors has been to engender a norm of guardedness and secrecy, and a deep suspicion of the possible adverse effects of a regime of public or political scrutiny.

Expanding civil service accountability

The modernisation of civil service accountability is partial and incomplete, and it has taken place in an ad hoc, piecemeal fashion, in typical British constitutional style. Despite a short-lived flurry of interest at the time of the Scott Inquiry (Treasury and Civil Service Committee, 1994; Public Service Committee, 1996; Public Finance Foundation, 1996), there has been no pause to consider the principles and to decide on a plan of action. The most recent argument in favour of such a plan came from the Commons Public Administration Committee (see below) when it renewed its call for a Civil Service Act as a means of regularising various aspects of the Whitehall system, including the accountability dimension. Nonetheless, significant changes have taken place, although they are attacked by adherents to the traditional Whitehall model who do not accept that the single channel of ministerial responsibility, however well it secured the accountability of the nineteenth-century system of government for which it was designed, should not continue to be appropriate for the complexities of the twenty-first century.

There has been a discernible expansion from the rather limited and impoverished concept of external accountability, with its focus on the provision of some basic factual answers (at second remove, via the conduit of ministers), to a richer and fuller concept of accountability that includes at least the possibility of redress of grievances and amendatory actions, in addition to a commitment to provide fuller explanations when requested to do so. Civil service accountability has expanded in a number of ways which, while overlapping, can be analysed under the broad headings that follow.

The accountability of officials to Parliament

The steady extension of parliamentary scrutiny mechanisms from the late 1960s, encapsulated by the advent of the Parliamentary Ombudsman and the emergence of the new forms of House of Commons select committee (all of which served to supplement the more traditional mechanisms of parliamentary scrutiny: questions, debates, standing committees and the financial probity secured by the Public Accounts Committee), brought fresh meaning to the concept of ministerial responsibility by effectively extending that doctrine to include (albeit in limited, strictly circumscribed, and officially unrecognised ways) the civil service.

Parliamentary Questions (PQs) provide a long-established mechanism of accountability to Parliament that has become more prominent in recent years, with the number of 'written answers' to MPs from ministers growing from 33,000 in 2000–01 to 52,000 in 2002–03 (data for financial years in Rogers and Walters, 2004: 302). Though MPs and peers can put 'oral' questions to ministers (answered on the floor of the Chamber), written answers obtain more information about departmental work. Departments handle PQs in different ways (some have a 'parliamentary branch', and some organise it directly from the Secretary of State's private office), but in essence the question triggers an examination of the department's work on that issue up and down the departmental hierarchy until the official responsible for the topic and the minister 'sign off' the answer that will be given to the MP or peer and printed in *Hansard* (the parliamentary record).

The PQs asked about the 'Single Farm Payment' system introduced in 2006 for making European Union (EU) grants to farmers (see Box 5.1) demonstrated graphically to MPs that the Rural Payments Agency was failing to deliver in England. (The Welsh and Scottish governments chose a simpler payment formula, and had paid 90 per cent and 86 per cent of the grant by March 2006, see NAO, 2006b: 28) The PQs put pressure on the Department for the Environment, Food and Rural Affairs (DEFRA) to speed up the administrative procedures – and dismiss the Agency's chief executive. Although the 'governance' thesis implies that MPs might have lost this lever over policy and implementation with the growth of 'quangocracy' and other delegated forms of government, ministers still answer PQs on governmental policies that are delivered at arm's length. For example, in May 2006 the Transport Minister published written answers on the effect of English councils' transport plans on greenhouse gas emissions; the Education Minister on numbers of children taken into care by local authorities; and the Health Minister on the government's independent inspection and regulation regime for social care in private care homes (*Hansard, HC Debs*, 445: 1735–69).

Yet there are limitations to this form of accountability. First, MPs could not tell what was going wrong in the Rural Payments Agency: the National Audit Office (NAO, 2006b) and parliamentary committees

---

Box 5.1   Parliamentary Questions: Single Farm Payments

A selection of questions and answers published in *Hansard* on 30 March 2006

MP 1	• How many, and what percentage of, Single Farm Payments have been made?
Minister	• 120,367 applications have been received; • By 17 March 10,116 (8.43%) claims had been paid.
Our comments	*The MP has established that only a small proportion of claims will be paid by the date of 30 March that ministers had promised.*
MP 2	• What assessment has DEFRA made of the effect of delays in Single Farm Payments on non-farming businesses in rural communities?
Minister	• Non-farming businesses may be affected by cash flow issues in some farming businesses. All sections of the rural community will have welcomed the positive action DEFRA is taking to ensure payments are made as soon as legally possible.
Our comments	*DEFRA has not made any assessment (or is not willing to reveal what it found). It adds a 'positive' note, but payments were in fact legally possible from 1 December 2005; indeed the Agency had said then that it was likely to start paying in February 2006 (NAO, 2006: 28, 32).*
Many MPs	• How many applications have been received to date from Devon/Lancashire/Somerset/Bath . . . and how many have been paid?
Minister	• As the scheme is not administered on a regional basis, the Rural Payments Agency does not hold records specific to Devon/Lancashire/Somerset/Bath.
Our comments	*To try to cut back on staff, processing in England had changed from being 'client-based' (each claim and local area dealt with by one office), to 'task-based' (any stage of any claim could be handled electronically by any office). MPs could no longer check the position in their constituency. Farmers could not check the progress of their claims. In 2006, the Rural Payments Agency took on more staff and went back to a client-based system (NAO, 2006: 2, 5).*

Source: Questions and answers from *Hansard HC Debs*, 444: 1102-5W (The Stationery Office).

---

are better at investigating such problems. Second, PQs are 'tabled' to ministers through the Commons 'Table Office', which imposes rules, such as rejecting PQs similar to PQs ministers have already refused to answer. Third, answers to PQs can be 'economical with the truth', in the sense used by Robert Armstrong, Cabinet Secretary, at the *Spycatcher* hearing in Australia, of conveying minimal information as advantageously for the government as possible without it being outright lies. The Scott Report concluded on PQs that 'in circumstances where disclosure might be politically or administratively inconvenient, the balance struck by the Government comes down, time and time again, against full disclosure' (Scott, 1996: D1.165). Answers to PQs from the DTI, the FCO and the MoD were described by Scott as 'inaccurate and misleading', 'not correct', and 'not true'; and the civil service drafters knew they were inaccurate (Scott, 1996: D4.25–42).

The many accusations of 'sleaze' in the early 1990s, including MPs being paid to ask PQs, helped to drive the tentative move towards 'open government' made by John Major (Pyper, 1995a: 158–62). One product was the 1994 Code of Practice on Access to Government Information – now replaced by Freedom of Information (FoI) procedures – which required departments to give one of several reasons, such as 'commercial confidentiality', as to why they were withholding information. The Cabinet Office issued 'Guidance to officials on drafting answers to parliamentary questions'. Its 2005 version (see Box 5.2), updated to take account of FoI, reminded officials of ministers' obligations to Parliament as laid down in the *Ministerial Code*, and their own duties both to help ministers and to give answers that were as full as possible and not misleading. It is easy to see the potential pressures on officials from ministers or political advisers when helping to present policies in 'a positive light' – though we must also remember that five civil servants asked their ministers to sign PQs that the civil servants but not the ministers knew to be untrue (Scott, 1996: D.4.25–42).

MPs' letters to ministers about departmental business became much more frequent after 1945 (Pyper, 1995a: 120), as MPs paid greater attention to their constituency role; and their number continues to grow. MPs sent 160,000 letters to ministers and agency chief executives in 2001, and 203,000 in 2005 (*Hansard HC Debs*, 386: 674W; 444: 75WS). MPs write to ministers on behalf of constituents who complain about being discharged too early from hospital, have relatives not being allowed to settle in the UK or being kept in poor conditions in prison, or who 'seek the MP's help in negotiating some tangle of bureaucracy' (Rogers and Walters, 2004: 309). Letters are more popular for

---

***Box* 5.2   Parliamentary Questions: instructions on drafting**

Guidance to officials on drafting answers to parliamentary questions

Ministerial responsibilities and rights

- 'It is of paramount importance that Ministers give accurate and truthful information to Parliament, correcting any inadvertent error at the earliest opportunity . . . Ministers should be as open as possible with Parliament and the public, refusing to provide information only when disclosure would not be in the public interest' (*Ministerial Code*).
- 'It is the Minister's right and responsibility to decide how to do so. Ministers want to explain and present Government policy and actions in a positive light. Ministers will rightly expect a draft answer that does full justice to the Government's position'.

Civil Service responsibilities and procedures

- Help Ministers fulfil their obligations to Parliament.
- Try to give relevant information fully but as concisely as possible, taking into account the cost of providing the answer.
- If full information cannot be given because it would be too expensive to obtain, nevertheless give any part of the information requested that is readily available.
- 'Do not omit information sought merely because disclosure could lead to political embarrassment or administrative inconvenience.'
- If there is a conflict between openness and non-disclosure to protect the public interest, consult the Freedom of Information liaison officer.
- If it is a fine balance and the outcome is non-disclosure, tell the Minister.
- If the answer gives information that is normally not disclosed, tell the Minister.
- If you must withhold relevant information, make it clear in the answer that it is withheld and give the reason, using terms similar to those in the Freedom of Information Act.
- Do not give answers that, even if literally true, could be misleading.

Source: Summarised from Cabinet Office document as published in Public Administration Committee, 2005b, Appendix A.

---

calling departments to account than PQs because they avoid the restrictions imposed in the Table Office, can be sent even if the House is not in session, and can address the issue at some length. They are treated with less urgency by departments than PQs, but when the Public

Administration Committee (1998b, para. 15) complained that, under FoI, 'the public' would receive more generous treatment than PQs, the government invited MPs to write letters, and this channel of accountability is now being organised more efficiently, no doubt because departments had in any case to gear themselves up to deal with 'the public'.

The speed of response to MPs is itself informative about departments' capacity to account for their work. In 2001, among departments with large post bags, the FCO answered 80 per cent of letters within a month, but the Department of Health (DH) and the Department of Work and Pensions (DWP) only about 65 per cent. DEFRA, the Department of Education (DES) and the Home Office (excluding the Prison Service) had a more ambitious target of three weeks, which DES achieved for 76 per cent of responses, but DEFRA and the Home Office for only 35 per cent. DEFRA said it was because of the foot and mouth outbreak; and the Home Office said it was taking steps to improve its performance. The DTI, to whom MPs are likely to write about business grants and forms, aimed to reply in two weeks, but only managed this half the time; it said it was reviewing its system for handling MPs' correspondence (*Hansard, HC Debs*, 386: 674W).

By 2005, with the Cabinet Office now reporting to Parliament on departments' performance, many had improved enormously: DH and DWP were answering 90 per cent of letters within a month. The DH had revised its system after the Independent MP, Dr Richard Taylor, brought its slow response to his letters to the attention of the Public Administration Committee (2004c: 233). The DES and DEFRA were answering more letters within three weeks than they had previously (86 per cent and 75 per cent, respectively). The Home Office had achieved 79 per cent by counting immigration letters separately – which at least identified the problem area. The IND introduced a new system in 2004 and was answering half the letters within three weeks by 2005. The DTI had launched a centralised response system to improve its performance (*Hansard, HC Debs*, 432: 137WS 444; 75 WS).

The variation in departmental performance offers more evidence of the differentiated nature of the apparently unified civil service. Despite the Cabinet Office's guidelines on PQs, departments decide their own organisational structures, issue their own guidelines, and apply them with varying assiduousness (Public Administration Committee, 2005b: para. 2). In 2003–04 the MoD systematically adopted the categories listed in the *Code of Practice* to explain clearly why it was withholding information, whereas the Home Office did so for only 10 per cent of refusals (Public Administration Committee, 2005b: para. 4).

The National Audit Office (NAO) has also criticised the Home Office. The NAO was introduced by W.E. Gladstone in 1866. Its traditional task is to audit departments' accounts to see that they have spent their money honestly and in accordance with the budgets Parliament voted for, and to report discrepancies to the Public Accounts Committee (PAC), established by Gladstone in 1861. This function has not lost its relevance: the NAO 'found that the Home Office had not maintained proper financial books and records' for 2004–05: it had a £3 million gap between its own records and the amount in its bank balance (though it should be borne in mind that the Home Office's total budget that year was £13,000 million!). The NAO and the PAC blamed a new accounting system, poor skills in the department's accounts branch and inadequate oversight from senior management. The criticism was aimed at 'the Home Office', not the Home Secretary, reflecting the fact that the Accounting Officer (the Permanent Secretary) was accountable directly to Parliament for financial management. The following year, NAO praised the progress made – even if there was still 'much to be done to embed a culture of strong financial management at the heart of the Department' (NAO, press notices, 31 January and 11 December 2006).

From 1983, with demands from parliamentarians and academics for the public audit to be modernised, the NAO's scope was extended from 'checking the books' to examining value for money, as the new Audit Commission was doing for local government. The NAO gradually changed its traditional ways (the Audit Commission, run by a former business executive, tended to be ahead of the NAO in its choice of topics and in presenting advice attractively in reports with catchy titles). The NAO's 2006 report on the Single Farm Payment compared the way it was implemented in the devolved administrations and other EU countries, and surveyed the impact on farmers. It stimulated the questions select committees asked officials and ministers when they tried to attribute responsibility. The whole accounting cycle can be illustrated by NAO's *Dealing with Pollution from Ships* (2002), which led to recommendations by the PAC in 2003 on what the Department for Transport (DfT) and its Maritime and Coastguard Agency should do to ensure that ports and local authorities could deal with emergencies, and that ship owners did not evade their responsibilities. The DfT then recorded in its 2004 Annual Report to Parliament the actions it had taken to implement PAC recommendations – which, it should be noted, required the DfT to bring into line the public, private and non-profit-making bodies that fall within the 'governance' network of this sector.

The Public Accounts Committee is the committee civil servants are said to fear most, though from the perspective of a Prison Service Finance Director who had once headed Sainsbury's internal audit, PAC was overly concerned with small procedural misdemeanours; ill-equipped to identify the serious weaknesses in the Home Office's financial management systems; not appreciative of savings that had been made and reinvested in prisons; and keener on making political points about agencies and performance bonuses (Landers, 1999: 196). The PAC is especially daunting in that it is the only parliamentary arena in which civil servants are legally held to account as themselves and cannot transfer the responsibility to a minister as they can in other committees. 'Being summoned before the PAC is the mandarinate equivalent to being told you are redundant . . . To suggest to someone that the PAC might take an interest in what they were doing was the direst of warnings' (Landers, 1999: 196).

If the Permanent Secretary as Accounting Officer considers that a minister's spending plans are financially irregular or poor value for money, he or she may send an Accounting Officer's Minute to the Treasury and the National Audit Office to avoid personal liability. Such actions are rare, but famously include the case of the Second Permanent Secretary in Tony Benn's DTI, Peter Carey, writing a Minute objecting to the financial implications of Benn's decision to fund the Kirkby workers' cooperative (Fry, 1985: 26). The move from 'probity' to 'value for money' has brought Accounting Officers closer to commenting publicly on ministers' policy choices. The Minute that Tim Lankester wrote as Permanent Secretary of the Overseas Development Administration (ODA), noting that subsidising the Pergau dam did not fulfil the ODA's aid objectives, called into question the government's trade-and-aid policy. The World Trade Movement argued that Thatcher's agreement to subsidise the dam was part of a deal with Malaysia to buy UK aircraft. The NAO and the Foreign Affairs Committee (1994), having investigated the affair, the World Trade Movement took the government to the High Court, which ruled that allocating aid to the dam was not of economic or humanitarian benefit to Malaysians. The government then had to change the way the aid policy worked (Marr, 1996: 248–9).

The *new forms of Commons select committee* introduced in 1979 were a significant advance in the systematic scrutiny of departmental activity. This form of accountability expanded in the twentieth century in an intermittent way. There was no systematic coverage of subjects, and the Agriculture Committee was 'wound up in 1969 after a campaign of opposition by government departments' (Rogers and Walters, 2004: 313). In the late 1970s, opposition members (Conservatives) were especially keen to introduce a comprehensive system of scrutiny. The Procedure Committee made recommendations for 'the different branches of the public service to be subject to an even and regular incidence of select committee investigation', and the new Conservative Leader of the House in 1979, the reformist-minded Norman St John Stevas, took the opportunity to introduce them before his colleagues in the new government had organised their resistance (Adonis, 1993: 158–9).

Civil servants soon lost their anonymity: over eighteen months, 652 officials gave evidence to the committees (Drewry and Butcher, 1991: 183). The work of the committees has become increasingly important in orientating departmental activities, and bringing officials as individuals into the limelight, even if, officially, they answer on behalf of their minister, who is able to determine the scope of the questioning. As was seen in Chapter 2, officials are formally limited in what they may say by the Osmotherly Rules, drawn up and circulated within Whitehall in 1967, after the Agriculture Committee violated the accepted conventions (Lee *et al.*, 1998: 240–1). Though updated in 1994 and 2005, the limitations remain the same. While the rules exhort civil servants 'to be as helpful as possible to Select Committees', restrictions are placed on the information that may be given: no exposure of inter-departmental discussion or policy advice to ministers, or indication of the level at which decisions were taken. The Commons itself has never accepted the validity of these rules, but neither has it demanded a wholesale review, because it prefers to keep rules that in practice do not impose serious constraints rather than risk a new set that government might impose more strictly. There are occasional acute points of conflict – in particular when a Committee wants to interview particular officials (those involved in the Westland Affair or Dr David Kelly, for example). Ministers can stop them attending or restrict the questions. A recent point of grievance is the more generous treatment given to inquiries: Scott (1996) was allowed to call civil servants to speak in their own name, and Hutton (2004) was provided with documents, e-mails and telephone records: committees have 'access to information' as written or oral evidence only.

The effectiveness of the committees is difficult to evaluate, especially where this concerns grand policy changes (which some argue is in any case a role better suited to parliamentary parties). Their usefulness is clearer where it concerns day-to-day accountability: scrutiny that improves implementation or modifies policy in the light of lessons from implementation. For example, the Transport Committee failed to stop radical policies it thoroughly opposed – such as Conservative rail privatisation (1993) and Labour's Public Private Partnership for London Underground (2002) – but succeeded when it demanded that the DfT produce more data on ports, especially about workers (employment, accidents), to inform national ports policy (Transport Committee, 2003). In retrospect, even committee inquiries that have little impact at the time, such as the parliamentary hearings on the Westland affair, move the accountability of ministers and the civil service forward, as did the Treasury and Civil Service Committee's 1994 report. Inquiries into specific activities such as the Home Affairs Committee (2006) on immigration control, or the Work and Pensions Committee (2006) on the Efficiency Savings Programme in Jobcentre Plus (see Chapter 7) provide food for thought not only for the officials they concerned but also for those who might also be in the Commons committee corridor one day. They provide more effective regular accountability of departmental activities than the traditional debates on the floor of the House of Commons, despite the folk memory of some historic parliamentary occasions.

The enhanced importance of this parliamentary line of civil service accountability was confirmed when the Next Steps executive agencies were established. Changes were introduced (following serious disputes between Parliament and the Thatcher Government) to facilitate the publication of written answers to PQs by the chief executives of the agencies; and the select committees took increased volumes of written and oral evidence from civil servants at all levels of these delivery bodies (see the contributions to Giddings, 1995). One negative aspect of this expansion of external accountability to Parliament was the confusion caused by the attempt to differentiate between particular strands of accountability. The flawed thinking that led to claims that absolute distinctions could be drawn between matters of 'policy' on the one hand, and matters of 'administration' and 'management' on the other (epitomised by some of the drive behind the establishment of the Next Steps executive agencies and the apparent determination to persist with a policy/management dichotomy) led to attempts to make accountability divisible. The managerialist philosophies that tease apart political, business, consumer, professional and other forms of accountability can lead in practice to serious gaps and confused lines of accountability. This was seen most obviously in the cases of two executive agencies (the Prison Service Agency for

England and Wales, and the Child Support Agency) where 'buck-passing' between ministers and senior officials, and arguments about whether the problems facing these agencies stemmed from policy or managerial failings, led to serious parliamentary and public unease, and effective breakdowns in accountability (Talbot, 1996; Hogwood *et al.*, 2000).

The Parliamentary Commissioner for Administration ('the Ombudsman') was another device added in the 1960s, but in this case to permit individual citizens to seek redress for problems of poor, unfair or incorrect administration (Gregory and Giddings, 2002). The role is now combined with that of the Health Service Commissioner for England, under the title of Parliamentary and Health Service Ombudsman (in the person of Ann Abraham in 2007), following (in part) the models in Scotland and Northern Ireland, and more recently in Wales. Unlike complaints to Ombudsmen in many other countries, in England they have to be submitted through an MP. The Ombudsman's Office investigates the complaint, reports back to the MP and to the relevant department's Permanent Secretary. It then prepares 'anonymised' syntheses and an annual report for the Public Administration Select Committee. This Committee considers whether there are general lessons for departments, and scrutinises closely those issues where the government rejects the Ombudsman's recommendations.

Our academic colleague, Professor Jack Hayward (2000, 2002, 2007), brought to the attention of the Ombudsman his case as one of a group of British civilians who were interned by the Japanese during the Second World War and who would have been entitled to compensation payments if the MoD had not 'maladministered' the compensation scheme by drawing it up too hastily, not announcing it clearly, changing the criteria after the scheme had started (without telling claimants), and setting criteria that excluded about 1,000 British internees. The case gained greater adverse publicity for the MoD than it might otherwise have done because the MoD at first refused Ann Abraham's recommendation to 'fulfil the debt of honour', which was the aim of the scheme (PHSO, 2005). Only when the Public Administration Committee decided to interview a defence minister did the MoD agree that errors had been made.

The caseload of the PHSO (2006: 9) is increasing; it examined nearly 2,000 'parliamentary' complaints in 2005–06. The departments or agencies most complained about were the Inland Revenue division dealing with Gordon Brown's working family tax credits (highly complex to administer and inappropriate for people whose incomes vary), of which 90 per cent of complaints were upheld; the Jobcentre Plus Agency (52 per cent upheld); and the Child Support Agency (83 per cent upheld). Nearly 90 per cent of the complaints against the Immigration and Nationality Directorate (IND) were also upheld. The Ombudsman's office has stronger formal powers to hold civil servants to account than have select committees, because it can interview individual officials (but not in public), and ask for searches of the relevant documents in departmental files. Yet joint working with Parliament is also important, because the refusal of departments to comply with the Ombudsman's recommendations can result in the Permanent Secretary and ministers being called to a Public Administration hearing – at which journalists will be present.

Reviewing the state of civil service accountability to Parliament in 2007, the Public Administration Committee argued against a 'formal separation of accountability' that would lead to officials being legally and personally accountable for the decisions they take (as in Sweden and Finland, for example), but

> Nonetheless, we believe that civil servants could be considerably more open with Parliament without threatening the doctrine of ministerial responsibility . . . we consider that increasing the expectation that civil servants will account honestly to Parliament does not undermine the principle of ministerial responsibility, but strengthens accountability as a whole. (Public Administration Committee, 2007, paras 56–7)

Internal accountability

Conventional 'internal' accountability through the departmental route up to the Permanent Secretary and to the Secretary of State expanded from the 1970s because of the growth in 'external' civil service accountability to Parliament. MPs' letters and questions from select committees and the Ombudsman forced senior officials and ministers to give increasing attention to what was happening further down the chain.

Yet conventional internal accountability also evolved in its own right, because post-1979 governments were determined to exercise control over the civil service and direct it towards their own objectives, as was shown in the previous chapter. The cumulative effect of the waves of financial management reforms that swept through government departments from the early 1980s onwards (the Financial Management Initiative, the management information systems and their successors) enhanced the internal accountability of officials to their departmental and agency superiors, and, ultimately, to ministers. Devolved budgeting systems, resource accounting (organising the division of departmental expenditure budgets to show how spending related to departmental objectives) and, under Gordon Brown as Chancellor, tying departmental budgets to specific policy outcomes in terms of Public Service Agreements, clarified to some extent the accountability relationships within government departments and agencies because they made transparent the object of the exercise and what officials were expected to achieve. The introduction of business planning systems, starting with the framework documents of the executive agencies, also contributed to this process.

Most of these schemes worked on the principle that responsibility for determining policy and setting targets could be separated from responsibility for delivering them. Ownership of responsibility is only clear when this separation can be reflected unambiguously in the organisational structure, as in the case of the DfT and its Highways Agency (the first advises on highly 'political' decisions such as new road projects; the second organises the technical building and maintenance of roads). As the Prison Service Agency and the Child Support Agency have shown, ministers and senior officials in the core departments can 'interfere' even in operational work. Pollitt (2003: 22, 50–1) thought the New Public Management solutions such as agencification and contracting-out were more likely to meet difficulties when applied to functions of a highly 'public' nature: subsidised; subject to complex legal constraints; involving the coercion of citizens; politically symbolic; and liable to political interference. It was therefore surprising that the solution John Reid offered in July 2006 for the problems of the Home Office's IND was for it to become an Executive Agency.

It would, however, be a mistake to think that the traditional structures provided better internal accountability. John Reid assured the Home Affairs Committee that 'if there are people culpable then they will have to bear responsibility', but his Permanent Secretary, David Normington, while confirming that he was 'completely clear that we have to have accountability of officials and we have to pin that on them', revealed that 'there was not someone who was responsible for foreign national prisoners. There were people responsible for the prisons and prisoners in general, but there were not people focused on this specific issue' (Home Affairs Committee, 2006: Q869). Moreover, of the officials appearing with John Reid (in post for two months), the Permanent Secretary had been there four months, the IND Director-General nine months and the Chief Executive of Offender Management (prisons) five months (ibid, Q866), leaving uncertain who might reasonably be considered responsible. It could be argued that the greater interest being shown by parliamentarians in the executive work of departments (one reason for governments trying to hive off the accounting for this work to the agencies themselves), has merely exposed the weak accountability of the traditional structures in practice, whatever the formal theory.

In 2007, the Public Administration Committee concluded that the internal accountability of civil servants remained problematic as 'there is no consensus about the respective responsibilities of ministers and civil servants' (Public Administration Committee, 2007: para. 23).

Consumerist accountability

Another external strand of accountability has also been extended. The strict constitutional statement that civil servants are not accountable directly to the public was challenged by the growth in consumerist accountability, or responsiveness to users. The implicit assumptions underpinning developments including the Citizen's Charter, Service First, the 'delivery agenda', 'Government Direct' and 'information age government' were that officials had a duty of accountability to service users, clients, customers or consumers.

Major's Charterism was part of the process of redirecting the preoccupations of senior officials and the ministers they advised from an overriding preoccupation with departmental budgets and inputs towards outputs, and moreover outputs determined to some extent by the service user. The shift came about partly because Major, thinking back to his time as the chair of Lambeth Housing Committee, was genuinely interested in ensuring that services met the wishes and needs of the people who used them, and partly because consumer satisfaction surveys were a relatively easy way to measure performance and thereby to put pressure on officials to do better. The Citizen's Charter Unit encouraged departments and agencies to produce audited performance standards and schemes for redress (financial compensation), and their Charters publicised the possibility of appeal, including to the Parliamentary Ombudsman (see Chapter 4).

The precise nature of these accountability relationships could be questioned. In its strongest forms, accountability must include allowance for amendatory or remedial actions and redress of grievances through various means (including financial compensation), and the compensation mechanisms available within the consumerist brands of accountability are often fairly limited. None the less, there is a real contrast between the culture and ethos of local branch offices of government departments in the 1970s, where the idea that those on the receiving end of service provision might be considered to have basic rights and expectations regarding the level of service being provided would have been viewed by all concerned as rather odd, and the customer orientation of modern offices as well as their online equivalents.

The devolved polities

The fourth category is in the sphere of the devolved polities. Whether because of their smaller population size (more akin to the Scandinavian democracies), different political cultures (seen, for example, in party systems that diverge from that of England), or merely the chance to consider the institutions afresh in an up-to-date context, the advent of devolution in both Scotland and Wales brought about a significant and marked change to the scale of civil service accountability.

Before devolution, officials working in the Scottish and Welsh Offices faced only basic scrutiny of their work, with a small number of ministerial superiors in each case, and a remote Parliament within which there were limited mechanisms of accountability (one select committee each to cover the full range of work in these multifunctional departments, plus the Public Accounts Committee to focus on financial matters). The coming of the Scottish Parliament and the National Assembly for Wales transformed this position, and brought elected representatives and an array of scrutiny mechanisms to the doorsteps of civil servants in Edinburgh and Cardiff.

As Keating observes for Scotland (2005: 98), the larger number of ministers increased ministerial control and policy direction over the work of civil servants. Paradoxically, however, 'the greater visibility and coverage of government in Scotland' – that is, the greater exposure of executive work to the general public – contributed to management problems and service delivery crises. As in Wales (Laffin, 2002: 40), Scottish ministers have strong contacts in local networks, meaning that 'they are better informed from outside the civil service', as a civil servant told researchers, 'so we have to be on our mettle' (Rhodes *et al.*, 2003: 96). Yet, if ministers and Parliament are uninterested in a policy sector, as seemed to be the case in Wales with community care (in Scotland, Parliament *was* making an input), civil servants can influence planning and strategy, with no need for ministerial support and therefore political oversight, because of their superior knowledge of the policy network (Rhodes *et al.*, 2003: 96, 125–7).

If MSPs (members of the Scottish Parliament) and AMs (Welsh Assembly members) were surprised by the formal convention that civil servants are accountable to, and answer to, ministers but not to other parliamentarians, civil servants were not used to such close and local scrutiny. MSPs and AMs of all parties have been encouraged to telephone or e-mail civil servants if they wanted to discuss matters directly, and have taken advantage of that opportunity. However, one MSP interviewed (in Pyper and Fingland, 2006) observed that there remained a tension for civil servants, exhibited in committee hearings, between the 'new openness' of the Scottish system and the inherited concept of accountability through ministers. In Wales, the tension seems to be lower, with civil servants tending in committees to reply directly to AMs without the genuflection traditional in Westminster to the authority of the minister (Laffin, 2002: 38).

The small number of parliamentarians to cover the normal range of ministries and subject committees has meant that many parliamentarians cover a number of committees, reducing the time they have for carrying out forensic scrutiny (the more so as the committees also prepare legislation), though this disadvantage is balanced to some extent by the presence of ex-ministers (with their 'inside knowledge') and up-and-coming future ministers on the committees. Some scrutiny reports from the Scottish committees are agreed to have made a real impact, such as the Enterprise and Lifelong Learning Committee's report on the prison estates review (Arter, 2004). Unlike the Westminster Parliament, the Scottish Executive is obliged to reply within a set time period to a committee report. Surveys of Welsh Assembly committees in 2001–02 found that accountability was weakened by AMs allocating little time to this function; and while subject committees were starting to spend more time discussing the monthly reports presented to them by ministers, there was little evidence that the Assembly Government had taken up their suggestions (Jones and Osmond, 2002). Indeed, the Richard Commission (2004) thought the number of AMs should be increased if Wales were to be given legislative powers, simply because the current committees have not demonstrated sufficient capacity for scrutiny and challenge (Osmond, 2005: 13–18).

A Public Service Ombudsman was established in Wales in 2005–06, combining into a 'one-stop shop' for citizens the Welsh Administration Ombudsman, the Health Service Commissioner for Wales, the Social Housing Ombudsman for Wales, and the Local Government Ombudsman. The same unifying convergence had already taken place in

Scotland in 2002, whereas the UK Ombudsman, while taking on the health role in 2005–06, deals with issues overlapping central–local boundaries only by collaborating voluntarily with Local Government Ombudsmen. The new Ombudsman institutions have followed more closely those of other countries in making them independent of government (nomination by Parliament, signed by the monarch) and freer access to citizens, who do not have to apply through their MP (Gay, 2005). Westminster MPs and peers have expressed their preference for similar changes to the UK Ombudsman (1993, 2000, 2003). A private member's bill introduced by Anthony Lester, a Liberal Democrat Peer, passed its Lords stages in 2004–05, but the government did not provide time in the legislative timetable to bring England up to date with Scotland and Wales.

Managing openness: freedom of information and the civil service

In the period since the 1980s, the civil service has been faced with the challenge of adapting to a slow but significant expansion of 'open government' and accommodating the long-delayed legislation that introduced a form of freedom of information. Given the comments made above regarding the underlying culture of secrecy within British government in general, and the civil service in particular, this new openness has been a major challenge.

The prevailing culture of secrecy imposed severe strain on some civil servants and contributed to crises of conscience in instances where officials believed they should be able to serve the public interest by disclosing sensitive information. These crises of conscience were best exemplified by the cases of Sarah Tisdall and Clive Ponting. The consequences of these cases included prosecution of the officials concerned (with mixed results – Tisdall was convicted but Ponting acquitted), a firm restatement of the limited nature of civil service accountability in the form of the Armstrong Memorandum, aspects of which were subsequently tested to destruction during the Westland affair in 1986, as was seen above (although this did not prevent the document's incorporation into the *Civil Service Code*), and a reinforcement of the secrecy legislation in the form of the 1989 Official Secrets Act. While this loosened the restrictions on certain categories of government information, it failed to meet the desire of reformers for a 'whistleblower's charter'.

The first signals of a changing climate of opinion within government came when the Major Administration published its 1993 White Paper on *Open Government*, and the subsequent 1994 *Code of Practice on Access to Government Information* put increased amounts of information automatically into the public domain. The Labour Party came to power in 1997 with a long-standing commitment to legislate for open government and freedom of information, but the policy became the subject of serious in-fighting between ministers, with senior civil servants playing their part in the lobbying and counter-lobbying surrounding the White Paper and draft bill. Eventually, the Freedom of Information Act was passed in 2000 (the Scottish equivalent being passed in 2002), but with a long delay before full implementation. From November 2002, government departments were required to produce publication schemes setting out the information they would publish proactively, and how this information could be accessed. This process occupied considerable amounts of time and energy for the civil service. The public's right of access did not come into force until January 2005, and even then there were exemptions covering information relating to national security, ongoing investigations, material whose release is prohibited by another law, or where the information can 'reasonably' be obtained elsewhere. Appeals can be lodged with the Information Commissioners (one in London and one in Edinburgh).

The FoI provisions represented a new and additional form of scrutiny for the civil service, although the final say on whether to release information remains with ministers. The flow of certain types of information from within government departments into the public domain has now become fairly routine, and for officials starting to make their careers within government departments there is now the certain knowledge that the documents they create and process might become the subject of freedom of information requests at some future point. The impact of this knowledge on the culture and working habits of the civil service remains to be seen, but it is likely to be significant. There have been occasional skirmishes, often precipitated by journalists eager to test the limits of the new 'freedom'. For example, days after the legislation came into force in 2005, access was sought to the Treasury papers relating to Britain's exit from the European Exchange Rate Mechanism in 1992, and there was a delay while former ministers (John Major and Norman Lamont) were consulted about the content of the documents. The papers were then published, and served to reveal (much sooner than would otherwise have been the case) the internal workings of this pivotal department at the height of the most significant financial crisis in modern times. Although there is continuing criticism of the operation of the Act, progress was demonstrated by the contrast with the publication later in 2005 of a letter from the Labour Chancellor, Denis Healey, sent in 1976 to the International Monetary Fund, asking for a loan of £2.3 billion to help Britain escape a sterling crisis. It revealed that he offered in return the budgetary reductions of £2.5 billion that started the cutbacks in the civil service. Published almost thirty years later (the standard time for opening up access to public records), it no longer had much relevance for contemporary policy-making (*Financial Times*, 10–11 December 2005).

Recommendations by the Public Administration Committee (2002) following the 'Jo Moore' affair stimulated the government into setting up the Phillis Review to review its system for communicating government information. Interest in the review was enhanced by the almost simultaneous and unprecedented flow of e-mails and other correspondence to the Hutton Inquiry, which 'lifted the veils on the inner workings of government' (Sue Cameron, *Financial Times*, 24–25 January 2004), rather than keeping it quiet for thirty years. The Phillis Review (2004: 4) found that a culture of secrecy and reluctant disclosure of information was at the root of the three-way breakdown in trust between government and politicians, the media and the general public. It suggested that the government should further liberalise the Act during implementation, in order to create a 'powerful tool to help rebuild public trust', by announcing that ministers would not use their veto; by making the default position one of disclosure; and by replacing the general exemption for policy analysis with a specific 'harm test', as in the Scottish FoI Act and the Open Government Code of the Welsh Assembly, which would permit information to be withheld only when it was likely to cause 'substantial harm'.

The UK government ruled out any speedy reconsideration, and its attitude can best be judged by its proposals at the end of 2006 to restrict departmental budgets for FoI work. Departments and the largest executive agencies and regulatory agencies (all staffed by civil servants), were together receiving about 1,200 requests a month at that time. For about 60 per cent of requests the information was provided in full; and for 20 per cent it was refused entirely. In the period June to September 2006, the FCO, the Departmental for Constitutional Affairs, and the Office of Gas and Electricity Markets were the least likely to grant the request in full; the MoD, the DfT and the DWP provided all the information requested in three-quarters of cases (Department for Constitutional Affairs, 2006). The most common reasons for refusal were that the request related to personal information; that [judicial] investigations were pending; or that the information had been provided in confidence. 'Formulation of government policy' and 'prejudice to the effective conduct of public affairs' were more controversial reasons for withholding information, and applied to about 13 per cent of cases.

Though the Information Commissioner for England, Richard Thomas, tried to settle disputes over non-disclosure amicably, he issued 187 formal decision notices in 2005–06, some ordering disclosure, some agreeing that the information need not be disclosed. The former group included a notice to the DES that it must supply minutes of some meetings (Information Commissioner's Office, 2006: 14). A journalist interested in an alleged schools funding crisis had asked for minutes of the meetings of the DES senior management group which discussed school budgets. The DES used the 'formulation of government policy' exemption to withhold them, and then appealed against the Commissioner's decision on disclosure. In what is likely to become a landmark decision, the Information Tribunal ruled that the reason for the exemption did not outweigh the public interest of disclosure. The former Cabinet Secretary, Andrew Turnbull, called as a witness for the government, said disclosure 'would strike at the heart of civil service confidentiality'. The Tribunal did not agree: it said understanding how government tackled important policy problems was more important; and that, though the names of the officials were unlikely to prove interesting, there was no public interest in their suppression either (Robert Verkaik, case report, *Independent*, 9 March 2007).

The expansion in freedom of information and transparency on departmental activities has benefited from the formal provisions on open government, which move the UK (especially in Scotland and Wales) nearer to the norms and practices of other liberal democracies. However, the many references in this chapter (and indeed throughout the book as a whole) to instances of 'scandals' or 'affairs' suggests that more can be learned about civil service behaviour and procedures from decisions that have unintended consequences than from the formal procedures.

Conclusion

In contrast to the evidence presented in some other chapters, notably those dealing with the internal management of the civil service

(Chapter 4) and the reward structure of officials (Chapter 6), the British civil service is at its least 'modernised' – certainly by comparison with the standards of other liberal democracies – when it comes to access to information. It would appear that the Whitehall model resisted change more effectively where its traditional conventions protected ministers and top officials from public scrutiny than where they protected junior officials from changes to their work and careers.

Yet there has been change and modernisation even in this domain. First, where it concerns officials accounting on their own behalf, we have seen that, whatever the Whitehall model said about ministerial responsibility, officials rather than ministers (or as well as ministers in the Crichel Down case), have long been held responsible (and even publicly) for departmental failures that come to light, and this trend seems to be growing. Modern management techniques have added to the numbers and types of ways in which civil servants find their work measured and reported. Second, some particular and hopefully exceptional events, which originated with ministers or their political advisers, have ended in high-profile public inquiries, to which government felt obliged to provide information that revealed not only the specific activities and circumstances of those events but also the minutiae and day-to-day functioning of the British civil service (the weaknesses of its personnel management; the incapacity of financial departments; the poor coordination between departments; the attitudes of some civil servants to MPs or shareholders, or to their duties to the courts). Hence the importance of the documents and testimonies placed in the public domain by such episodes as the 1996 Scott inquiry into the DTI's management of export licences for the sale of defence equipment to Iraq; the Hutton inquiry into the circumstances surrounding the death in 2003 of Dr David Kelly; and the 2004 Butler inquiry into the government's handling of intelligence information relating to weapons of mass destruction.

These incidents related directly to the debate about improving conventional parliamentary accountability, because the documents available to the inquiry teams made MPs realise just how much they had fettered their own capacity for scrutiny by accepting the 'traditional' obstacles put in their way by ministers and civil servants. The Butler report, which showed beyond all speculation on 'sofa government' that the mechanisms underpinning formal accountability were undermined fundamentally by the 'unscripted' meetings of crucial decisions, indirectly intensified and justified the demand already present from Charter 88, Liberty and other groups for better general and direct access to the information that existed. The media debate on the inquiries exposed the fact, as the Phillis Review recognised, that the public had lost trust in the traditional mechanisms for reporting and accounting for government decisions. People were no longer prepared to accept that 'the gentlemen in Whitehall' know best, but wanted to judge for themselves.

In this area, as in others covered by this book, the story is one of a civil service evolving to meet the challenges of an increasingly complex polity within a context of gradual, progressive modernisation. The adaptation to a changing environment has been flawed, and the consequences of changes to civil service accountability, as well as the expansion of freedom of information, sometimes problematic and partial. None the less, the need for change (contrary to the view held by the defenders of the Whitehall 'tradition') has been clear, and the acceptance of change, albeit often on negotiated terms, very much in line with the historical development of this institution.

6

The Human and Managerial Dimension

Today's civil service shares features with the civil service of a century ago, and yet there have been profound changes. Whether these changes are interpreted as undermining the Whitehall model, adapting it to the new demands of civil and political society, or 'hollowing-out' the central state, they have had a practical impact on the working lives of individual civil servants.

The principles of civil service recruitment, which are integral to the Whitehall model, derive from the Northcote–Trevelyan Report of 1854. This report recommended selection on merit on the basis of fair and open competition in 'literary' examinations, followed by advancement within the service (see Drewry and Butcher, 1991: 41–6; Pyper, 1991: 9–12). The Fulton Committee (1968), appointed by Prime Minister Harold Wilson to examine such questions, expressed postwar concerns about whether people recruited in this way had the right skills for a modern civil service, but its recommendations for more technical expertise and training were not fully implemented. However, the New Public Management reforms of the 1980s (see Chapter 4) addressed other weaknesses it saw in civil servants with 'new people management' (Horton, 2000: 212) that copied private sector management techniques. In other ways, such as its approach to social diversity, the civil service is a model employer, in advance of the private sector.

Rules on civil service careers can be brought into line with ministers' wishes more easily than in many other countries because they do not need to be agreed by Parliament. The government makes most changes to the *Civil Service Management Code* by Orders in Council that are approved automatically by the Queen. Nevertheless, if changes are proposed that are unacceptable to trade unions, ministers may have to be prepared to take the consequences, as the Chancellor,

Geoffrey Howe, did on public-sector pay in 1980 (Hoskyns, 2000: 196). These consequences may be painful, as Tony Blair admitted in 1999 when he talked about 'the scars on his back' from his battles over the modernisation agenda, a comment which most took as referring to the civil service (Gillman, 2001: 71).

Recruitment of civil servants

Nearly all civil servants are recruited into the 'main stream' by departments, whose adherence to the principle of 'fair, open and on merit' is audited by the Civil Service Commissioners, first appointed in 1855. It is possible to reach the highest posts from the bottom – as did John Herbercq, in charge of civil service management in the 1980s, and Terry Heiser at the Department of Environment in the 1990s – but such promotion is rare. For most entrants, the civil service is not a career. A third of civil servants who left in 2003–04 were aged under 30 (29 per cent of men, 38 per cent of women; the statistics on staffing in this chapter come from the annual *Civil Service Statistics*, unless stated otherwise).

The classic Whitehall profile belongs to the small minority recruited into the 'fast stream', selected for their potential to reach the Senior Civil Service (see Table 6.1). They are helped to progress quickly by showing what they can do in posts close to ministers and top officials. Other senior officials join by 'direct' or 'lateral entry', through open competition to posts needing particular skills. This method was highlighted in 1984 after Michael Heseltine, without consulting the Civil Service Commission, appointed Peter Levene, a defence company executive, as head of defence procurement. The controversy led to a ruling that departments could make short-term (five-year) appointments without competition, but that longer or very senior appointments had to involve the Commission (Pyper, 1995a: 36–7).

Ministers now use this 'temporary civil servant' route to appoint 'special advisers' and pay them from public funds (see Chapter 2 for a full discussion). Technical specialists such as Tom Burke, Green Alliance member and adviser to the Conservative Environment Minister, Chris Patten, or Keith Hellawall, former Chief Constable of West Yorkshire Police, as UK Anti-Drugs Coordinator in the first Blair term, can be brought in quickly. In personnel management terms, special advisers pose problems when they move from advising ministers to giving instructions that clash with the civil servants' *Code of Conduct*, as Jo Moore did in the Department of Transport, Local

Table 6.1 Steps in civil service grade classification

Administration Group	Science Group	Open structure (1972)	Unified structure (1987)	Senior civil service (1996)	Responsibility levels (1996)	New titles (2002)	Pay bands (2002)	Salary band (£000s) (2005)
Permanent Secretary		*	1					130–264
Deputy Secretary		*	2	*	JESP 19–22	Director General	3	93–198
Under Secretary		*	3	*	JESP 13–18	Director	2	76–160
Executive Directing grade	Chief Scientific Officer (B)		4	*	JESP 11–14		1a	64–127
Assistant Secretary	Deputy Chief Scientific Officer		5	*	JESP 7–12	Deputy Director	1	55–116
Senior Principal	Senior Principal Scientific Officer		6				A	
Principal	Principal Scientific Officer		7		6	Assistant Director	A	
Senior Executive Officer	Senior Scientific Officer				5		B2	
Higher Executive Officer (D) ('fast stream' – internal)							special	
Higher Executive Officer	Higher Scientific Officer				4		B2	
Administration Trainee (AT) ('fast stream' – recruits)							special	
Executive Officer	Scientific Officer				3		B1	
Administrative Officer					2		C2	
Administrative Assistant	Assistant Scientific Officer				1		C1	

Notes: JESP = Job Evaluation for Senior Posts; Administrative Officers and Assistants were called Clerical Officers and Assistants until 1987.
* An asterisk means these grades were or are part of the open structure (1972–87) or SCS (1996 to date).
Sources: Cabinet Office, *Civil Service Statistics*, 1984, 1996; www.civilservice.gov.uk, 'SCS Pay System' (accessed 18 November 2006); Cabinet Office pay bands are given in *The Government's Expenditure Plans 1999–00 to 2001–02*, Cm 4221 (Stationery Office, 1999).

Government and the Regions (see Chapter 2). The department's Permanent Secretary found his powers to discipline civil servants did not apply to special advisers, who could be dismissed only by their minister. The subsequent politically-charged dispute about temporary civil servants overshadowed longer-term issues about permanent officials.

Fast stream recruitment

Fast-stream recruitment has long been criticised by those who thought it gave 'preference to those with a certain type of social background and educational history' (Kelsall, 1956: 169). The Fulton Committee found that 71 per cent of recent recruits into the Administrative Class (the fast stream of its time), had been to fee-paying schools, and 80 per cent to Oxbridge (Oxford and Cambridge). The Committee also worried about the strong presence of arts graduates at a time of rapid technological change.

Some recent figures for the general (now 'graduate') fast stream (GFS) are presented in Table 6.2. There are other fast streams, but the question of 'social exclusivity' is particularly associated with the general fast stream, because it is a surer way to the top than specialist fast streams. The proportion of GFS recruits from Oxbridge has halved since 1982. Degree subjects are spread more evenly. Men are not always in the majority, and more people from ethnic minority groups and/or with physical disabilities are being recruited. The successful candidate is still likely to have attended a fee-paying school (in 1997, 50 per cent had attended independent schools; *Hansard, HC Debates*, 308: 272). The civil service always defends the selection process (to do otherwise would undermine senior officials), but revises it constantly in the light of criticism and the changing possibilities of IT (see Table 6.3 for a summary of the reviews).

Fast-stream assessment is rooted in a two-stage selection process introduced after the Second World War (Drewry and Butcher, 1991: 105), which enabled middle class, public-school, Oxbridge, 'literary' graduates to perform better than others. The system was changed in 1971, although not to the extent recommended by Fulton. The first stage became a written qualifying test (QT) of intellectual abilities, marked anonymously. The second stage of interviews, paper-drafting and committee activity mirrored civil service work. When the Oxbridge dominance continued, critics suggested there was unconscious bias, but Oxbridge candidates did even better at the anonymous QT stage than during the second stage. Reviews in 1979 and 1983 therefore concluded that the process was sound.

Table 6.2   Successful candidates to the graduate (general) fast stream

Percentage of successful external candidates	1988 (%)	1993 (%)	1998 (%)	2002 (%)	2005 (%)
Men	67	61	56	43	55
Oxbridge	42	59	52	36	37
Arts	68	48	70	45	38
Social sciences	18	18	n.a.	29	30
Science and technology	11	24	n.a.	23	22
Other subjects	3	10	n.a.	2	10
From minority ethnic groups	n.a.	n.a.	5	7.4	3.6
Declared a disability	n.a.	n.a.	2	4.7	8.9
Total number of successful external candidates (= N)	**97**	**119**	**136**	**256**	**336**
Number of Oxbridge successes among external candidates	41	70	67	91	124
Internal candidates					
Number of internal applicants	n.a.	n.a.	48	92	107
Number of places offered	n.a.	n.a.	12	29	53
Internal scheme success rate (%)	n.a.	n.a.	25	32	50

Notes: n.a. = data not available. University and degree subject are for first degree.
Sources: 1988–93 Compiled from Cabinet Office (1994b); 1998–2005 Cabinet Office (2006e).

In 1992, none of the 452 applicants with ethnic minority backgrounds passed the second stage (*The Independent*, 22 October 1992). The Civil Service Commission said that half the failures could be explained by candidates' weak academic qualifications (white candidates with the same qualifications would fail too), but that it had not identified the remaining causal factors. The Commission for Racial Equality (CRE) announced it would undertake a formal investigation for possible indirect discrimination, which it suspended while the Cabinet Office introduced changes to marketing, tests and assessment. Questions in the QT which seemed to disadvantage women and/or ethnic minority candidates were 'weeded out'. Applicants with disabilities such as dyslexia were offered an interview instead of the QT. The QT mark was weighted with 'biodata' useful to the civil service (candidates' achievements and interpersonal skills), without introducing new bias. A preliminary 'self-assessment' test was introduced to help candidates familiarise themselves with the procedures (and filter out unrealistic applications). Assessors were advised about indirect discrimination, and scrutinised for potential bias, including formal warnings. Finally, a competence-based method of assessment was adopted for the second stage in 1999, weighing candidates' behaviour against a 'fast stream person specification', and the CRE withdrew its objections. Assessors are now looking for candidates who demonstrate delivery skills (drive for results, learning and improving); intellectual capacity (decision-making, constructive thinking), and interpersonal skills (building productive relationships, communication with impact).

Marketing the GFS changed following a review of its procedures as part of the *Civil Service Reform* programme (Cabinet Office, 1999b). The review of the GFS said that it ought to send the same messages about diversity as the civil service as a whole (Cabinet Office, 2001b: paras 1.6–1.9). More effort (including open days, internships and work placements) was made to reach a wider range of universities, ethnic minority undergraduates and students with disabilities. The presence of only 4 per cent of recruits from ethnic minorities in 2005 implies there is still work to do (13 per cent of first-year students in 1998–99 were from these groups. Cabinet Office, 2001b: Annex 2). Further, although the 'Headline Figure' promoted in 2006 was that 'successful candidates graduated from over 50 universities', two universities produced 37 per cent of these: there were no successful candidates from a further 52 universities.

Recruitment on merit by fair and open competition will always bring high success rates for Oxbridge students, since Oxbridge itself selects from a pool of strong candidates on similar principles. Indeed, most private companies are fishing in the same pool. On the other hand, candidates of equivalent merit, but disadvantaged by social and educational factors, are currently lost to the fast stream. These candidates often lack the support of middle-class or 'civil service' families, fee-paying schools, tutors and careers advisers who are equipped to direct good candidates towards the fast stream. While 'some top universities with high Fast Stream success rates provide intensive coaching for potential Fast Stream candidates' (Cabinet Office, 2001b: para 7.36), students and careers advisers in other universities 'remained sceptical' about the value of applying (para. 6.32). Oxbridge's tutorial-based teaching increases the advantages of candidates (Cabinet Office, 1994b). More fundamentally, there is a symbiosis between Oxbridge and 'Whitehall', one turning out graduates trained in researching, writing and debating papers with their tutors, the other preparing White Papers and briefs for ministers, and made manifest in a recruitment

Table 6.3   Official reports on 'fast stream' recruitment

Findings	Recommendations	Actions
1968 Fulton Committee		
Dominance of the 'amateur' and 'generalist', with a classics or arts degree	More emphasis on 'relevant' qualifications Select by specialist exams (Method I) not by tests of general skills (Method II) Recruit to specific posts	'Relevance' rejected Method II and general stream kept, some special streams Open recruitment increasing from late 1980s Selection criteria lowered
Social and educational exclusiveness in recruitment	Inquire into selection process Widen graduate entry	More fast-stream places offered to internal candidates
1969 Davies Committee		
Found no evidence of bias; commended Method II	Qualifying IQ test with objectively-marked cognitive tests; tests of relevant skills	Recommendations implemented in recruitment of Administrative Trainees (i.e. fast-stream)
1977 House of Commons Expenditure Committee		
Selection process biased in favour of independent schools and Oxbridge	Abolish Administration Trainee Scheme; recruit from inside Appoint majority of Commission from outside civil service	AT Review Committee set up Minority of outsiders appointed to Commission (balanced by 1994)
1979 Allen Committee		
Selection process fair; Civil Service must have graduate scheme like other employers	Keep Administration Trainee scheme Introduce parallel scheme for internal candidates	Fast stream introduced with tougher criteria Half the fast stream to come from internal candidates
1983 Atkinson Committee		
Selection system had a high reputation; should look for more candidates outside Oxbridge	Strengthen links with non-Oxbridge universities Increase lateral entry Bring on mainstream insiders	Visits to many universities Age limits relaxed Departments to identify more internal candidates

(Continued)

Table 6.3   (Continued)

Findings	Recommendations	Actions
1994 Cabinet Office, Review of Fast Stream Recruitment		
Perceptions of bias towards Oxbridge and against serving officials damages civil service	External audit of selection process Make scheme more accessible to internal candidates	Commissioners audit selection process Number of internal applicants continues to decline
1998 Civil Service Commissioners, Audit of General Fast Stream		
Cabinet Office and Capita RAS take considerable care to ensure fair, open, objective recruitment	Introduce internal checks Set up complaints procedures Devise policy on surplus successful candidates	Implemented Commission for Racial Equality lifts threat of court action
2001 Cabinet Office, Redefining the Fast Stream		
Fast stream still essential, but to be aligned better with overall civil service reform agenda	Market to ethnic minorities and broader range of universities Develop In-Service Scheme Use web to inform and select	Outreach programmes, training, work placements for students In-Service Scheme re-launched; publicity, seminars

scheme devised by senior civil servants to select people for this work. These talents are less useful when the government needs officials able to manage a diverse set of people, programmes and technologies. The 'Bringing In and Bringing On Talent' group of the Civil Service Management Committee said it wanted 'to bring in new entrants to the civil service from a more diverse group … to broaden horizons, improve innovative thinking and increase the breadth of the skill base' (Cabinet Office, 2001b: para. 1.2).

The in-service fast stream competition has expanded in the last few years to 'bring on' more 'mainstream' officials. The Fulton Report, several reviews and civil service unions had called for serving officials who showed merit to advance to senior posts (see Table 6.3) but to little effect. While Britain is not the only country to bring in new recruits at the training grade of senior officials (France does too), it is not universal. Australia, though adopting Britain's Northcote–Trevelyan reforms, by 1959 had already rejected proposals for a direct entry training grade on the grounds that it was incompatible with Australia's egalitarian principles, and it directed its attention to educating serving officials (Halligan, 2003: 95–6).

The Thatcher Government introduced in 1981 a new internal 'fast stream' scheme that was intended to produce half the annual intake 'in-house' from officials nominated by departments. This aim was never remotely reached (Drewry and Butcher, 1991: 105–8). Departments did not nominate officials; they wanted the 'quality' they thought they obtained through external competition. Only 9 per cent of GFS recruits in 1998 came through the internal scheme (see Table 6.2). *Civil Service Reform* committed departments to 'talent spotting' internal candidates (Cabinet Office, 1999b: key action 16 xxi); website information was provided matching that for the external scheme. The first year of marketing 'revealed a pent-up demand', and places were offered to all who met the fast-stream standard. Ethnic diversity was not monitored until 2004, but in the following two years, 13–15 per cent of the officials nominated and accepted were from ethnic minorities, 48–68 per cent were women, and 4–7 per cent of the new recruits were disabled (Cabinet Office, 2006e). A non-graduate official in the Foreign and Commonwealth Office (FCO) who was promoted to fast stream grade and potentially ambassador level by passing similar tests to those of the GFS, said: 'If you pass the assessment centres you can compete with everyone' (Gillman, 2001: 104).

Despite these successes, the internal recruits still remain a small percentage of the fast stream (9 per cent in 1998; 16 per cent in 2005), because the number of external recruits has also expanded. Equalisation and diversification in the fast stream have in effect been accomplished by adding people from under-represented groups without disturbing the incumbent groups (the number of Oxbridge recruits increased from 67 in 1998 to 124 in 2005). Recruiters already stress that applicants must not be led to expect that promotion will follow automatically. The test case on whether the SCS really has embraced diversity will be when recent entrants seek advancement through what is a rapidly narrowing funnel.

Qualifications, training and experience

The Fulton Committee and others worried about populating the higher ranks of Whitehall with Oxbridge arts graduates because they thought this system produced a civil service with an insufficient understanding of people, business or modern technology. During the Second World War, Harold Wilson, Director of Economics and Statistics at the Ministry of Fuel, and his fellow ex-academic, John Fulton, 'used to grumble together about the amateurishness of the civil service and the need for an injection of professional skills' (Ziegler, 1993: 37). Fulton found the civil service was dominated by the 'generalist' or 'all-rounder', while 'scientists, engineers and members of other specialist classes were given neither full responsibilities nor 'the corresponding authority'. It recommended that specialists be given management training and opportunities, while generalists should specialise in economic or social administration: all officials should receive professional training at a Civil Service College. There should be greater mobility between Whitehall and outside employment (Fulton, 1968: 104).

Specialists and generalists

Bevir and Rhodes (2003: 146–67) argue that the concept of the 'generalist' who could offer advice in any field from accumulated wisdom was a Tory ideal. The Socialist or Fabian preference for an expert bureaucracy was expressed in the Fulton Report, and more explicitly by Kellner and Crowther-Hunt (1980), who blamed generalists for not implementing the recommendations. A liberal critique of the 'generalist administrative class' came from Thatcher's former adviser, Hoskyns (1983, 2000) and the academic Fry (1993), who wanted more specialists and outsiders to be recruited. The Whig view was in the title of Major's White Paper *The Civil Service: Continuity and Change* (Cabinet Office, 1994a), which defended 'the defining principles and standards' of the Whitehall model yet agreed that 'new blood' was needed.

The lowly position of the scientist was corroborated by the Hutton Inquiry (hearings: 11 August 2003) into the death of Dr David Kelly CMG, the government's expert on chemical and biological proliferation. The Ministry of Defence's personnel director agreed that the scientist was promoted to Grade 5 in 1992, that those at Grade 5 'in general' joined the new SCS, and that the 'pay [Kelly] had … is well within the band of pay that would be available for a senior civil servant … It is just that he [was] not managed as a member of the Senior Civil Service, he [was] not part of its corporate programme'. Fulton in 1968 had recommended that all specialist and administrative 'classes' be merged into a single unified grading scheme. The structure introduced in 1972 (see Table 6.1 on page 194) covered only the top three grades, which generalists continue to dominate. Despite his earlier scepticism about the quality of the civil service, Harold Wilson's experience of Whitehall also made him deferential to the senior generalists he rather admired (Ziegler, 1993: 184–5), and 'Whigs' thought generalists were needed to synthesise specialists' advice for ministers. However, in other developed countries (for example, Australia, Denmark, France, Sweden), ministers receive advice from top specialists directly. Indeed, according to Foster (2001: 741), Labour ministers in 1997 were disappointed to find that they did not have immediate access to 'a specialist civil servant who knew everything known on a particular topic'.

Foster (2001: 729–31) suggests that officials of all types lost 'power and authority' when Thatcher's ministers, keen to make savings (see Chapter 4), and with their own policy ideas, let professional expertise run down. He ascribes the failings of the poll tax, the Dangerous Dogs Act and the Child Support Agency to inadequate professional consideration of implementation. A prominent study of the poll tax decision clarified the terms 'generalist' and 'specialist' when it noted that the Department of Environment (DoE) officials involved, from Heiser downwards, had specialised in local government policy and lacked the detachment of 'all-rounders', yet they were not 'specialists' in the Fulton sense of being trained to evaluate the evidence and likely outcomes, a problem made worse by their failure to consult the real professionals in local government finance (Butler *et al.*, 1994: 206–23, 71).

In the Blair Government, civil service recruiters started to stress that they need generalists familiar with scientific issues and the interpretation and presentation of numerical data. The prime minister's Performance and Innovation Unit (PIU, 2000: 5–6) urged the recruitment of more specialists, to improve evidence-based policy-making. Yet the government experienced great difficulty in attracting them. Job satisfaction is low for specialists cut off from policy-making and from higher-level posts. The proportion of SCS economist posts had dropped sharply in the 1990s; and the top posts for social and operational researchers just reached the lowest SCS level (PIU, 2000: 17–18). The civil service needs to be made more attractive to specialists, by greater use of personal promotion if they want specialist careers (without administrative responsibilities), and higher pay to show their expertise is valued (PIU, 2000: 6; see also OECD, 2002). Recruitment to the specialist fast-stream schemes has improved recently, but 20–30 per cent of these posts remain unfilled each year (Cabinet Office, 2006d).

In 2004 (as noted in Chapter 2), the group leading *Civil Service Reform* announced that the generalist/specialist dichotomy would be replaced by three 'career groupings': policy expert (evidence-based advice), operational delivery (expertise in customer service, large-scale management); and corporate services (finance, human resources, IT, procurement). A 'Professional Skills for Government' Programme would place posts and people into one of three 'careers' defined by the competences required. The Cabinet Office insisted that the groupings would not create new silos; and that all routes could lead to the top (see www.psg.civilservice.gov.uk). Levitt and Solesbury (2006: 11) were sceptical, seeing the programme as a defensive reaction of traditional policy-making civil servants to the influx of specialist outsiders being recruited though open competition. None the less, this belated recognition of the need for evidence-based policy should be welcomed.

Training, development and professional skills

The Fulton Committee described Whitehall as 'amateur' because it recruited graduates of any discipline, and gave them little formal training. Officials in other countries studied subjects related to government (law in Japan and Italy, law plus another subject in Germany; social or natural sciences or economics in Denmark). Fulton made much of the French Ecole Nationale d'Administration (ENA), yet many other countries with competent officials, such as Denmark and the Netherlands, prefer 'on-the-job' training. The current emphasis internationally is on 'flexible people' (Horton and Farnham, 2000: 314), and British casualness has some advantages over the French pattern of fixing on a public service career at the age of 18, which is a straight-jacket, not least for the person involved.

The Civil Service College that Fulton hoped would emulate the ENA was set up in London, Sunningdale and Edinburgh (the last fell victim to cutbacks but was partially revived after devolution). Departments trained most staff, while the College's role was to 'professionalise' graduate recruits (Duggett, 2001: 99). However, its courses on economics, social science and statistics were rejected by fast-streamers, especially as (unlike ENA students) their careers were not determined by a final examination. Thatcher's 'managerialism' (see Chapter 4) incited generalists to learn financial and performance management; and specialists felt it worthwhile taking generalists' courses after the unified grading structure was extended in 1987 (see Table 6.1 on page 194). A rare compulsory training scheme, the six-week Top Management Programme for those entering grade 3, where officials were mixed with private-sector managers, was designed by the Cabinet Office in 1985 and initially resisted by the College (Hennessy, 1990: 527). Similar but briefer management courses were then introduced for more junior staff. In the 1990s, *Development and Training for Civil Servants* (Cabinet Office, 1996: 2) sent messages about 'greater numeracy skills' and 'better managerial skills' that could have come from Fulton and would be heard again under New Labour. Individuals and departments were asked to take responsibility for their own 'personal development', as happened in the private sector and local government; but it was not a 'laissez-faire' approach, because departments were simultaneously being pushed to acquire 'Investors in People' status.

Modernising Government portrayed the public service as 'a learning organisation' (Cabinet Office, 1999a: 56). The Civil Service College was brought into a new Centre for Management and Policy Studies in the Cabinet Office. In the first few years there were only modest changes, despite devolution leading to a reopening of the College in Edinburgh, and the College collaborated with Cranfield and other universities (in Glasgow, Birmingham and elsewhere) in promoting public-sector MBAs or Master's degrees in Public Administration. After 2004, civil service training moved into a 're-centralising' phase, with all officials pressed to identify and acquire the 'Professional Skills for Government' they needed. The Civil Service College was re-created in 2005 as the National School of Government (a non-ministerial department). It soon offered modules from 'Brush up your grammar' to a 'Developing Top Management' programme (£6,500 for two weeks) for SCS aspirants, and lunchtime seminars for the SCS. 'Professionalisation' from the top is a new goal in the Fulton image, but the College itself is likely to remain 'peripheral' (Theakston 1995: 103) when compared with ENA, whose students use their 'old boy' networks to dominate public- and private-sector affairs, not to mention political life.

Experience

The traditional training method in Britain is experience, for senior officials through service in a variety of posts. The Oughton Report (Efficiency Unit, 1993: 3) repeated the Fulton criticism that officials (like ministers) moved offices and jobs too frequently for performance to be assessed. The Southgate review of the Treasury concurred: 'No sooner do staff begin to come to terms with a new area than they are whisked off to do something else' (Southgate, 1994: 20). By 2004, there was 'an expectation of a four-year term for SCS postings' (Cabinet Office, 2006f: 38), balancing depth and breadth of experience.

Civil servants of the 'Whitehall' model had little experience of other sectors: 'No senior official in the DoE responsible for the poll tax had ever worked in local government' (Butler *et al.*, 1994: 221). In Britain, national and local careers are separate (unlike in France or Germany, where national, regional and local careers interleave). The Oughton Report found that a quarter of senior officials had spent some time in an outside post, but only about one in ten had ever worked in industry or business (Efficiency Unit, 1993: 46–7). In 1996, the Major Government asked for a 10 per cent increase per year in secondments to business (Cabinet Office, 1996: 30); and this modest aim was continued under Blair. By 2005 (Cabinet Office, 2006e: 38) more than half the SCS had spent at least a year outside the sector, and senior recruits from other sectors were being given a higher profile in official publications, conveying different expectations, inside and outside the civil service, of what was needed to become a top 'Whitehall' official.

New people management

Traditional management of civil servants was highly centralised because it was a way of unifying departments through common conditions of service. It was in the hands of the Treasury because of the impact of the wages bill on the national budget. Then Wilson followed Fulton's recommendation to assign corporate direction to a specialised department: 'the Civil Service Department (CSD) marked the zenith of centralised civil service management' (Maor and Stevens, 1997: 533). Employment practices were standardised and industrial relations paternalistic and collectivist; the government negotiated with trade union leaders on pay and other conditions of employment. Staff had high security of tenure and remuneration; it was a system that rewarded loyalty, conformity and long service (Horton, 2000: 211).

Margaret Thatcher abolished the CSD. Its future was already in question, and 'the CSD's apparent inclination to appease the unions during the civil service strike of 1981 ensured its death later that year' (Fry, 1985: 91). Pay-related functions went to the Treasury, and the rest to a Management & Personnel Office which from 1983 and under various names has been part of the Cabinet Office (see Lee *et al.*, 1998: 134–40, 238–40). In 1983, departments were given power to recruit their own clerical and other junior staff, and other career policies, such as training, soon followed. From then on, the conditions of service associated with the Whitehall model were challenged by new policies, such as competition for jobs, individualised contracts and performance pay. In 1994, a decision to 'reduce the Treasury to its core business' encouraged the transfer of its remaining civil service functions to the Cabinet Office civil service unit (see Bevir and Rhodes, 2003: 179; Southgate, 1994: 94–5). Thus a special department was again responsible for managing the civil service – but with far fewer powers than the CSD had to ensure a unified service, because so much had meanwhile been delegated to departments, as we shall see below.

Open competition for jobs

The creation of executive agencies (see Chapter 4) inaugurated a new way of appointing senior civil servants: by competition between officials and outside candidates. Michael Bichard, later Permanent Secretary of the Department of Education and Employment, was among the first to be selected as chief executive of an Agency in open competition, after managing successfully two large local authorities. Early criticisms centred on the role of ministers in influencing the appointment process: when Derek Lewis was chosen as Prison Service chief executive in 1992 the selection criteria included 'successful management of change' but not experience of prison management or Whitehall. Career officials would probably not have transferred IRA prisoners closer to home at a critical stage in Anglo-Irish negotiations, as Lewis did. On the other hand, ignorance of Home Office ways was seen as advantageous by ministers, who thought the problems with prisons lay with the Prison Service. Disquiet was increased by two Orders in Council of 1991: one abolished the Civil Service Commission (directed largely by civil servants) and created an Office to support the new Commissioners (mainly human resources experts from outside); another allowed departments to recruit their own staff to just below grade 7, within a code written by the Minister for the Civil Service (that is the prime minister). 'Since 1991 the Civil Service Commission has not existed,' said one academic (Chapman, 1997: 29).

For 'NPM' supporters, freeing-up recruitment would add new talents and flexibility. The Canadian public service already used lateral entry from industry, commerce and academia to a significant extent (Pyper, 1995a: 21). Iceland, Sweden, the Netherlands and New Zealand have gone even further than Britain in delegating and opening up recruitment (OECD, 2003: 11; 2004: 4). For others, the demise of the Commission presaged a return to Victorian corruption and partisan influence (Chapman, 1997: 29). O'Toole (1993: 2–3) speculated whether people brought in through open competition would feel frustrated by 'inefficient' democratic accountability. The Major Government half-accepted such arguments and gave responsibility for the Recruitment Code to the Commissioners, but reduced their direct intervention to appointments to the SCS made by open competition or as exceptions to the Code. By 1997, over two-thirds of chief executives had been selected through open competition, with more than a third of those appointed coming from outside the civil service (Public Service Committee, 1998: para. 196).

After *Continuity and Change* (Cabinet Office, 1994a), some traditional SCS posts were also opened to external candidates: David Clark, Minister for the Public Service in the first Blair Government, defended the principle, saying 'people from the outside … gingered up and added a new dimension, new blood' (Public Service Committee, 1998: para. 196). Numerous studies had found that traditional 'mandarins' were interested in policy advice, but not business-style management (Campbell and Wilson, 1995: 42–3). Open competitions for SCS posts expanded under Labour: from 83 in 1997–98 to 158 in 1999–2000, with only a third won by civil servants (Civil Service Commissioners, 2000). Of the twenty top posts opened up in 2005–06, just over half went to Civil Servants (Civil Service Commissioners, 2006). Nevertheless, we should bear in mind the increase in all SCS grades under Labour, which means that external recruits have added to, and not replaced, the number of traditional promotions.

As numbers of both competitions and SCS posts grew, the Commissioners started to delegate to departments those without particular significance. The Scottish Executive, the Welsh Assembly and departments now organise their own recruitment of most SCS posts, in conformity with the Code. The range of posts in which the Commissioners played a direct role was reduced officially in 2002 to open competitions for 'Top 200' posts (former grades 1 and 2). For the 'Top 200', the Senior Leadership Committee (formerly the Senior Appointments Selection Committee), chaired by the Head of the Home Civil Service, and attended by the First Civil Service Commissioner, decides whether there should be open competition. After Gus O'Donnell became Head of the Home Civil Service in 2005, all appointments at this level (not just open competitions) involved the Civil Service

Commissioners (letter from First Commissioner to *The Independent*, 9 January 2007).

In her 2006 report, the new First Civil Service Commissioner raised the issue of the more traditional form of internal appointment to posts in the SCS, and suggested Commissioners should monitor internal transfers and promotions:

> I find it somewhat incongruous that public assurance about appointment on merit is not given here in a way comparable to external recruitment ... Our approach does not allow Ministers the opportunity to express a preference among candidates ... Our role would be to ensure the appointment on merit of the most suitable candidate for any senior position in an impartial Civil Service. (Civil Service Commissioners, 2006: 3)

Contracts

Fixed-term contracts were proposed by Fulton for a few policy advisers, but it seems they were resisted by the civil service (Winstone, 2003: 12). They have been used in Australia since 1983 to encourage people from the private sector to enter the Senior Executive Service through open competition (Halligan, 2003: 98). The unorthodox appointment of Levene, having been authorised retrospectively, made it easier for others. Fixed-term contracts were then used for agency chief executives, because remuneration could then be adapted to attract external candidates and incorporate performance pay.

Continuity and Change (Cabinet Office, 1994a: 35) extended the concept to individualised contracts for all SCS officials apart from Permanent Secretaries. In practice, 'individualisation' is limited because departments and agencies use 'model contracts' with minor variations. None the less, contracts moved the civil service away from the traditional 'career-based structure' towards the 'position-based structure' of private-sector employment (OECD, 2003: 13). They enabled salary increases to be decided by the line manager (for example, on the basis of performance or extra responsibility) instead of automatic annual increases. On the other hand, the special nature of 'Crown employment' remained in principle, even if features such as 'the power of the Crown to dismiss at will' are in practice accompanied by conventional procedures for dismissing officials, similar to those in private-sector employment (*Civil Service Management Code* – Cabinet Office, 2006a; ch. 11).

Fixed-term contracts pose several problems. First, widespread use of fixed-term contracts and thus a high staff turnover might harm the efficient coordination of departmental and interdepartmental business, which relies on a common culture built up over decades (Pyper, 1995a: 40). Second, fixed-term contracts undermine not only the morale of current officials, but also the attractiveness of a Whitehall career. Third, as the Public Service Committee (1998: para. 206) concluded, fixed-term contracts might weaken 'the traditional political impartiality of Senior Civil Servants'. Would officials on fixed-term contracts be honest advisers? Would they curb their objections to ministers' proposals for fear of not being reappointed?

There are two further points. First, there is no solid evidence that contracts improve performance. Virtanen (2000: 56–7) has shown empirically for Finnish officials that the only well-proven relationship is that during the final years of a contract both commitment and performance decline. There are even counter-arguments: officials might do only what the contract requires; or refuse to take the blame for ministers' mistakes (see Pollitt, 2003: 48).

Second, if officials are to be employed on fixed-term contracts they must be free to seek employment elsewhere, which raises ethical questions. It has long been the practice for retiring top officials to collect directorships: Andrew Turnbull was appointed to Prudential, British Land, Frontier Economics, Booz Allen Hamilton and Arup within nine months of retiring as Head of the Home Civil Service (*Financial Times*, 7 April 2006; and see other examples in Pyper, 1995a: 86–7). It is usually argued that such 'interchange' is in the public interest (Robin Butler, Head of the Home Civil Service, letter to the *Guardian*, 12 September 1992), and that senior civil servants have to seek permission from a Cabinet Office committee, especially if they used to negotiate contracts. However, the restructuring of the 1980s changed the number of such appointments dramatically. Applications to the Committee from MoD officials quadrupled between 1979 and 1992 (David Pallister and Richard Norton-Taylor, the *Guardian*, 10 September 1992), when MoD 'downsized' from 247,000 to 139,000 officials. Will officials be firm in negotiating with contractors when their future livelihood might depend on a job with these firms? An early warning came when Bob Ayling, a Department of Trade and Industry (DTI) civil servant helped to privatise British Airways (BA) in 1987, was then recruited as BA legal director, and became its chief executive (*Financial Times*, 25 January 1999). Whitehall now seeks wide, relevant experience, such as in the appointment to the head of an executive agency (UK Trade & Investment) of Andrew Cahn who had previously worked in Whitehall, the European Commission and BAA the airports operator. However, there are potential problems as well as advantages from mixing public and private careers, leading the First Civil Service Commissioner (2006: 3) to propose that the Commission be given a regulatory role on business appointments too.

Pay and performance

The traditional civil service offered a lifelong career with pay and other conditions of service largely determined by age and number of years in each grade (Maor and Stevens, 1997: 534). By the time Labour arrived in government in 1997, the national collective pay bargaining system in place since 1919 (the National Whitley Council) had been replaced by one structure for the SCS and a diversity of systems for other officials.

In 1985, a trial performance-related pay (PRP) scheme had been introduced at Principal to Under-Secretary level, consisting of a lump sum added to the year's pay for up to 20 per cent of these officials. Despite a mixed reception (Farnham, 1993: 112) it was extended to all but the top grades from 1990. Even if there are strong doubts about its role as a performance incentive, there were other arguments for PRP: it rewarded individual achievement in what was otherwise a structure dominated by grades and years of service; it could attract talented outside candidates earning higher private-sector salaries; it could hold wage bills down by substituting PRP for automatic salary rises (and give higher rewards now without adding to future pension bills); and it signals that civil servants are not unaccountable and overpaid, by demonstrating that their performance is monitored (OECD, 2005a: 2).

Surveys in the early 1990s showed that agency chief executives wanted to be able to introduce similar variable pay systems. The Civil Service (Management Functions) Act 1992 enabled ministers to delegate personnel functions to any official. *Taking Forward Continuity and Change* announced that department heads would have to devise pay systems that took into account 'performance, the level of responsibility and the marketability of their skills and experience' (Cabinet Office, 1995: para 4.14). They were made responsible for managing their SCS staff, including defining which were SCS posts, but they had to work within a common SCS framework, use the same criteria for defining the level of the post (Job Evaluation for Senior Posts (JESP); see Table 6.1 on page 194), a centrally determined set of pay bands, and a common system of pay and performance appraisal. This new system was intended to combine the unifying 'cohesion' that concerned the traditionalists, with NPM 'flexibility', seen in the profusion of new job titles that soon appeared in the *Civil Service Yearbook*.

Below SCS level, there was less concern with cohesion. Departments developed their own systems, following the principles of performance, responsibility and marketability, but within Treasury budgetary control. Her Majesty's Stationery Office (HMSO), which was part of the Cabinet Office, with 'trading fund' status (its budget came from its sales, not the Treasury), introduced its own pay and appraisal system in 1991. The Cabinet Office developed a nine-band pay structure for its junior staff (A, B, C, see Table 6.1 on page 194), like that of the SCS. At the Benefits Agency in 1994, chief executive Bichard had responsibility for pay arrangements but within Department of Social Security (DSS) guidelines (James, 2003: 82). Pay was linked to the agency's performance targets (set by ministers), but it became clear that managers pushed harder on targets that were of political interest to ministers (such as turnaround time) than the main targets, such as accuracy of assessment (James, 2003: 102–3).

The Labour government does not seem to have made up its mind about pay delegation or PRP. In 1999, Bichard chaired the Performance Management Group, one of the Permanent-Secretary-led groups set up to implement *Modernising Government*. It concluded that 'most of the existing departmental and agency arrangements for appraisal and pay, including those for the SCS ... need to change ... There is little evidence that they have helped to confront poor performance ... The performance pay system is not perceived to offer significant rewards for excellence' (Cabinet Office, 1999c: 7). The 'Bichard group' recommended making individuals in the SCS responsible for their performance; and rewarding the most those who 'made the biggest contribution' relative to others, such as taking on difficult tasks. It thought these principles could be applied by departments and agencies, probably to teams rather than individuals, while still meeting their business needs (Cabinet Office, 1999c: 9).

The Cabinet Office introduced a pay system for the SCS in 2002, implementing 'the Bichard principles'. Departments assess a senior official's annual salary increase within a formula set centrally. In 2005, for example, they had to give rises of 5–9 per cent of salary to the 'most effective' quarter of their SCS staff; from 0–2 per cent to the 5–10 per cent of officials with the 'least effective' performance; and 2.5–4.5 per cent to the broad 'tranche' of officials in the middle.

The Cabinet Office adjusts each department's assessments to ensure that the SCS as a corporate body achieves this same distribution of PRP. Though very few officials receive no salary increase at all, the lesson is clear when they do. The government did not formally re-centralise pay structures for other staff, but required departments and their agencies to revise their pay systems and put pressure on them to model their system on that of the SCS (Cabinet Office, 2001c: 11). It wanted pay structures that gave the 'rate for the job' (especially with reference to the local job market), plus a team or individual bonus for performance, which could be a non-pay-related reward (funding for training courses, gym membership or paid leave, for example).

However, a review of departments and agencies by the prime minister's Office of Public Services Reform (OPSR) found that they thought 'authority, rewards, incentives, penalties or opprobrium bear no relation to performance' (OPSR, 2002: 13). There is evidence now across many civil services in developed countries that PRP is divisive, and far less important as an incentive to public-sector employees than job content and career development prospects; though it could help performance by providing a reason for more effective procedures, such as discussions between line managers and staff; or to stimulate other changes, such as encouraging team working by offering collective bonuses (OECD, 2005a: 6). The OPSR also wanted pay systems to be decentralised: 'Agency management must be able to recruit and reward all staff, including senior civil servants, according to local needs and to plan and manage within broad financial parameters in order to deliver effectively' (OPSR, 2002: 14). The Department of Work & Pensions (DWP), when set up in 2002, had recentralised the pay bargaining that had previously been delegated to its agencies, in order 'to provide easier movement for similarly skilled staff across their businesses'. The OPSR warned that pay levels in agencies were lower than in parent departments. Re-centralised pay bargaining was therefore likely to lead to staff shortages and service reductions; 'geography and cultural issues' were far more significant than differential pay structures in restricting transfers (OPSR, 2002: 43).

Civil service human resource management

The complexity of the issues and procedures described above draws attention to the specialist skills now required of civil service personnel managers. The first four 'Capability Reviews' of departments found 'strong evidence that whilst our managers think they are good managers of people, their people do not always share that view' (Prime Minister's Delivery Unit, 2006: 22). Civil service personnel management has traditionally been 'amateur' in the Fulton sense, with departmental personnel officers assigned to this role as a 'generalist' posting: the MoD personnel director who interviewed David Kelly in 2003 about his discussions with the media was previously MoD's policy director. What may have worked when officials followed steady paths up departmental ladders is inadequate for 'new people management', as the Hutton Inquiry illustrated (see Hutton, 2004, especially the oral and documentary evidence on its website: www.the-hutton-inquiry. org.uk). Though this was only one case, it showed the potential effects of delegation, secondment, agencies and 'marketisation', if excellent human resource structures are not in place.

The MoD's Permanent Secretary had overall responsibility for staff in the Defence Science and Technology Laboratory (Dstl; see the Framework Document in Box 4.1 on page 130). Yet the 'Personnel Director for the Ministry of Defence as a whole' did not know how Dstl 'levels' related to MoD grades, nor Dstl's full name. He could 'not quite understand, to be honest', Dstl's guidelines to staff on media activities, nor was able to provide the Inquiry with the more recent 'detailed instructions' from the MoD that he thought Kelly should have read. He did not know why the FCO had been reimbursing the MoD for Kelly's staff costs since 1996 (Hutton Inquiry evidence: 11 August 2003). When the MoD created the executive agency DERA in 1995, transferring to it Dr Kelly's unit while he was working for the UN in Iraq (UNSCOM), Kelly was downgraded by mistake: he 'had not been properly assimilated within the DERA salary scale' (Hutton, 2004: 4). A colleague who took up the matter found that Kelly 'fell into a black hole' because the personnel department was divided between those who would not deal with it because Kelly had an SCS-level grade, and those who said he was not a member of the SCS (Hutton Inquiry evidence: 16 September 2003). When Dr Kelly pursued the claim he found that there 'were no personnel records for him on file'.

Further complications derived from DERA 'marketing' its research, to make it easier to sell DERA later. Dr Kelly's secondment in 1992 from the MoD to the UN had been organised through the FCO and his salary paid by the MoD. Then DERA started to charge customers, including 'profit', and UNSCOM complained. Transfer to the 'core' MoD would have resolved the problem, but the 'core' MoD was unwilling; and the FCO was not willing to pay the MoD. 'A financial fix' was arranged for 'a notional secondment' to MoD that was never formalised, and Kelly's salary was funded by the FCO (Hutton Inquiry evidence: 11 August 2003; 16 September 2003; Document mod_ 2_0009). Dr Kelly therefore had four employers (Dstl, MoD, FCO, and the UN), but none of them properly managing his career. Asking himself whether the government took 'the proper steps to help and protect Dr Kelly in the difficulties in which he found himself', Lord Hutton considered that the MoD's actions 'must have given rise to a feeling that he had been badly let down by his employer' (2004: 324).

Modernising Government (1999: 20) had recommended that the fragmentation of public services needed to be counteracted by 'a more corporate approach' ... 'to ensure that the principles of better policy making are translated into staff selection, appraisal, promotion, posting and pay systems'. Its follow-up 'newsletter' acknowledged that the civil service encouraged people to go on secondment, but 'sometimes make it difficult for them to find their way back' (Cabinet Office, 1999d: 3). In 2002, SCS officials started to be managed for 'pay and rations' more closely and more consistently; and the Cabinet Office had asked departments to implement similar systems for non-SCS staff. In 2006, the civil service 'Human Resources Profession' was recognised and organised as such by the Cabinet Office, which appointed a 'Director General, Leadership and People Strategy' from the consultants Accenture.

The civil service as a model employer

Before the arrival of the Thatcher Government, the civil service had tried to be a model employer (Corby, 1997: 60). *Modernising Government* indicated it would return to that position: 'The government has a particular responsibility as employer. We will value the public service and make sure that it is properly equipped to rise to the challenge and properly rewarded when it does well' (1999: 55). Public organisations have tended to operate at higher than national minimum standards in order to attract and retain staff, and to be an exemplar of good employee relations (Horton, 2000: 211). Until 1980, the characteristics of the civil service were 'job security, relatively generous sick pay and pension arrangements, encouragement of union membership and effective grievance machinery' and national collective bargaining arrangements that set pay by 'fair comparison' with other sectors (Corby, 1997: 70).

Few of these features have survived, as this and previous chapters have shown. From 1979, job security was undermined by staff cuts and privatisation, and then by recruiting 'new blood'. Pay comparability was eroded in 1981, after Thatcher's advisers noticed that different sets of public workers had pay reviews at different times, comparing their pay with the increases achieved by others, thus making it difficult to stop the cycle of rises (Hoskyns, 2000: 144). Following the ensuing strike, in which union members at the Government Communications Headquarters (GCHQ) participated, the government banned union membership at GCHQ, further polarising the relationship between the government and the unions (see Pyper, 1995a: 16).

The restructuring of the civil service has had an impact on the size, composition and power of unions. The effects of privatisation and contracting-out fell first on industrial and scientific staff, and their unions have grouped together to maintain organisational strength. The Institute of Professional Civil Servants, formed in 1918, became the Institute of Professionals, Managers and Specialists in 1989, and then joined with the Engineers & Managers Association in 2001 to form Prospect (102,000 engineers, scientists, managers and specialists in the civil service and privatised agencies). It campaigns vigorously against further privatisation, and defended the Vehicle and Operators Services Agency in 2006. The Public and Commercial Services Union (PCS), also formed from a merger in 1998, has 325,000 members in 'governmental services in both the public and private sectors' (www.pcs. org.uk). The 16,000 members of the First Division Association (FDA) now comprise not only senior generalists as in the past, but also economists, lawyers, diplomats and NHS managers in 100 departments and agencies.

The FDA's membership gives it a subtle influence, but the PCS is the more openly militant; it initiated an employment tribunal hearing in 2003 which ruled that former agriculture officials had been entitled to the same pay as former environmental officials at the same responsibility level in the merged Department for Environment, Food and Rural Affairs. The officials' case was that they ultimately shared the same employer, the Treasury (representing the Crown), but this argument was overturned by the Employment Appeal Tribunal (*Financial Times*, 18–19 January 2003). Some single-department unions, such as the Prison Officers Association (POA), remain formidable opponents to change; Home Secretaries found it easier to establish new prisons in the private sector than to reform public provision (see Chapter 4).

The unions were split on the issue of executive agencies; although the largest union was opposed, the association for junior and middle managers saw some advantages (James, 2003: 63–4). In their weakened condition, the unions agreed to performance-related pay in exchange for a say in the performance criteria (Pyper, 1995a: 17). Since pay and other pay-related conditions, such as sick pay, were fully delegated to departments and agencies in 1996, fragmentation has hampered union mobilisation and put legal obstacles in the way of taking industrial action 'in sympathy' with colleagues in another part of the civil service.

The arrival of Labour introduced a more conciliatory period, and the Blair government consulted the PCS more frequently (Mark Serwotka, PCS, *Financial Times*, 6 April 2001). The Cabinet Office, under Mo Mowlem, signed an agreement in March 2000 on *Partnership Working in the Civil Service* with the three cross-departmental unions and the long-standing umbrella body, the Council of Civil Service Unions (CCSU). The agreement said nothing remarkable (it promised joint action on the key themes of *Modernising Government*) but it *was* remarkable after the previous two decades. The new spirit was exemplified in 2001, when Dstl's staff representatives negotiated over the agency's pay system and expressed themselves as being content with terms that related pay transparently to 'worth' and rises 'were no longer linked to how a business area had performed (or not)' (Dstl, 2002: 6).

Yet, by 2006, the unions were at best sceptical about reforms, and in direct conflict with the government on some issues. The PCS and Prospect said they would have welcomed the 'Professional Skills for Government Programme' had it offered something concrete for non-SCS people; the FDA's SCS members 'generally had a view that it was a passing fad' that would be gone in three years (Public Administration Committee, 2006). The 'Gershon' plan for efficiency savings by cutting 70,000 posts brought the industrial action many predicted (see Chapter 4). PCS members led a mass one-day strike in November 2004, which was especially intense at Jobcentre Plus offices; they were to lose many posts and had not yet absorbed the merger between Job Centres and Benefit Offices. The government took more notice of a generalised threat of strikes in 2005 over its proposal to change the pensionable age from 60 to 65, to bring it into line with the private sector. Officials were indignant that one of the few remaining advantages of civil service employment had been terminated. The Cabinet Office entered negotiations with the CCSU and in January 2006 announced that existing staff would retain existing rights though new entrants would have new arrangements.

The civil service had been in advance of the private sector in according equal pay for men and women. Equal pay for the same grade was

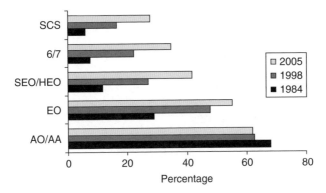

Figure 6.1   Women in the civil service
Notes: The bar chart shows the percentage of non-industrial civil servants at each responsibility level who are women. In Figures 6.1 to 6.3, the abbreviations AO/AA refer to administrative officers and administrative assistants; EO to executive officers, SEO/HEO to senior and higher executive officers; and SCS to Grades 5 and above. The data are headcount figures (not full-time equivalents).
Sources: Data from Cabinet Office (1998c) and Cabinet Office (2006).

accepted by the Conservative government as a principle in 1952, though not implemented until 1955, and then only by stages, on grounds of cost. However, few women reached the higher grades. Moreover, until 1970, the government refused to extend the equal pay principle to 'industrial' civil servants, arguing that it could not take the lead over other industrial employers, rather diminishing any claim to be a model (Theakston, 1995: 77). Despite criticisms by Thatcher's ministers of the equality agenda being set by the Greater London Council under Ken Livingstone, and by other local authorities, the Cabinet Office in 1984 introduced a 'Programme of Action' to achieve gender equality in promotion opportunities, including to part-time work at the highest grades (Figure 6.1 shows the changes since 1984). The Cabinet Office collected data systematically on ethnicity from 1989 (see Figure 6.2), which meant that it was available for monitoring when John Major gave his personal backing to equality policies: a Programme of Action to achieve equal opportunities of employment and promotion for people from ethnic minority backgrounds was adopted in 1990, a new programme for women in 1992, and one for people with disabilities in 1994 (see Figure 6.3).

Figures 6.1 and 6.2 show that much had already changed before the arrival of the Labour government in 1997. In 1997, nearly half the

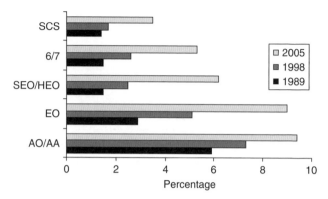

Figure 6.2   Civil servants from minority ethnic backgrounds
Notes: The bar chart shows the civil servants at each responsibility level who
have identified themselves as being from an ethnic minority background as a
percentage of civil servants at that level who have stated their background.
The graphs are only approximate, since about a quarter of officials do not
supply this information. See Figure 6.1 for other details.
Sources: Data from Cabinet Office (1998c) and Cabinet Office (2006).

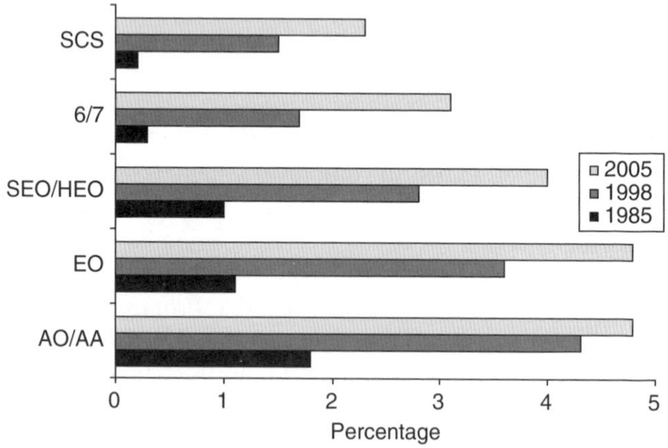

Figure 6.3   Disabled civil servants
Notes: The bar chart shows the percentage of civil servants at each
responsibility level whom departments report as disabled. The 1985 data
used different criteria for defining disability and so are not directly
comparable with the 1998 and 2005 data, but they show a similar pattern of
there being relatively few disabled people in senior positions. See Figure 6.1
for other details.
Sources: Data from Cabinet Office (1998c) and Cabinet Office (2006).

Executive Officers (EO, the first management level) were women (up from just over a quarter in 1984). While only 15 per cent of officials in the SCS were women, this proportion had more than doubled since 1984. The proportion of officials from ethnic minority groups had risen at EO level too, but was still very small at the SCS level. While the proportion of people from ethnic minorities was overall a little higher in the civil service (5.7 per cent in 1997) than in the British workforce, their regional presence was not representative of the ethnic minority active population: for example, there were fewer civil servants from ethnic minorities in London and Yorkshire than might have been expected, and rather more in the East Midlands and East Anglia (Cabinet Office, 1998c).

Modernising Government (1999: 59–60) added the benefits of 'diversity' to the traditional 'fair, equal and merit' ethos. Together with the CCSU, it announced a set of diversity targets for 2004–5 for the SCS (adding that of disabled people in 2000):

- 35 per cent to be women (18 per cent in 1998);
- 25 per cent of the top two grades to be women (13 per cent in 1998);
- 3.2 per cent to be from ethnic minority backgrounds (1.6 per cent in 1998); and
- 3.0 per cent to be made up of disabled people (1.5 per cent in 2000).

Target-setting and monitoring are useful basic contributions to the government's diversity agenda, as are the instructions in the *Civil Service Management Code* on legislation and the civil service's programmes for 'equality of opportunity' (Cabinet Office, 2006a; Section 2). Yet the more significant action after 1997 was the attention paid to the processes underlying recruitment and promotion, such as the efforts on Fast Stream Recruitment and a series of inquiries into the way the performance of staff is appraised. In 1999, an initial survey of a dozen departments found that staff from ethnic minority groups, or with disabilities, or who were men, were consistently more likely to receive lower performance ratings than white or non-disabled people, or women. The Cabinet Office (under Mo Mowlem) and the CCSU jointly commissioned more comprehensive quantitative and qualitative research from the Institute for Employment Studies, which in 2001 confirmed these statistical findings. It showed they were not related to objective facts about officials, such as their length of service, nor to the performance review system itself. It seemed that the main issues were about how people were managed, valued and developed, and how the performance management systems were operated (Cabinet Office, 2003: 5).

Richard Wilson, as Head of the Home Civil Service, reported to Tony Blair that, from the civil service side, departments would become accountable for their diversity objectives, and all managers would be trained in diversity awareness, but that leadership had to come from ministers as well as Permanent Secretaries (Wilson, 2000). The Civil Service Management Board, chaired by Wilson, agreed departments would check the quality of performance appraisals and 'equality proof' their performance management procedures. By 2003, nearly all departments and agencies had audited their appraisal systems; only 11 per cent had found statistically significant differences between minority and majority groups; most had made diversity training mandatory; and nearly all had reviewed their performance management procedures in consultation with staff, trade unions and equality experts. On the other hand, the minority groups that were supposed to be the beneficiaries, while acknowledging that efforts had been made, thought progress had been limited – it was 'window-dressing'; but they found it hard to complain for fear of affecting their careers. They thought in particular that the 'momentum' given in 2000–01 by the ministers and top officials of the time (such as Mo Mowlem and Richard Wilson), which had helped to 'ensure that managerial values match the stated values', had gone with them when they left (Cabinet Office, 2003: 5–9).

It was soon clear that women would not occupy the targeted 35 per cent of SCS posts by 2005 (the figure was in fact 29.4 per cent), though the promotion of women into a quarter of the top two grades should be acknowledged as an achievement. In 2005, only 2.9 per cent of SCS staff were from black and minority ethnic groups, and the percentage of disabled people decreased to 2.8 per cent, having reached a higher level the year before, as people moved in and out of the service (Cabinet Office, 2006f: 41). A new impetus had been provided in 2004 in the Public Spending Review produced by the Treasury, under Gordon Brown as Chancellor but, probably more importantly, with Gus O'Donnell as Permanent Secretary. The lack of progress on appointing women to the SCS was rather obscured by pushing all targets further ahead to 2008 under the guise of a new '10-point plan' launched by O'Donnell when he became head of the Home Civil Service (Cabinet Office, 2005b):

- 37 per cent to be women (from 29.4 per cent in 2005);
- 4 per cent to be from ethnic minorities (2.8 per cent in 2005);

- 3.2 per cent to be disabled people (2.9 per cent in 2005); and
- 30 per cent of the top two grades to be women (25 per cent in 2005).

O'Donnell was undoubtedly committed to improving diversity representation at all levels within the civil service. Departments were set diversity targets and delivery plans for improving diversity in the grades from which people are promoted into the SCS (Cabinet Office, 2006f: 20, 40). There was a clear and strong commitment to ensuring that 'in the longer term' the civil service at all levels reflects Britain's diverse population.

Finally, the regional location of civil servants (see Figure 6.4) has been seen as an element of diversity but also of equality. This has been an important consideration for British governments for at least half a century, but the underlying concerns have varied. For post-war governments, relocation of offices relieved London of traffic congestion and housing shortages. Then decentralisation from the South East was a way to provide employment in regions where it was lacking.

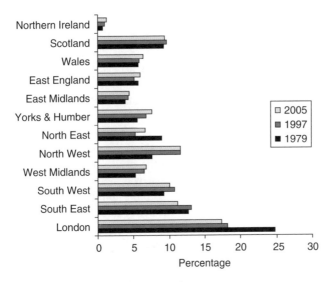

Figure 6.4   Civil servants in the regions
Notes: The bar chart refers to permanent non-industrial civil servants (full-time equivalents) in the Home Civil Service. The figures for Scotland and Wales include staff in the devolved executives.
Sources: Data for 1997 and 2005 from Cabinet Office (2006); and calculations for 1979 from data in Cabinet Office (1998).

For the Thatcher Government, relocation promised cost savings by enabling large-scale administrative processing to take place in towns where labour and office space were cheaper, especially once the delegation of pay systems enabled a move away from national pay scales. The proportion of civil servants who worked in London and the rest of the South East fell from to two-fifths in 1976 to under a third in 1997. By contrast, there has been only incremental change during the Blair Government to 2006, though that was expected to change as a result of the Lyons and Gershon reviews (see Chapter 4). Less than one-fifth of civil servants now work in London, a figure that reminds us that 'Whitehall' is not where most civil servants are to be found.

Conclusion

There is evidence in this chapter to support the 'decline of Whitehall' thesis, but on a limited scale and mainly at lower levels in the service. Aspects of recruitment that mattered most to the Whitehall model – recruitment to the career civil service that was 'fair, open and on merit' of people with a broad education and advanced negotiating skills – produced (and reproduced), for social, cultural and educational reasons, the dominance of the Oxbridge arts graduate. Thus the gradualist reforms to the classic recruitment procedures, widening the intake while retaining the essential selection criteria and goals, have not damaged the 'Whitehall' model; indeed, in absolute numbers the Oxbridge arts graduate is more in evidence than ever.

However, the demands by successive governments that outside experience should be brought into the civil service posed a bigger challenge to the model, coupled as it was with the downsizing and 'privatisation' of the Civil Service Commission. It seems unlikely that market values, such as financial efficiency and customer responsiveness, have not affected to some extent traditional Whitehall administrative values (accuracy and due process, for example). Yet claims of damage to the public sector ethos need 'considerably more context-specific empirical research into values and value change than has yet been undertaken' (Pollitt, 2003: 141). Similarly, the fears that civil servants working interchangeably with the private sector would undermine Whitehall's code of ethics seem to have been overplayed – it seems that ethical standards may be more specific to society or generation than to sector (Doig, 1997: 95–6, 105–6), and top civil servants always had post-retirement private careers which (they claimed) were in the public interest. Nevertheless, the Commissioners' offer to extend their remit to former civil servants' business careers seems prudent.

Yet, the personnel management reforms that appeared to undermine the Whitehall model also drew attention to characteristics that had previously gone unremarked. Commissioners from outside Whitehall spotted that internal promotions also needed monitoring, a procedure that could reduce inequalities in performance assessment as well as sustain political impartiality. Agencification and open competition certainly called into question the unified, socialised, culture of the civil service; but it also revealed (as did the Hutton Inquiry) that senior specialists can run research or law agencies of a few thousand officials but not be treated as a member of the SCS. That is, it is clearer now than under the older 'unified grade structure' that the careers of specialists and managers do not lead to the top. To the extent that the unified Whitehall model of personnel management was a model that applied best to senior generalists, it would seem to have survived rather well.

The changes in employment practices that applied to the civil service as a whole, and that accompanied the organisational restructuring described in other chapters, are not well analysed by reference to the Whitehall model. The starting point was characteristic of a rather old-fashioned hierarchical system typical of large organisations and not specific to the Whitehall–Westminster context. A career structure in which officials most years received a standard incremental annual salary rise related to their grade but not to merit scarcely fitted the Whitehall ideal, except in its 'conservative' form in which one year older was one year wiser. Rather, the changes are explained more easily within the framework of reforms called 'new public management', or specifically here, 'new people management', even if there is no academic or international consensus on what these reforms comprise.

Horton (2000: 213) describes 'new people management' in the British public sector as the use of more open recruitment, and more diverse modes of employment and working patterns, instead of planned career pathways with job and employment security. Public-sector jobs are opened up to recruits from the private sector; job demarcation is removed and people are expected to move between posts and tasks. Pay and benefits are more flexible; related more frequently to performance; and person-related – linked to the market worth of the individual employee. All these reforms have been implemented to a greater or lesser extent in the civil service according to the grade and the department or agency – decentralisation of human resources responsibilities is yet another feature of 'modern public employment', according to the OECD (2005b: 6).

The OECD promotes these changes as 'modernising public employment', on the basis that most of the developed countries it represents, especially those with sound economic performance, have adopted some or all of these reforms since the 1980s (encouraged by the OECD itself, it must be said). How 'modernised' is the British civil service in these terms, in relation to developments in other countries? The national government service in Sweden changed further and earlier than in Britain (more use of contracts of different types, more variety in working patterns, more local determination of pay and/or performance pay, more career mobility), but Britain is, with Finland and the Netherlands, among a group of countries that have introduced far more of these types of changes than Germany, for example, where there is general satisfaction with the outcomes of current arrangements (Farnham and Horton, 2000: 317). The contribution of the Conservative market ideology to British reforms, and the reasons for the 'scars' on Blair's back, can be judged by a double comparison with France and Sweden. In France, governments have found personnel reforms difficult to achieve because of the absence of a strong free market ideology; the presence of strong resistance among trade unions, who have a statutory place in negotiations; and because the top civil service *corps* (well-represented in the political class), are uninterested in a reform from which they will not personally profit, and who are too distant from delivery to see the problems faced by citizens (Burnham, 2000). In contrast, Sweden had never had a special or unitary civil service, special recruitment competition, tenure, or professional civil service *corps*, and therefore there were no institutional barriers to change.

Finally, the more recent developments in human resources management described above can also be interpreted in the context of a similar rethinking of policies in other countries: the pendulum has swung back a little as disadvantages emerge (OECD, 2005b: 4). *Modernising Government* was concerned with improving coordination from the centre to counteract the fragmentation of policy conception and delivery between agencies, and to achieve corporate goals, such as diversity, for the civil service itself. Delegation to agency chief executives to improve performance management and economy had to be balanced against a lack of accountability and control from the centre to achieve departmental and, in the end, national targets. In that sense, the warnings about the dangers of 'hollowed-out government' have been heeded.

7

Conclusion: The Modernised Civil Service

There is more than one way to interpret current developments in the British civil service, depending on the eye of the observer and where he or she chooses to look – and therefore more than one way to predict where the British civil service might be going. However, there is no disputing that the civil service has undergone significant internal change over recent decades, of a form that is recognised internationally as 'modernisation'. It has had to adapt to external developments too, such as the UK's membership of the European Union (EU), the devolution of substantial power to Scotland and Wales, and the intermittent progress towards new institutions in Northern Ireland. There is no denying that traditional features of the civil service have experienced some erosion during the course of that modernisation. Nevertheless, the departures from the classic norms are less drastic than is often portrayed, because much of what went on in Whitehall was not well described by the Whitehall model. While the principles of the model were useful guides to civil service behaviour, they should always be set alongside other interpretations of the civil service (see Chapter 1). Looking at issues from more than one angle helps us to assess the forces driving the civil service, whether discussing the triangular power relationships between ministers, civil servants and policy advisers (considered in Chapter 2); the potential divergences between officials at different territorial levels following devolution (see Chapter 3); or the actual divergences between central departments and agencies that have resulted from 'new public management' (NPM) (Chapter 4). We have seen (in Chapter 5) how these forces changed the ways in which civil servants account for their actions and (in Chapter 6) their effect on civil service careers.

Yet the emphasis on recent changes should not obscure the longer-term, gentler and more organic transformation of the civil service. It evolved in parallel with British political structures, as seen in the separateness of the Northern Ireland Civil Service, or the absence (in 2007) of a parliamentary statute for the civil service, despite many official recommendations by reformers from the Northcote–Trevelyan Report of 1854 to the Committee on Standards in Public Life in 2003. Like the Constitution within which it is located, no historic occasion has until now forced a fundamental, back-to-basics analysis of the role and functioning of the civil service in the UK polity (although the advent of devolution to Scotland and Wales might have provided such an opportunity).

This pragmatic development of the civil service does not mean there were no guiding principles: some were enunciated in the Northcote–Trevelyan Report; others set out in the Fulton Report of 1968. The civil service, as a large and ponderous organisation not fully controlled by its own or its political leaders, takes its time to match up to the principles that others announce for it. Nevertheless, the civil service has progressed from the levels of corruption and inefficiency that Gladstone asked Northcote and Trevelyan to address in the nineteenth century and from the entrenched departmentalism that the Treasury Permanent Secretary Warren Fisher started to correct after the First World War. It is even, perhaps, with the Professional Skills for Government programme, finally implementing some of the recommendations of the Fulton Report, in response to the criticisms of the incoming Labour government in 1997 (see Chapters 2 and 6).

Out of this hesitant process emerged a specifically British civil service operating within the British political context, which differs in one way or another from the equally specific civil services of other liberal democracies. Unlike the situation in many parts of Europe (Slovenia and Sweden are two examples), civil servants are distinct from local government officials and, in a rather indeterminate way, from the National Health Service. Unlike in France, no particular qualifications or training are required before starting work as a civil servant; and unlike in Australia, the British civil service still recruits and grooms senior officials from a highly-selective set of untried graduates. Unlike in the United States, Germany, France or Italy, top civil servants are non-partisan and expect to remain in place when one government departs and another arrives (see Chapter 2). Unlike many other European bureaucracies, the British civil service adopted very early the 'administrative modernisation' or New Public Management techniques being promoted by other English-speaking countries (Chapters 4 and 6).

Three views on the evolution of the British civil service

A variety of 'stories' exist about the British civil service. We identified three contrasting strands of explanation that are relevant to analysing the civil service (see Chapter 1). The first is the traditional view, expressed in the Northcote–Trevelyan Report. It argued for a career civil service of officials recruited young in 'literary' competitions, trained in-house and promoted on merit. It would be divided hierarchically by function, but fragmentation between departments would be counteracted by the interchange of some officials, facilitated by uniform pay scales. Much of this 'Whitehall model' was put into effect, though for significant elements – such as uniform pay scales – only after 1920. For observers who see the Whitehall model as being almost fully implemented, or who admire it as a goal (the 'Tory tradition'), the changes introduced by the Thatcher Government therefore signalled 'the end of Whitehall', and the decline of the British civil service. Others, whether or not approving the model as an aspiration, point out the ways in which it does not describe the British civil service very well. The model might exist at the level of discourse or even in guiding officials' behaviour, but the outcome has been different. Other critics thought the Westminster–Whitehall model was always inadequate, whether as a description or a normative concept, because it ignored the complexities of the policy process.

From the 'governance' approach, the attention to 'government' actors was too narrowly conceived. Policy network theory suggests that policies are made and implemented within a larger arena that includes interest groups, local authorities and other service-deliverers. Yet this larger arena is also segmented into policy sectors, each centred on an individual department, making coordination difficult across the civil service. One aim of the Conservatives' delegation of service delivery (see Chapter 4) was to give ministers and senior officials more time for their control and coordination functions. However, proponents of the 'hollowed-out state' thesis thought it led instead to power being transferred to the delivery bodies, emptying departments of their capacity to drive policy. Less pessimistically, the 'multilevel governance' variant supposes that national, sub-national and international actors are sharing a joint policy-making process. Putting these different components together, the 'differentiated polity' thesis replaces the unitary state, centralised authority and command bureaucracy assumed by the Westminster–Whitehall model with political and administrative decentralisation, fragmentation into sectors and interdependence between a more diverse set of policy actors in a global context.

The third thesis is that the civil service is being modernised: the changes are part of a progressive reform process taking place over a very long period (see the Introduction). Bevir and Rhodes (2003: 146–54) make a philosophical distinction between three different kinds of reformers: 'Whigs' (incremental change while guarding core values); Fabian Socialists (larger role for specialists and 'managerial accountability'); and neo-Liberals (replacement of inefficient bureaucracies with market solutions). In practice, these 'modernisation' strands are mixed together within the writings of individual authors, and we made a simpler division (see Chapter 1), between radical programmes (New Labour's modernisation and the New Right's managerial and market revolution), and gradualist or progressive approaches (the Whigs and Fabians).

New Labour slogans ('joined-up government', 'information age government', 'partnership') differed from the free market rhetoric of the neo-Liberal Conservatives. Yet there were many similarities of views and programmes: a strong antagonism to the existing civil service; a desire to remove the barriers between it and organisations in other sectors; a willingness to challenge traditional civil service procedures (whether appointments or written records); certain reform actions (market testing, *Citizen's Charter*, the Public Finance Initiative, external recruitment). While New Labour's constitutional programme was more radical than that of the New Right (devolution, freedom of information, proposed Civil Service Act), in the end it had a very limited impact on the civil service. This finding would have been anticipated by 'gradualist' academic-practitioners, who are professionally sceptical about the extent of change achieved by the new ways of managing the public sector (Pollitt, 2003: 26, 40). Progressive reformers may admire some aspects of the 'Whitehall' model but judge that it has still not adapted to the demands of ministers in the twenty-first century, and therefore needs considerable modification (Hennessy, 1990: 730–40; Foster, 2001). The conclusion of modernisers is that the contemporary civil service is the outcome of a continuous, if rather jerky, process of evolutionary reform, following somewhat at a distance the movements in the role of the British government and the state.

Such a conclusion seemed particularly appropriate after our examination of the challenges facing the civil service in relation to policy work (see Chapter 2), despite some apocalyptic media comment about the powers wielded by New Labour's special advisers.

Current issues for debate

Ministers, civil servants and special advisers

Certain sequential issues have structured the debate about the role of civil servants in advising ministers on policy or on policy presentation:

- How to ensure that civil servants are not politicised, because – though ministers may like to receive advice from people who are known to be sympathetic towards their political agendas – British governments have usually regarded it as more useful to ensure that advice is seen by Parliament and the public as being independent, and that an expert support system is permanently available.
- How to ensure that a self-selecting group of civil servants does not become a non-elected policy-making force, pursuing its own interest or its own conception of the 'common ground' (Fry, 1985: 27).
- How to accommodate the temporary political advisers to ministers who add the party dimension that civil servants are unable and unqualified to offer. The 'people who live in the dark' (Blick, 2004) or 'night visitors' (Attali, 1993: 616), can cause friction between ministers (Margaret Thatcher and her economic adviser, Alan Walters, brought about the resignation of her Chancellor, Nigel Lawson) or between ministers and civil servants (Stephen Byers and his adviser, Jo Moore, discredited the government and the civil service before they both resigned).

In the nineteenth century, the Westminster–Whitehall principle that 'civil servants advise: ministers decide' had shielded civil servants from partisan debate and helped to establish a permanent service that could serve alternating governments. With the growth in state intervention, reserving decisions to ministers was no longer plausible. As Chapter 2 explains, civil servants so outweighed ministers in numbers, time, experience and access to information that Socialist radicals (Tony Benn, Barbara Castle, Norman Crowther-Hunt, Richard Crossman, Brian Sedgemore) and neo-Liberals (Geoffrey Fry, John Hoskyns) were increasingly outspoken about bureaucratic power, whether it concerned corporate interests (pay settlements) or policy advice ('consensus-seeking', 'negative'). Not all ministers were worried, but Harold Wilson, as prime minister, 1964–70, 1974–76, was sufficiently concerned to choose his own top civil servant for No. 10, and to appoint special policy advisers (Burnham and Jones, 2000: 83–5). The neo-liberal modernisers of the Conservative years restructured the bureaucracy with the aid of such advisers (see Chapter 4) but 'think tanks' and consultancy firms were the great beneficiaries of their search for independent advice.

After eighteen years of Conservative government, New Labour in 1997 was particularly wary. It had modernised its own media machine, and by contrast was dissatisfied with government press officers and the level of civil service expertise (Foster 2001; and see Chapter 6 of this volume). On the other hand, few Labour ministers or special advisers had previous knowledge of Whitehall, and Blair's own lack of ministerial, or even managerial, experience led him to have unrealistic expectations of the speed of implementation. These factors fuelled New Labour's reliance on political advisers. In consequence, among the 'risks of politicisation' (see Chapter 2), those relating directly to the career civil service are important but currently do not rank as highly as those concerning special advisers:

- Individual acts of opposition by civil servants are relatively rare, though they have appreciable side-effects in the form of hardening codes of conduct, or by opening up procedures to the public gaze (see Chapter 5).
- Appointments of career officials on political grounds are limited to a very few cases close to top government leaders, but some prime ministers (Thatcher, Blair) have introduced new selection criteria ('can do' enthusiasm, professional skills).
- There is a significant risk of civil servants being pressured by special advisers to slant their reports, advice or actions towards political priorities.
- Increasingly large numbers of political appointees are moving into an increasingly wide range of civil service roles (media, policy units, 'task forces', 'blue-sky' thinking, public service reform). Though their number is tiny in proportion to the size of the civil service, they make up a substantial proportion of the aides in ministers' private offices; and a few can now give orders to civil servants.

The behaviour of 'spin doctors' led to a Code of Conduct for Special Advisers (see Box 2.3 on page 83) being introduced in 2001 under pressure from the Committee on Standards in Public Life (2000) and the Commons Public Administration Committee (2001). These committees recommended that a Civil Service Act should be prepared, and meanwhile that people appointed to short-term posts should be trained in ethical issues. In the 'Jo Moore' affair of 2001–02, both temporary and permanent civil servants breached the *Codes of Conduct*. The Public Administration Committee (2002, 2004b), and the Committee on Standards in Public Life (2003), called on the government to make a clear legal distinction between the civil service and special advisers, including via a Civil Service Act, to avoid more cases that harmed the civil service as a whole. Ministers and shadow ministers too were to have a clear code of 'custom and practice', and given training. However, the draft Civil Service Bill has failed to progress, with top civil servants apparently disagreeing on its value. The Commons Public Administration Committee renewed its call for legislation in March 2007, in a report examining the nature of the ministerial–civil service relationship (Public Administration Committee, 2007). Rejecting the notion that the civil service has become politicised, this report none the less recommended a 'new public service bargain', to be underpinned by a governance code, in order to give ministers full confidence that Whitehall is responsive to their requirements, while assuring civil servants that they have the right to proffer honest advice without fearing adverse consequences, and to be judged in relation to their legitimate areas of responsibility.

A unified but differentiated service

The principal issues for the British civil service of operating at more than one territorial level are less clearly-defined, not because they are new, but because they do not receive much attention in Westminster and Whitehall (see Chapter 3). They include:

- the challenge of serving different executives with divergent goals and varied procedures;
- the challenge of promoting British government goals in a European Union of twenty-seven states; and
- these multilevel challenges to a unified civil service.

Given that Britain is conventionally analysed as a unitary state with a unitary, or at least unified, civil service, devolution in the 1990s seemed to herald a radical departure. In fact there was already some decentralised decision-making – strongest (at times) in Northern Ireland, weakest in Wales. The new settlements produced a variety of departmental patterns for civil servants to operate: for a time, Scotland aimed at 'joined-up ministries' that did not replicate ministerial portfolios (although there was a move in the direction of aligning ministerial and departmental remits following the establishment of the SNP minority administration in 2007); the Welsh civil service incorporated previous agencies and quangos; Northern Ireland had ten ministries and six intergovernmental committees, administered by the Northern Ireland Civil Service (NICS), not the Northern Ireland Office. The new institutions created additional and different work for civil servants: there are more ministers, more parties in government, an active local Parliament, and intense interest by groups, the media and the public. Provision for accountability and scrutiny is more constraining than when their ministers accounted only to Westminster. Only in 2007, however, with the emergence of an SNP minority government in Edinburgh, did the occasion finally arise for testing the question posed by John Mackintosh (1976: 108) at the time of Labour's earlier half-hearted attempt at devolution: 'Can UK-recruited civil servants looking to eventual promotion to top jobs advising the Secretary of State or other UK Ministers be loyal to a different set of Ministers at an earlier stage in their careers?'

Just as civil servants supporting devolved governments did not start from scratch, those active in supranational EU negotiations built on previous intergovernmental practice. They found ways to satisfy the 'Westminster–Whitehall' norm of ministerial responsibility, even for hasty, last-minute decisions. The views of devolved governments were integrated as before: indeed, the more frequent use of the Joint Ministerial Committee in relation to the EU provides an example to follow in other domains now that political majorities have changed (Constitution Committee, 2002). Whitehall has reorganised itself incrementally to meet the challenges of the EU, but individual officials take their cue from ministers and the public in seeing no career advantage from gaining European experience or 'representing' Britain in the European Commission. Yet a large number of senior British civil servants have negotiated with their European equivalents. Though they remember national interests by bringing to the table the aims of their domestic 'policy community', the EU decision-making process tends to segment policy-making between sectors, adding to the risk that civil servants will coordinate their positions more closely with their counterparts in other states than with other departments in Whitehall (see Chapter 3).

Examining EU relations drew attention to the separation between the Foreign Office and the Home Civil Service. Devolution, similarly, stimulated researchers to demonstrate the historical distinctiveness of the Scottish Office from the Welsh Office, and to make comparisons with the organisationally separate Northern Ireland Civil Service (Rhodes *et al.*, 2003). The Blair Government's plans for devolution did little more with regard to the civil service than stress its continuing unified nature, and to reassure civil servants with concerns about their career prospects. Mackenzie's point was answered with an amendment to the *Civil Service Code*, stating that 'civil servants owe their loyalty to the Administrations in which they serve', that is, the UK government, Scottish Executive or Welsh Assembly (the Northern Ireland Civil Service has a similar code). The Constitution Committee (2002: paras 168–9) thought, on balance, that there were advantages to retaining the single Home Civil Service, while recognising that eventually the devolved governments might think differently. There was already a contrast between Scottish Executive civil servants, who are self-confident enough to combine their strong professional and national identity with the benefits of remaining in the wider unified service, and the officials of the former Welsh Office, who, without a distinctive identity, could plausibly dissolve into an innovative 'Welsh public service'. Only in Northern Ireland is there a frank separation between a bureaucracy serving the regional government and legislature, and the regional presence of a federal UK service; they form one possible model for a federal UK in a future that looked remote after the failure of English regional reform.

Restructuring the civil service

The British civil service has been reformed since 1979 by policies that are summed up loosely but usefully in the term 'New Public Management' (NPM). Marr (1996: 254), considered the 'changes merit the over-used term of "revolution"; they help Britain return to an era where state servants will do less'. Horton (1993: 144), contrasting them with the 'incremental', 'pragmatic' and 'reformist' changes before 1979, saw them as 'more radical and more far-reaching than any since the Northcote–Trevelyan reforms of 1854'. Labour added its own flourishes with the Lyons relocation programme (2004), the Gershon programme of 'efficiency savings' (2004) and the merger of HM Revenue & Customs (2005), which together were 'the most significant restructuring of public services for a generation' (Work Foundation, 2004: 4).

Pollitt (2003: 26) reminds us that the various elements that make up NPM have all been seen before in one country or another, and that the benefits in performance are difficult to demonstrate (mainly for methodological reasons). He thinks it likely that NPM works best when applied to activities of low 'publicness', such as issuing vehicle licences. In contrast, functions of a highly 'public' nature (subsidised; subject to complex legal constraints; involving coercion of citizens; politically symbolic; subject to political interference) are much less likely to achieve through NPM the improvement leaders envisage (Pollitt, 2003: 22, 50–51). The Thatcher Government embarked on NPM without benefit of evidence, pursuing anti-bureaucracy ideas from William Niskanen, Milton Friedman and the Institute of Economic Affairs (Jackson, 2001: 9). Many civil service functions that were contracted-out, privatised or delegated to agencies without raising serious problems (except for the staff involved), had low 'publicness' – industrial production, ship maintenance, printing, property services and routine processing of data or pensions all have parallels in the private sector. In contrast, there was considerable opposition to applying NPM to prisons, the Civil Service Commission's recruitment agency (RAS), the Benefits Agency (now part of Jobcentre Plus), and the Child Support Agency. These functions have no private equivalents – the private recruitment agencies, for example, lack an understanding of the concept of public service, or so former civil service leaders argued (D. J. Trevelyan, former First Commissioner, letter to *The Independent*, 6 March 1996).

The restructuring process has met a wide and varied range of criticisms, such as the impact of private-sector methods on public-service ethics (for a summary of the evidence and references, see Pollitt, 2003: 134–9); the outright loss of some past functions (such as data collection and other sources of expertise, according to Foster, 2001); the storing up of debt for future generations in public–private partnerships; the fragmentation of a formerly cohesive civil service (though its former unity can be exaggerated), and the impact of all these things on lines of accountability.

Jobcentre Plus encapsulates the mixed quality of the strategy and its outcomes. The Work and Pensions Committee of the House of Commons (2006: 3) drew up the balance sheet at a critical moment in the agency's restructuring programme. It said that Jobcentres were far more welcoming than Benefits Offices, and that the vast majority of officials worked very hard for their clients and often in stressful conditions (dealing with people without a job or money), but the performance of the new call centres was inadequate and occasionally 'truly appalling'; there were not enough staff, telephones went answered and the computer system did not work. Senior officials and ministers had imposed too many simultaneous changes: new computer programmes; relocation of offices; a major reform of procedures; the Gershon staff cuts; and annual budgetary cuts of 5 per cent. Yet, while the performance record of Jobcentres is mixed, it is far better than critics of agencies imagine. The seven main indicators listed in Table 7.1 show overall progress. While the choice and measurement of performance indicators always raise questions, it is 'an advance from simply measuring the number of schools, or of hospital beds, or of miles of railway track', and in particular from the traditional focus on departments' annual budgetary and staffing inputs (Marr, 1996: 255).

Expanding civil service accountability

Civil service modernisation has required officials to adapt to new regimes for accountability and open government. The converse is also true, according to reformers, from Mikhail Gorbachev preaching *glasnost* (openness) in order to 'restructure' the Soviet Union to Thatcher's

Table 7.1   Performance Indicators in the Jobcentre Plus Agency

Target	2003–4		2004–5		2005–6	
	Aim	Outcome	Aim	Outcome	Aim	Outcome
Jobs – points	7,681,000	7,459,000	7,295,000	7,647,000	6,659,000	6,467,000
Jobs – people		1,184,000		1,117,000		861,000
Employer outcome	82.0%	84.9%	84.0%	85.5%	84.0%	87.5%
Customer service	83.0%	83.4%	81.0%	83.2%	81.0%	85.2%
Business delivery	88.0%	90.9%	89.6%	91.6%	90.3%	91.7%
Benefit processing unit cost	–	–	£28.18	£28.07	£28.24	£29.18
Job brokering unit cost	–	–	£191.49	£197.65	£217.03	£204.03
Fraud and error	6.9%	6.4%	6.0%	5.4%	5.2%	5.0%

Note: 'Business delivery' combines accuracy of processing benefits and success at bringing lone parents to a 'job-benefits' interview; see 'About us' page on www.jobcentreplus.gov.uk.
Source: Data from Jobcentre Plus Annual Reports and Accounts (The Stationery Office).

policy adviser, John Hoskyns (1983), who thought 'open government' would reveal public-sector inefficiency. More broadly, as Karl Popper put it in *The Open Society and its Enemies* (1945), a pluralist democratic system requires a government open to challenge. The 'enemies of democracy' are the 'tribal taboos' that go unquestioned, such as the conventional wisdom and practices of the 'Whitehall village'.

The conventional argument is that officials' advice to ministers is secret so that policy options can be explored, dropped or refined before they cause unnecessary public anxiety – 'it is a prerequisite to free and frank exchange between officials and ministers' (Barberis, 1997b: 148). It is said that secrecy underpins a permanent bureaucracy by not identifying officials with policies unacceptable to another government (a redundant argument, because 'ministers decide'); that it reduces lobbying (but some groups are involved in any case and the pluralist democratic solution is to involve all interests); and that it enables officials to put a case to ministers that goes against a group's interest while continuing its good relationships with the group. It also saves officials and ministers from embarrassment when policy decisions go wrong. These rationales, which supported the 'culture of secrecy' in a civil service developed by the nineteenth-century elite (Vincent, 1998, and see Chapter 5 in this volume), have weakened with the development of a more highly-educated and less deferential electorate, a more participatory style of democracy, and 'the information age'.

A similar conclusion could be drawn about the related principle that ministers and not civil servants are accountable to Parliament. The formal exception – the departmental accounting officer's responsibility for the legality of public spending – opened the way for Accounting Officer Minutes dissenting from ministers' decisions, of which the classic case was Tony Benn's decisions to fund the Kirkby workers' cooperative and other initiatives around the UK led by redundant workers (Fry, 1985: 26). The extension of the accounting officer's remit to ensuring 'value-for-money' produced a Minute revealing disquiet in the Overseas Development Administration at subsidising the Pergau Dam. The resulting parliamentary inquiry (Foreign Affairs Committee, 1994) into the link between Pergau and the sale of weapons to Malaysia showed why it is politically convenient for officials' advice to remain secret.

Chapter 5 showed that the accountability of civil servants has expanded incrementally since the 1960s, in the following ways:

- *Parliamentary scrutiny*: through the Parliamentary Ombudsman; stronger forms of select committee that question officials in public – though they 'should as far as possible avoid being drawn into discussion of the merits of alternative policies where this is politically contentious' (see Chapter 2); and the addition of Executive Agency chief executives to the list of 'Accounting Officers' who can be summoned to give evidence – though this extension of accountability was based on the false distinction between 'administration' and 'policy'.

- *Internal accountability to line superiors and ministers*, enhanced extensively by the Conservatives' financial management systems in the early 1980s, devolved budgeting systems, executive agency framework documents and business plans and Labour's Public Service Agreements (Chapter 4) and by diversity targets (Chapter 6).
- *Consumerist accountability*, implicitly assumed by the Major and Blair reforms to service delivery (*Citizen's Charter*, 'Government Direct' and customer-focused performance indicators), though not explicitly set out as doctrine.
- *Devolved accountability of civil servants working for the Scottish Executive and Welsh Assembly.* In the place of limited scrutiny before 1999 of one or two ministers by a single select committee that met rarely, officials have the close attention of local parliamentarians (and TV) across the full range of policy committees dealing with both scrutiny and legislation, even if the quality and quantity of scrutiny in the small Welsh Assembly has disappointed many observers (Jones and Osmond, 2002; Richard Commission, 2004); and even though almost half of the Scottish Nationalist MSPs thought civil servants were still too remote and unaccountable (Pyper and Fingland, 2006).
- *Judicial accountability*, through the growth of judicial review, and quasi-judicial inquiries into policy failures; the latter revealing to the public gaze the actions of officials in close and forensic detail. 'Scott' (1994) and 'Hutton' (2004) examined officials in public and published their internal communications; 'Butler' (2004) inquired into the work of the officials of the Joint Intelligence Committee and its Assessments Staff.
- Finally, we have to note *the role of the media* in publicising the names and activities of civil servants. Whether it concerns reportage on the civil service itself, explanations by the government's specialists or lurid reports of the Hutton proceedings, civil servants are no longer the anonymous officials of the traditional principle.

The media are also, for their own purposes, pushing out the frontiers of freedom of information. Civil servants now have to bear in mind the constraints of open government as well as of parliamentary accountability. The Hutton Report showed that officials have not (yet) begun to avoid using paper or e-mail. However, the 'excellent quality papers' they prepared before the Iraq war were not circulated to ministers, nor discussed in Cabinet or Cabinet Committee (Butler, 2004: para. 610). Key decision-making discussions, whether on Iraq or Dr David Kelly, were taken in the absence of the Cabinet Secretary and the relevant senior officials. Blair's 'informal' and 'unscripted' style of government was a hindrance to political accountability (paras 606–11).

Whereas the Whitehall–Westminster model made ministers responsible for departments, it is now clear that there is no solid doctrine, let alone practice, of ministerial responsibility (Pyper, 1987a; Barberis, 1997b). Civil servants are no longer (if they ever were) anonymous, and they are increasingly likely to be called to account, whether they are policy aides to ministers or in delivery agencies where all is measured and counted in detail.

The Oxbridge generalist and the administrative assistant

All these changes have had an impact on the work and careers of individual civil servants, with inferences for human resources management – though the 'human resources profession' was only recognised as such in the civil service from 2006 in Whitehall (slightly earlier in Wales). Overall, the Whig formula of 'change and continuity' has ruled in the British civil service, whether we consider recruitment and qualifications, training and outside experience, NPM methods of managing personnel, or the ambition of the civil service to be a model employer. Yet this formula applied differently to junior and senior grades (see Chapter 6).

The Whitehall concept of the official recruited for life did not fit junior staff. Even before NPM, four or five administrative assistants left each year for each one that retired at the age of 60 (even among men); though scarcely any SCS left before retirement. Privatisation, redundancies and early retirement hit all grades in the 1980s, but the reductions, even in the 'de-layering' reforms 1994–97, were proportionately smaller for the SCS; and the SCS was soon larger than before. 'De-privileging the civil service' applied first to the industrial and scientific civil service and disproportionately severely to those earning least, not to the Whitehall generalist. Parallel conclusions can be drawn on analyses of the CVs of those now recruited: a smaller proportion – but still the same number – of fast stream recruits are from the classic 'arts, Oxbridge, white, male' mould; a higher proportion of them are recruited from inside the service, but without reducing the number of graduate recruits. The generalists of the Whitehall model remain at the core of the civil service, even if now surrounded by a more diverse set of people.

Recruitment has opened up in all parts of the British civil service, but the Welsh Assembly has gone further in bringing in organisations and their staff from other parts of the public sector, having recognised the Welsh Office's limited delivery experience. Experts have continued to play a minor role compared with the generalists, and much 'in-house' expertise was lost during the Thatcher years. However, the dissatisfaction of Labour ministers with the lack of direct briefing by specialists, in London (Foster, 2001) or in Cardiff (Laffin, 2002: 40–1), has stimulated a greater emphasis on 'professional skills for government'. Yet civil servants will continue to be sceptical about the ever-changing initiatives until they see the outcomes (Public Administration Committee, 2006: evidence, 30 November 2006).

Though senior officials were relatively protected from privatisation and outsourcing, they were the first to be transferred from a uniform grade-based pay structure to individual contracts and performance pay. However, performance-related pay (PRP) quickly spread to other staff, whose pay, recruitment and promotion were moreover delegated to departments, whereas SCS staff in main departments, agencies and devolved administrations are still part of a centrally-managed elite. The civil service had been a 'role model' employer after the Second World War on equal pay for women but the NPM methods of the 1990s followed harsher private-sector trends. The Major Government was nevertheless in advance of the private sector (though behind local government) in showing concern for broader aspects of equal opportunities. Under New Labour, certain ministers and top officials made a new effort to understand and correct indirect discrimination, so that the civil service would reflect and benefit from diversity. Within the traditional reward package offered to the British civil servant – job security, common pay scales, retirement at 60, inflation-proofed pension – each in turn has come under threat. The planned withdrawal of 'retirement at 60' that civil servants had been promised at the time they were recruited was one theme that united all civil servants in the twenty-first century. It led to mass strike action, which only postponed the loss of one of the few remaining features that distinguish a public-sector career.

Interpretations and future directions

Though retirement at 60 and inflation-proofed pensions were not the prime aims of the Whitehall model, they underpinned the development of a permanent civil service. Chapman used the issue of pay to structure his thesis on the 'end of Whitehall'. He reminded us that 'the classic definition' of the British civil service – that given by the Tomlin Royal Commission in 1931 – is based on pay; civil servants are 'those servants of the Crown, other than holders of political or judicial offices, who are employed in a civil capacity, and whose remuneration is paid wholly and directly out of moneys voted by Parliament' (Tomlin Report quoted in Chapman, 1997: 23). As Chapman goes on to argue, the remuneration package of civil servants: the 'Queen's birthday' holiday, the 'attractive non-contributory pension arrangements', the 'jobs for life' were the benefits of being a 'servant of the Crown' that enabled the British civil service to be built up in the early and middle years of the twentieth century as a service of high standards with a sense of belonging and of loyalty to a distinctive service (Chapman, 1997: 25). On this basis, Chapman concludes logically that 'the British civil service, as defined by the Tomlin Royal Commission, no longer exists' (Chapman, 1997: 36).

Yet, for other analysts, the current diversity in remuneration, depending where the official is located (in which grade, department, agency, devolved administration, regional office, in London or the provinces), is evidence not of an end to the civil service but of a decentralised civil service. In the particular case of pay in the devolved administrations, the differentiation on pay was found in fact to be limited because, while fully delegated to ministers for Scotland and Wales even before devolution (apart from the SCS), freedom to depart from UK norms is still constrained by the *Civil Service Management Code* and by the [UK] 'government's policy stance on public sector pay' (Rhodes *et al.*, 2003: 85).

In addition, or alternatively, the 'modernising thesis' would interpret changes to traditional remuneration principles as part of the *Modernising Public Employment* (OECD, 2004) strategies being implemented in most developed countries to adapt employment policies to demographic and other social trends. The higher age of retirement now applying to new recruits to the British civil service recognises that it is politically as well as financially unrealistic to increase the pensionable age for everyone except public servants. Paying similar wages in regions with very different house prices (to the extent that

Welsh civil servants are inhibited from applying for posts in London), can also be harmful to creating a unified service (Laffin, 2002: 35).

How do these three different ways of looking at the evidence interpret other issues treated in the previous chapters, such as in policy-making; responses to devolution and European integration; organisational restructuring; changes to accountability regimes and open government, or indeed in human resources management? What insight does each give into the future of the British civil service?

The Whitehall model and the end of the unified service?

The Westminster–Whitehall model seems to work best where it describes the role and characteristics of the small group of career officials who work close to ministers. Those who analyse the civil service in terms of this model are worth heeding most when they debate problems relating to this group. The traditional concept of civil servants as ministers' sole advisers – and its recent evolution – was acknowledged in 2005 by the then Head of the Home Civil Service, Andrew Turnbull, when he said that the civil service 'no longer claim[s] a monopoly over policy advice. Indeed we welcome the fact that we are much more open to ideas from think tanks, consultancies, governments abroad, special advisers, and frontline practitioners' (quoted in Heffernan, 2006: 20). In practice, ministers have long received advice from many sources. All prime ministers since Benjamin Disraeli had politically-sympathetic advisers in No. 10 (Jones, 1976), but their presence was small-scale and usually discreet. However, the type of media-enhanced friction generated by Thatcher's economic adviser in 1989 (Lee *et al.*, 1998: 127), became frequent in the Blair Government because there were more advisers and they were accustomed to operating a party machine. For analysts in the 'Whitehall model' mode, such as O'Toole, the impact of special advisers on the policy role of the civil service, as demonstrated in the reports by Hutton (2004) and Butler (2004), hastened the 'ethical decay' and general decline of the traditional model. His ironic suggestion to future governments is that they agree new Codes of Conduct which recognise that civil servants are no longer advisers but managers, and that the crucial ethical relationship to be regulated is now that between ministers and special advisers (O'Toole, 2006: 45).

Others, such as Campbell and Wilson, see 'the end of Whitehall' approaching because they had defined the 'Whitehall paradigm' as 'a professional civil service [which] provides politicians with both fearless advice … and a smooth running machine for implementing decisions once they had been made' (1995: 5). This paradigm has been undermined by short-term contracts and by the Blair Government expanding 'the "can do ethos", the administrative willingness to say "yes, minister" rather than "no, minister", pioneered by the Thatcher governments' (Heffernan, 2006: 20). Instances of Cabinet Secretaries or Permanent Secretaries not saying 'no, minister' have accumulated since the 1980s. However, Plowden (1994: 102–9) blamed not 'mandarins' but [Conservative] ministers for not wanting to hear unwelcome advice. Labour politicians are responsible for the 'unrecorded government' and poor accountability that comes from taking vital decisions when their officials are out of earshot (Butler Review) or out of London (Hutton Report). These failings will sustain Campbell and Wilson's prognosis of 'the end of Whitehall', if they are not corrected.

Yet accountability as conceived by the Whitehall model has always been rather 'one-dimensional' (Barberis, 1997b: 148), valuing only direct accountability through ministers to Parliament and eschewing communication between civil servants and MPs. The 'folkways of Whitehall and the conventions of the constitution' caused a Scottish First Minister, Henry McLeish, to abandon his idea of civil servants briefing all MSPs (Keating, 2005: 103), though most MSPs have now come 'to see the civil service as at least reasonably accountable' (Pyper and Fingland, 2006). In Wales, the construction of the Welsh Assembly and Government as one corporate body has facilitated direct contact between AMs and officials, whether in committee or in writing. The Whitehall model is not helpful in debating the future impact of devolution or European integration on the British civil service, because its basic assumption is of a unitary civil service within a unitary United Kingdom and a sovereign Westminster. It has always failed to take into account existing diversity, or of those parts of the civil service that fall outside the 'Home Civil Service'.

A civil service model developed at a time when central government intervened very little also does not seem well suited to interpreting trends in delivering large-scale services. The discussion of the Thatcher structural reforms exposes the gaps in the model when it comes to industrial civil servants, specialists or Jobcentres. Nevertheless 'new public management', especially executive agencies and the turning (or returning) to private or voluntary sector delivery, is greatly criticised for its undermining of civil service unity and public-sector values. For O'Toole, NPM reforms are to be welcomed for challenging the 'elitism and insularity' of senior officials, but they take insufficient account of the risks to the ethos of public service: 'the concept of public duty is dead' (1997: 94). However, Mellon's research on executive agencies established that chief executives (whether recruited from inside or outside the civil service) 'appear to espouse the normative civil service value of integrity, alongside the more proactive, private sector approach to change' (Mellon, 2000: 220); moreover, agency chief executives were less willing than other senior civil servants 'to bend the rules to achieve results' (ibid.: 204–5). Two decades after the Next Steps report (Efficiency Unit, 1988), claims of the 'death of the civil service' seem exaggerated, and must be balanced by other experts' views that the NPM reforms are non-revolutionary and with little proven effect on bureaucratic culture any more than on economy, efficiency and effectiveness (Pollitt, 2003: 26, 40).

Governance and the differentiated polity: a network of civil services?

For proponents of the governance thesis, the Whitehall model is inadequate because it does not take into account the wider context in which civil servants make or implement policy. They argue that, while ministers and civil servants may have been the dominant policy actors in a past era of top-down, hierarchical government, the UK executive is now only one member, even if a crucial one, of a much larger policy network of actors that includes local service organisations and 'allies in Brussels' (Smith and Richards, 2002: 3–10). The outsourcing of civil service work in the 1980s and 1990s added layers to an existing complexity, by grafting on the need for civil servants to 'steer' policy delivery through private and voluntary-sector agents not directly within the state's control. Devolution added further complexity.

In the 'multilevel governance' narrative, British civil servants at national and sub-national levels, together with their favoured domestic interest groups, now embark routinely on negotiations with civil servants from other European countries, together with *their* networks. The fragmentation of policy-making between different UK departments (which unification of the civil service has never managed to overcome) now extends into European policy-making too.

The 'differentiated polity' version of governance emphasises the increasing differentiation within the civil service as a result of devolution. Examination of devolution drew attention to the existing diversity between the civil service(s) in the UK, previously obscured by the Westminster–Whitehall narrative of a unitary state and a unified civil service (Rhodes *et al.*, 2003: 9). The new political powers may well lead to a more distinctive devolved civil service and possibly a separate Welsh civil service or even a separate Welsh public service. In Scotland, for the time being at least, senior officials seem more able to defend their preference to remain part of the British civil service. Putting the Thatcher reforms, globalisation and devolution together, Bevir and Rhodes (2003: 58) assert that 'the British core executive ... has been further hollowed out internally by the unintended consequences of marketisation, which fragmented service delivery, multiplied networks and diversified the membership of those networks', and 'externally ... by membership of the EU and other international commitments'.

The proposed solutions to 'hollowing out' and 'fragmentation' diverge. Smith and Richards (2002: 9, 210, 240–50) argue that the Blair Government tried to remedy this weakness with 'joined-up government'. New units were added to the Cabinet Office, and departments were encouraged to work together, with some success (the apparently harmonious working relationships of Social Security and Employment officials), but also failures (the reluctance of Agriculture and Defence to work together during the foot-and-mouth crisis of 2001). Rhodes *et al.* (2003: 157) are pessimistic about these institutional remedies; they contend that the increase in size of the Cabinet Office shows only that the centre sensed it was weak, thus proving it was indeed 'hollowed-out' (but it also shows that the centre identified a former weakness that it took steps to correct!). Holliday (2002: 106) makes a more balanced assessment: on the one hand, the Whitehall executive dispersed power to devolved executives and to advisers in those parts of the policy process hitherto dominated by civil servants; and on the other hand, the long-term 'creeping centralisation of power in the core executive' looks set to continue. Our chapters have shown that what the centre has given away it has made up for in new 'steering' controls: contractual obligations for the private sector, performance targets for agencies and local government; Public Service Agreements for departments; and strict budgetary control. Bevir and Rhodes, however, expect this 'command operating mode' to fail. 'Trusting devolved governments, local authorities and, indeed, any decentralised agency to deliver the services people want and to be accountable to those whom it serves' would be a better strategy, but it is not one that British central government is accustomed to following (2003: 61).

The progressive modernisation of the British civil service

Dunleavy (2006: 317–41) draws a contrast in attitudes towards the Westminster–Whitehall model between radical postmodernists and orthodox political scientists. The first group, such as Rhodes and his colleagues, think the model is irrelevant to contemporary ways of governing, while the second group use the model in their analysis because they believe it describes reasonably well the contemporary world *and* that it is a valuable role model. For these orthodox analysts, according to Dunleavy, the British civil service model has not only remained among the least corrupt and most esteemed public service in the world, but has also shown itself to be capable of adapting to reform measures, whether on freedom of information or new career patterns. Between these two approaches comes that of the modernising reformers, who acknowledge that there have been changes, such as to civil service culture, but consider that the reforms are only partly achieved. For example, there is more openness of information – but not where confidential advice to ministers is concerned. There are new and revised *Codes of Conduct* – but as yet no Civil Service Act.

The catalogue of recommendations for Whitehall produced by Hennessy (1990: 730–40), a 'Whiggish' or moderate reformer, neither radical nor orthodox (according to Bevir and Rhodes, 2003: 150), provides a fitting benchmark for comparing the evidence on how much the civil service has changed with what there still might be to do.

Senior civil servants have traditionally seen themselves first as policy advisers and only second as managers, but whereas their neglected managerial role was forcibly modernised by the Thatcher and Major Governments, improving their policy advice has proved to be more problematic. Hennessy's view was that policy analysis and advice was 'not as good as it should be', because it came from the same small groups of civil servants in the same policy circuits. Authoritative studies have shown that these closed communities gave ministers poor advice on the poll tax (Butler *et al.*, 1994); on addressing the problem of salmonella in eggs (Smith, 2004); 'mad cow disease' (Phillips, 2000); and the foot-and-mouth outbreak (Anderson, 2002), and in assessing correctly the validity of intelligence on Iraq (Butler, 2004), to cite just a few well-known policy failures. Turnbull told the members of the First Division Association of senior officials in 2003 that they had to face 'some uncomfortable issues, such as whether we are sufficiently customer-focused, and whether we are sufficiently insistent on evidence-based policy' (Winstone, 2003: 23).

Open recruitment may improve policy capabilities in the longer term, but Hennessy proposed that, meanwhile, the civil service's 'best people' should be assigned to thinking about the big issues appearing over the horizon; and that commissions or task forces (with civil service members) should feed in fresh ideas and develop policy on contentious issues. Government would have to take their recommendations seriously or nothing would change. As we saw in Chapter 4, the Blair Government created central policy units of civil servants and people from other sectors, such as the Social Exclusion Unit, to tackle cross-departmental social issues; the Strategy Unit, to help departments improve their policies; and the Performance and Innovation Unit to conduct more rigorous analysis of aspects of government policy that contribute to policy delivery, such as how to recruit policy specialists. Yet some 'task forces' (for example, the 'drugs tsar') were dismantled before the relevant issue was resolved; and important 'over-the-horizon' issues were assigned to 'cronies' without relevant expertise (Lord Birt's 'blue-sky' thinking on transport and crime, for example). The '10 Year Transport Plan' (an unusually intensive effort to forecast and modify travel patterns) was quickly forgotten by ministers, and the 'Stern Review' (2007) of the economics of climate change by the Head of the Government's Economic Service was not followed by carbon taxes but by Stern's departure from the Treasury.

A different question is about whom the civil service should advise, and a pointer to the future is given by the practices introduced in Wales. Because there was no distinction between the Assembly and those AMs who formed the government, it has been easier to leave behind the 'Whitehall' norms that restrict contact with the opposition; Welsh civil servants answer committee questions directly and can brief MPs individually, as in local government. In Wales, special advisers are an openly-recruited joint resource across all ministers, and of both parties during the coalition period (Laffin, 2002: 38–41).

Hennessy, like Fulton, recommended that recruitment policies should be changed to improve both policy-making and management. There has been a great reliance on a narrow stream of generalist graduates and a failure to make full use of the human capital the civil service already possessed in its specialist and executive officer grades. Hennessy suggested that, rather than trying to guess which fast stream candidates would make good Permanent Secretaries in thirty years' time, when the world will have changed, the fast stream intake should be cut back drastically. Departments should bring in outsiders at senior level through open competition, entice back those who had left earlier and had gained other experience, and use the existing pool of talent. As we saw in Chapter 6, the civil service has since 1990 succeeded in recruiting and promoting a much wider range of talent, but it has done so by expanding the fast stream, not by cutting back on its traditional recruits. Future decades will show whether the more diverse entry to junior manager grades, and the current pressure on civil servants to acquire professional skills for government, have produced a more diverse and capable group of top officials.

In contrast, the civil service has already modernised its management systems and achieved substantial organisational reform. It has given good managers more freedom to manage, with block annual budgets, and allowed them to pay and recruit against agreed performance targets. There is central supervision by a civil service management board (in devolved administrations too). The role of Head of the Home Civil Service is still combined with that of Cabinet Secretary, a joint role that Hennessy thought could not be performed effectively. But whereas Robin Butler chose to give up his 'sherpa' role (advising the PM at summits), to give extra attention to a civil service apparently under threat, Blair undercut the role of the Cabinet Secretary in security and intelligence, and in coordinating the Cabinet secretariats (Butler, 2004: 607–8). However, while the civil service leadership is now well aware that it is at the head of a vast public business (Hennessy, 1990: 738), it remains to be seen whether managing this business is recognised in the Whitehall culture as an equally valid route to the top.

The final area for reform was in improving accountability, because, as we said earlier in this chapter, there is a need for 'the kind of openness and public accountability that keep bureaucracies constitutional, clean, efficient and responsive' (Hennessy, 1990: 739). Hennessy's 'Whiggish' proposal was to go with the constitutional grain, and take the parliamentary route, with the publication of a code of practice on openness to be agreed between the government and Parliament, and monitored by an 'Information Ombudsman'. From the first official governmental moves in this direction in 1993 to the full implementation of the Freedom of Information Acts in the UK took twelve years, but civil servants as well as journalists and citizens are now becoming used to its operation. Whereas students of government used to have to wait thirty years or profit from the rare public inquiry into government failure to observe civil service activity 'at first hand', documents on significant policy decisions are now in the public domain. Civil servants now have to bear in mind the constraints of open government, just as they have always borne in mind the possibility that ministers, and increasingly themselves, might one day have to account for their actions in Parliament.

The Whitehall model that harked back to the Northcote–Trevelyan Report is too narrow and incompatible with the evidence to be a realistic basis for analysing the modern British civil service, yet it is a present and future reminder to officials of the ethical standards that are expected of civil servants, but not necessarily of the private sector (albeit with exceptions in practice on both sides). The governance model draws attention to the complexity of the policy-making in which civil servants are engaged, within a political and economic world in which both decision-making and policy delivery are highly pluralist. Analysts using this model have revealed the multilevel and differentiated nature of the diverse communities within the civil service. They have shown that the civil service is highly diversified.

The modernisation perspective recognises all these features, but also emphasises the progress over time of the British civil service, noting its development from the collection of corrupt, inefficient and unaccountable aides to ministers in the nineteenth century; through the twentieth century's meritocratic, hierarchical, anonymous officialdom, whose chief pride was in its confidential advice to ministers; to a twenty-first-century organisation that is still evolving but looks set to become a federalised system of civil or public services, unified but adapted and accountable to the citizens it serves.

References

Adonis, A. (1993) *Parliament Today*, 2nd edn, Manchester: Manchester University Press.

Allen Committee (1979) *Report of the Committee on the Selection Procedure for the Recruitment of Administrative Trainees*, Basingstoke: Civil Service Commission.

Allen, G. (2003) 'The Private Finance Initiative (PFI)', *House of Commons Research Paper 03/79*, London: House of Commons Library.

Anderson, I. (2002) *Foot and Mouth Disease 2001: Lessons to be Learned*, HC 888, London: The Stationery Office.

Armstrong, R. (1985) 'The Duties and Responsibilities of Civil Servants in Relation to Ministers', reprinted in Marshall (1989a).

Armstrong, R. (2002) 'Daylight Jobbery', *The Spectator*, 2 March.

Arter, D. (2004) 'On Assessing Strength and Weakness in Parliamentary Committee Systems: Some Preliminary Observations on the New Scottish Parliament', *Journal of Legislative Studies*, 8: 93–117.

Atkinson Committee (1983) *Selection of Fast Stream Graduate Entrants*, London: Management and Personnel Office.

Attali, J. (1993) *Verbatim, I. 1981–1983*, Paris: Fayard.

Baines, P. (1995) 'Financial Accountability: Agencies and Audit', in P. Giddings (ed.), *Parliamentary Accountability. A Study of Parliament and Executive Agencies*, London: Macmillan, 95–117.

Barberis, P. (1997a) '*An Era of Change*', in P. Barberis (ed.), *The Civil Service in an Era of Change*, Aldershot: Dartmouth, 1–22.

Barberis, P. (1997b) 'The Accountability of Ministers and Civil Servants', in P. Barberis (ed.), *The Civil Service in an Era of Change*, Aldershot: Dartmouth, 131–49.

Bekke, H. A. G. and van der Meer, F. (eds) (2000) *Civil Service Systems in Western Europe*, London: Edward Elgar.

Bekke, H. A. G., Perry, J. L. and Toonen, T. A. J. (eds) (1996) *Civil Service Systems in Comparative Perspective*, Bloomington, Ind.: Indiana University Press.

Benn, T. (1987) *Out of the Wilderness: Diaries 1963–67*, London: Arrow Books.

Benn, T. (1989) *Office Without Power: Diaries 1968–72*, London: Arrow Books.

Benn, T. (1990) *Against the Tide: Diaries 1973–76*, London: Arrow Books.

Bevir, M. and Rhodes, R. A. W. (2003) *Interpreting British Governance*, London: Routledge.

Blackstone, T. (1979) 'Helping Ministers Do a Better Job', *New Society*, 19 July.

Blick, A. (2004) *People Who Live in the Dark: The Special Adviser in British Politics*, London: Politico's.

Blunkett, D. (2006) *The Blunkett Tapes: My Life in the Bear Pit*, London: Bloomsbury.

Bogdanor, V. (1996) 'Nobody's Fault: An Analysis of the Scott Report', in Public Finance Foundation, *Government Accountability: Beyond the Scott Report*, London: CIPFA, 27–33.

Bostock, D. (2002) 'Coreper Revisited', *Journal of Common Market Studies*, 40: 215–34.

Bulmer, S. and Burch, M. (1998) 'Organizing for Europe: Whitehall, The British State and European Union', *Public Administration*, 76: 601–28.

Bulmer, S. and Burch, M. (2000) 'The Europeanisation of British Central Government', in R. A. W. Rhodes (ed.), *Transforming British Government*, *I*, London: Macmillan, 46–62.

Bulmer, S. and Burch, M. (2005) 'The Europeanization of UK Government: From Quiet Revolution to Explicit Step-change?', *Public Administration*, 83: 861–90.

Burnham, J. (2000) 'Human Resources Flexibilities in France', in D. Farnham and S. Horton (eds), *Human Resources Flexibilities in the Public Services*, London: Macmillan, 98–114.

Burnham, J. and Jones, G. W. (2000) 'Innovators at 10 Downing Street', in K. Theakston (ed.), *Bureaucrats and Leadership*, London: Macmillan, 68–72.

Burnham, J. and Maor, M. (1995) 'Converging Administrative Systems: Recruitment and Training in EU Member States', *Journal of European Public Policy*, 2: 185–204.

Burns, J. P. and Bowornwathana, B. (eds) (2001) *Civil Service Systems in Asia*, London: Edward Elgar.

Butcher, T. (1997) 'The Citizen's Charter: Creating a Customer-Orientated Civil Service', in P. Barberis (ed.), *The Civil Service in an Era of Change*, Aldershot: Dartmouth, 54–68.

Butler, D., Adonis, A. and Travers, T. (1994) *Failure in British Government: The Politics of the Poll Tax*, Oxford University Press.

Butler, R. (1996) *The Duties and Responsibilities of Civil Servants in Relation to Ministers*, London: Cabinet Office.

Butler, R. (2004) *Review of Intelligence on Weapons of Mass Destruction*, HC 898, London: The Stationery Office; www.thebutlerreview.org.uk.

Cabinet Office (1988) *Service to the Public*, London: Cabinet Office.

Cabinet Office (1991) *The Citizen's Charter: Raising the Standard*, Cm 1599, London: HMSO.

Cabinet Office (1994a) *The Civil Service: Continuity and Change*, Cm 2627, London: HMSO.

Cabinet Office (1994b) *Review of Fast Stream Recruitment*, London: HMSO.

Cabinet Office (1995) *The Civil Service: Taking Forward Continuity and Change*, Cm 2748, London: HMSO.

Cabinet Office (1996) *Development and Training for Civil Servants: A Framework for Action*, CM 3321, London: HMSO.

Cabinet Office (1998a) *Devolution and the Civil Service: Staff Guidance*, London: Cabinet Office.

Cabinet Office (1998b) *Next Steps Briefing Note*, London: Cabinet Office.

Cabinet Office (1998c) *Equal Opportunities in the Civil Service: Data Summary 1998*, London: Cabinet Office.

Cabinet Office (1999a) *Modernising Government*, Cm 4310, London: Stationery Office.

Cabinet Office (1999b) *Civil Service Reform: Report to the Prime Minister*, London: Cabinet Office.

Cabinet Office (1999c) *Performance Management: Civil Service Reform*, London: Cabinet Office.

Cabinet Office (1999d) *A Civil Service for the 21st Century*, London: Cabinet Office.

Cabinet Office (2000) *Citizen's First: Modernising Government Annual Report*, London: Cabinet Office.

Cabinet Office (2001a) *Code of Conduct for Special Advisers*, London: Cabinet Office.

Cabinet Office (2001b) *Redefining the Fast Stream: Review Report*, London: Cabinet Office.

Cabinet Office (2001c) *Civil Service Reform 2001: Making a Difference*, London: Cabinet Office.

Cabinet Office (2003) *Equality in Performance Review: Progress Report*, London: Cabinet Office.

Cabinet Office (2005a) *Departmental Evidence and Response to Select Committees* [the 'Osmotherly Rules'], London: Cabinet Office.

Cabinet Office (2005b) *Delivering a Diverse Civil Service: A 10-Point Plan*, London: Cabinet Office.

Cabinet Office (2006a) *Civil Service Management Code* (Cabinet Office website); www.civilservice.gov.uk/publications/code.

Cabinet Office (2006b) *Civil Service Code*, London: Cabinet Office.

Cabinet Office (2006c) *Professional Skills for Government* (Cabinet Office website); www.civilservice.gov.uk/skills.

Cabinet Office (2006d) *Capability Reviews: The Findings of the First Four Reviews*, London: Cabinet Office.

Cabinet Office (2006e) *Civil Service Fast Stream Recruitment Report 2005–06*, London: Cabinet Office.

Cabinet Office (2006f) *Departmental Report 2006*, Cm 6833, London: Stationery Office.

Campbell, C. and Wilson, G. K. (1995) *The End of Whitehall: Death of a Paradigm?*, Oxford: Blackwell.

Carmichael, P. (2002) 'The Northern Ireland Civil Service: Characteristics and Trends since 1970', *Public Administration*, 80: 23–49.

Castle, B. (1990) *The Castle Diaries 1964–76*, London: Macmillan.

Chapman, L. (1978) *Your Disobedient Servant*, London: Chatto & Windus.

Chapman, R. A. (1992) 'The End of the Civil Service?', *Teaching Public Administration*, 12/2: 1–5.

Chapman, R. A. (1997) 'The End of the Civil Service', in P. Barberis (ed.), *The Civil Service in an Era of Change*, Aldershot: Dartmouth, 23–37.

Chapman, R. A. and O'Toole, B. J. (1995) 'The Role of the Civil Service: A Traditional View in a Period of Change', *Public Policy and Administration*, 10/2: 3–20.

Civil Service Commissioners (various dates) *Annual Report*, London: Office of the Civil Service Commissioners.

Clarke, C. (2006) 'Charles Clarke statement in full', 5 May; http://news. bbc.co.uk/1/hi/uk_politics/4976620.stm.

Committee on Standards in Public Life (1995) *Standards in Public Life: First Report* [Nolan Committee] Cm 2850, London: HMSO.

Committee on Standards in Public Life (2000) *Sixth Report: Reinforcing Standards*, Cm 4557, London: Stationery Office.

Committee on Standards in Public Life (2003) *Ninth Report: Defining the Boundaries of the Executive: Ministers, Special Advisers and the Permanent Civil Service*, Cm 5775, London: Stationery Office.

Constitution Committee of the House of Lords (2002) *Devolution: Inter-institutional Relations in the United Kingdom*, HL28, London: Stationery Office.

Constitution Unit (2002) *Devolution Monitoring Programme: Northern Ireland Report*, 13; www.ucl.ac.uk.

Constitution Unit (2005) *Devolution Monitoring Programme: Northern Ireland Report*, 23, www.ucl.ac.uk.

Corby, S. (1997) 'Industrial Relations in the Civil Service', in P. Barberis (ed.) *The Civil Service in an Era of Change*, Aldershot: Dartmouth, 69–81.

Crossman, R. H. S. (1975) *The Diaries of a Cabinet Minister: Minister of Housing 1964–66*, London: Hamish Hamilton.

Crossman, R. H. S. (1976) *The Diaries of a Cabinet Minister: Lord President of the Council 1966–68*, London: Hamish Hamilton.

Crossman, R. H. S. (1977) *The Diaries of a Cabinet Minister: Secretary of State for Social Services 1968–70*, London: Hamish Hamilton.

Davies Committee (1969) *Report of the Committee of Inquiry on the Method II System of Selection*, Cmnd 4156, London: HMSO.

Defence Science and Technology Laboratory (Dstl) (2002) *Annual Report and Accounts 2001/2002*, HC930, London: Stationery Office.

Denham, A. (2003) 'Public Services', in P. Dunleavy, A. Gamble, R. Heffernan and G. Peele (eds), *Developments in British Politics 7*, Basingstoke: Palgrave Macmillan, 282–301.

Department for Work and Pensions (DWP) (2005) *Departmental Framework*, London: DWP.

Department of Constitutional Affairs (2006) *Freedom of Information Act 2000: Statistics on Implementation in Central Government: July–September 2006*, London: Department of Constitutional Affairs.

Dicey, A. V. (1959) *An Introduction to the Study of the Law of the Constitution*, 10th edn [first published 1885], London: Macmillan.

Doig, A. (1997) 'People or Positions? Ensuring Standards in the Reformed Public Sector', in P. Barberis (ed.), *The Civil Service in an Era of Change*, Aldershot: Dartmouth, 95–113.

Donoughue, B. (1987) *Prime Minister: The Conduct of Policy under Harold Wilson and James Callaghan*, London: Jonathan Cape.

Draper, D. (1997) *Blair's Hundred Days*, London: Faber & Faber.

Drewry, G. and Butcher, T. (1991) *The Civil Service Today*, 2nd edn, Oxford: Basil Blackwell.

Duggett, M. (2001) 'Cross-Channel Perspectives on British Civil Service Training 1980–2000', *Public Policy and Administration*, 16/4, 96–105.

Dunleavy, P. (1991) *Democracy, Bureaucracy and Public Choice*, Hemel Hempstead: Harvester Wheatsheaf.

Dunleavy, P. (2006) 'The Westminster Model and the Distinctiveness of British Politics', in P. Dunleavy, R. Heffernan, P. Cowley and C. Hay (eds), *Developments in British Politics*, 8, Basingstoke: Palgrave Macmillan, 315–418.

Dyson, K. (2000) 'Europeanization, Whitehall Culture and the Treasury as Institutional Veto Player', *Public Administration*, 78: 897–914.

Economist (2006) Leader, 'Corruption and the Law: Barefaced', 23 December. Economist.

Efficiency Unit (1988) *Improving Management in Government: The Next Steps* [Ibbs Report], London: HMSO.

Efficiency Unit (1991) *Making the Most of Next Steps: The Management of Ministers' Departments and their Executive Agencies* [Fraser Report], London: HMSO.

Efficiency Unit (1993) *Career Management and Succession Planning Study*, London: HMSO.

Expenditure Committee of the House of Commons (1977), *The Civil Service*, HC 535, London: HMSO.

Falconer, P. K. (1999) 'The New Public Management Today: An Overview', Paper presented to ESRC Seminar on 'Recent Developments in the New Public Management', Imperial College, London, May.

Farnham, D. (1993) 'Human Resources Management and Employee Relations', in D. Farnham and S. Horton (eds), *Managing the New Public Services*, London: Macmillan, 99–124.

Farnham, D. and Horton, S. (eds) (2000) *Human Resources Flexibilities in the Public Services*, London: Macmillan.

Finer, S. E. (1956) 'The Individual Responsibility of Ministers', *Public Administration*, 34: 377–96.

Flynn, N. and Strehl, F. (eds) (1996) *Public Sector Management in Europe*, Hemel Hempstead: Prentice Hall/Harvester Wheatsheaf.

Foreign Affairs Committee (1994) *Public Expenditure: The Pergau Hydro-electric Project, the Aid and Trade Provision and Related Matters*, HC 271, London: HMSO.

Foster, C. D. (2001) 'The Civil Service under Stress: The Fall in Civil Service Power and Authority', *Public Administration*, 79/3: 725–49.

Foster, C. D. and Plowden, F. J. (1996) *The State Under Stress: Can the Hollow State be Good Government?*, Buckingham: Open University Press.

Franks Report (1983) *Falkland Islands Review: Report of a Committee of Privy Counsellors*, Cmnd 8787, London: HMSO.

Fry, G. K. (1981) *The Administrative 'Revolution' in Whitehall*, London: Croom Helm.

Fry, G. K. (1985) *The Changing Civil Service*, London: George Allen & Unwin.

Fry, G. (2000) 'Three Giants of the Inter-war British Higher Civil Service: Sir Maurice Hankey, Sir Warren Fisher and Sir Horace Wilson', in K. Theakston (ed.), *Bureaucrats and Leadership*, London: Macmillan, 39–67.

Fry, G. K. (1993) *Reforming the Civil Service*, Edinburgh: Edinburgh University Press.

Fry, G. K. (1995) *Policy and Management in the British Civil Service*, Hemel Hempstead: Prentice Hall/Harvester Wheatsheaf.

Fulton, Lord (1968) *The Civil Service: Report of the Committee of Inquiry into the Civil Service 1966–68*, Cmnd 3638, London: HMSO.

Garrett, J. (1980) *Managing the Civil Service*, London: Heinemann.

Gay, O. (2005) *The Public Services Ombudsman (Wales) Bill (HL)*, Research Paper 05/26, London: House of Commons Library.

Geddes, A. (2004) *The European Union and British Politics*, Basingstoke: Palgrave Macmillan.

George, S. and Bache, I. (2001) *Politics in the European Union*, Oxford University Press.

Gershon, P. (2004) *Releasing Resources to the Front Line*, London: The Stationery Office.

Giddings, P. (1995a) 'The Treasury Committee and Next Steps Agencies', in P. Giddings (ed.), *Parliamentary Accountability: A Study of Parliament and Executive Agencies*, London: Macmillan, 55–70.

Giddings, P. (ed.) (1995b) *Parliamentary Accountability: A Study of Parliament and Executive Agencies*, London: Macmillan.

Gillman, S. (2001) *Politico's Guide to Careers in Politics and Government*, London: Politico's.

Glaister, S., Burnham, J., Stevens, H. and Travers, T. (1998) *Transport Policy in Britain*, London: Macmillan/Palgrave.

Glaister, S., Burnham, J., Stevens, H. and Travers, T. (2006) *Transport Policy in Britain*, 2nd edn, Basingstoke: Palgrave.

Greenwood, J., Pyper, R. and Wilson, D. (2002) *New Public Administration in Britain*, 3rd edn, London: Routledge.

Greer, S. L. and Sandford, M. (2006) 'The GLA and Whitehall', *Local Government Studies*, 32/3: 239–54.

Gregory, R. and Giddings, P. (2002) *The Ombudsman, the Citizen and Parliament*, London: Politico's.

Halligan, J. (2003) 'The Australian Civil Service: Redefining Boundaries', in J. Halligan (ed.), *Civil Service Systems in Anglo-American Countries*, Cheltenham: Edward Elgar, 70–112.

Hayward, J. E. S. (2007) *Fragmented France: Two Centuries of Disputed Identity*, Oxford University Press.

Hayward, J. E. S. and Wright, V. (2002) *Governing for the Centre: Core Executive Coordination in France*, Oxford University Press.

Hayward, J. E. S., Barry, B. and Brown, A. (eds) (2000) *The British Study of Politics in the Twentieth Century*, Oxford University Press.

Heath, E. (1998) *The Course of My Life*, London: Hodder & Stoughton.

Heclo, H. and Wildavsky, A. (1981) *The Private Government of Public Money*, 2nd edn, London: Macmillan.

Heffernan, R. (2006) 'The Blair Style of Central Government', in P. Dunleavy, R. Heffernan, P. Cowley and C. Hay (eds), *Developments in British Politics 8*, Basingstoke: Palgrave Macmillan, 17–35.

Hennessy, P. (1989) *Whitehall*, London: Secker & Warburg.

Hennessy, P. (1990) *Whitehall*, London: Fontana.

Hennessy, P. (1996) *The Hidden Wiring: Unearthing the British Constitution*, London: Indigo.

Hennessy, P. (1999) *The Blair Centre: A Question of Command and Control?*, London: Public Management Foundation.

Herdan. B. (2006) *The Customer Voice in Transforming Public Services*, London: Cabinet Office.

Heseltine, M. (1990) *Where There's a Will*, 2nd edn, London: Arrow Books.

HM Customs & Excise (1997) *Traveller's Charter*, London: HMSO.

HM Treasury (1991) *Competing for Quality: Buying Better Public Services*, Cm 1730, London: HMSO.

HM Treasury (1993) *Breaking New Ground: The Private Finance Initiative*, London: HM Treasury.

HM Treasury (1994) *Fundamental Review of Running Costs*, London: HM Treasury.

HM Treasury (1998) *Modern Public Services for Britain: Investing in Reform: Comprehensive Spending Review: New Public Spending Plans 1999–2002*, Cm 4011, London: The Stationery Office.

HM Treasury (2003) *PFI: Meeting the Investment Challenge*, London: HM Treasury.

HM Treasury (2004) *Financing Britain's Future: Review of the Revenue Departments*, Cm 6163, London: The Stationery Office.

HM Treasury (2006a) *Budget 2006: Economic and Fiscal Strategy Report*, HC 968, London: The Stationery Office.

HM Treasury (2006b) *Releasing the Resources to Meet the Challenges Ahead: Value for Money in the 2007 Comprehensive Spending Review*, Cm 6889, London: The Stationery Office.

Hogwood, B., Judge, D. and McVicar, M. (2000) 'Agencies and Accountability', in R. A. W. Rhodes (ed.), *Transforming British Government, I*, London: Macmillan, 195–222.

Holliday, I. (2002) 'Executives and Administration', in P. Dunleavy, A. Gamble, I. Holliday and G. Peele (eds), *Developments in British Politics 6*, Basingstoke: Palgrave, 88–107.

Home Affairs Committee (2006) *Immigration Control*, HC 775, London: Stationery Office.

Horton, S. (1993) 'The Civil Service', in D. Farnham and S. Horton (eds) *Managing the New Public Services*, Basingstoke: Macmillan, 127–49.

Horton, S. (2000) 'Human Resources Flexibilities in UK Public Services', in D. Farnham and S. Horton (eds), *Human Resources Flexibilities in the Public Services*, London: Macmillan, 208–36.

Horton, S. and Farnham, D. (2000) 'Evaluating Human Resources Flexibilities: Comparative Perspective', in D. Farnham and S. Horton (eds), *Human Resources Flexibilities in the Public Services*, London: Macmillan, 313–36.

Hoskyns, J. (1983) 'Whitehall and Westminster: An Outsider's View', *Parliamentary Affairs*, 36: 137–47.

Hoskyns, J. (2000) *Just in Time: Inside the Thatcher Revolution*, London: Aurum Press.

Hughes, M. and Newman, J. (1999) 'From New Public Management to New Labour: From "New" to "Modern" ', Paper presented to Third International Symposium on Public Management, Aston University, March.

Hutton, Lord (2004) *Report of the Inquiry into the Circumstances Surrounding the Death of Dr David Kelly, C. M. G.*, London: Stationery Office; www.the-hutton-inquiry.org.uk.

Hyndman, N. and Eden, R. (2001) 'Rational Management, Performance Targets and Executive Agencies: Views from Agency Chief Executives in Northern Ireland', *Public Administration*, 79: 579–98.

Information Commissioner's Office (2006) *Annual Report 2005–2006*, HC 1228, London: Stationery Office.

Jackson, P. M. (2001) 'Public Sector Added Value: Can Bureaucracy Deliver?', *Public Administration*, 79: 5–28.

James, O. (2003) *The Executive Agency Revolution in Whitehall*, Basingstoke: Palgrave.

Jeffery, C. (2006) 'Devolution and the Lopsided State', in P. Dunleavy, R. Hefferman, P. Cowley and C. Hay (eds), *Developments in British Politics 8*, Basingstoke: Palgrave Macmillan, 138–58.

Jennings, I. (1966) *The British Constitution*, 5th edn [first published 1941], Cambridge University Press.

Jones, G. W. (1976) 'The Prime Ministers' Secretaries: Politicians or Administrators?', in J. A. G. Griffith (ed.), *From Policy to Administration: Essays in Honour of William A. Robson*, London: George Allen & Unwin, 13–38.

Jones, G. W. and Burnham, J. (1995) 'Modernizing the British Civil Service', in J. J. Hesse and T. A. J. Toonen (eds), *The European Yearbook of Comparative Government and Public Administration*, Baden-Baden: Nomos Boulder: Westview Press, 323–45.

Jones, G. W., Burnham, J. and Elgie, R. (1995) 'The Environment Agencies', in P. Giddings (ed.), *Parliamentary Accountability: A Study of Parliament and Executive Agencies*, London: Macmillan, 155–90.

Jones, J. B. and Osmond, J. (2002) *Building a Civic Culture*, Cardiff: Institute of Welsh Affairs/Welsh Governance Centre.

Jones, N. (2000) *Sultans of Spin: Media and the New Labour Government*, London: Orion.

Jones, N. (2001) *The Control Freaks: How New Labour Gets Its Own Way*, London: Politico's.

Jones, N. and Weir, S. (2002) 'The Masters of Misinformation: Behind the Jo Moore Affair Lies a Spin Machine That Has Corrupted the Senior Civil Service Itself', *New Statesman*, 25 February.

Jordan, A. G. (1990) 'Sub-governments, Policy Communities and Networks. Refilling the Old Bottles?', *Journal of Theoretical Politics*, 2: 319–38.

Jordan, A. G. (1994) *The British Administrative System: Principles Versus Practice*, London: Routledge.

Jordan, A. G. and Richardson, J. J. (1987) *British Politics and the Policy Process: An Arena Approach*, London: George Allen & Unwin.

Keating, M. (2005) *The Government of Scotland: Public Policy Making after Devolution*, Edinburgh: Edinburgh University Press.

Kellner, P. and Lord Crowther-Hunt (1980) *The Civil Servants: An Inquiry into Britain's Ruling Class*, London: Macdonald.

Kelsall, R. K. (1956) 'Selection and the Social Background of the Administrative Class: A Rejoinder', *Public Administration*, 34: 169–71.

Kemp, P. (1990) 'Next Steps for the British Civil Service', *Governance*, 3/2: 186–96.

Kemp, P. (1993) *Beyond Next Steps: A Civil Service Guide for the 21st century*, London Social Market Foundation.

Kirkpatrick, I. and Pyper, R. (2001) 'The Early Impact of Devolution on Civil Service Accountability', *Public Policy and Administration*, 16/3: 68–84.

Kirkpatrick, I. and Pyper, R. (2003) 'Modernisation and Civil Service Accountability: The Case of Scottish Devolution', in T. Butcher and A. Massey (eds), *Modernising Civil Services*, London: Edward Elgar.

Klöti, U. (2001) 'Consensual Government in a Heterogeneous Polity', *West European Politics*, 24/2: 19–34.

Knoke, D. and Kuklinski, J. (1982) *Network Analysis*, Beverly Hills, Calif.: Sage, 9–21; reproduced in G. Thompson, J. Frances, R. Levačić and J. Mitchell (1991), *Markets, Hierarchies and Networks*, Buckingham: Open University Press, 173–82.

Kooiman, J. (1993) *Modern Governance*, London: Sage.

Laffin, M. (2002) 'The Engine Room: The Civil Service and the National Assembly', in J. B. Jones and J. Osmond (eds), *Building a Civic Culture*, Cardiff: Institute of Welsh Affairs/Welsh Governance Centre, 33–42.

Landers, B. (1999) 'Encounters with the Public Accounts Committee: A Personal Memoir', *Public Administration*, 77: 195–213.

Lang, I. (2002) *Blue Remembered Years*, London: Politico's.

Lawson, N. (1992) *The View from No. 11*, London: Bantam.

Leach, R. and Percy-Smith, J. (2001) *Local Governance in Britain*, Basingstoke: Palgrave Macmillan.

Le Cheminant, P. (2001) *Beautiful Ambiguities: An Inside View of the Heart of Government*, London: Radcliffe.

Lee, J. M., Jones, G. W. and Burnham, J. (1998) *At the Centre of Whitehall*, London: Macmillan.

Legg, T. and Ibbs, R. (1999) *Report of the Sierra Leone Arms Investigation*, London: Stationery Office.

Lequesne, C. (2000) 'The Common Fisheries Policy', in H. Wallace and W. Wallace (eds), *Policy-making in the European Union*, Oxford University Press, 345–72.

Levitt, R and Solesbury, W. (2006) 'Outsiders in Whitehall', *Public Money & Management*, 26/1, 10–12.

Lewis. J. (1998) 'Is the "Hard Bargaining" Image of the Council Misleading?', *Journal of Common Market Studies*, 36: 479–504.

Lijphart, A. (1984) *Democracies: Patterns of Majoritarian and Consensus Government in Twenty-One Countries*, New Haven, Conn. and London: Yale University Press.

Likierman, A. (1998) 'Resource Accounting and Budgeting – Where Are We Now?', *Public Money & Management*, 18/2: 17–21.

Linklater, M. and Leigh, D. (1986) *Not With Honour: The Inside Story of the Westland Scandal*, London: Sphere.

Loughlin, J. (1992) 'Administering Policy in Northern Ireland', in B. Hadfield (ed.), *Northern Ireland: Politics and the Constitution*, Buckingham: Open University Press.

Lowe, R. and Rollings, N. (2000) 'Modernising Britain, 1957–64: A Classic Case of Centralisation and Fragmentation?', in R. A. W. Rhodes (ed.), *Transforming British Government, I*, London: Macmillan, 99–118.

Ludlow, P. (1993) 'The UK Presidency: A View from Brussels', *Journal of Common Market Studies*, 31: 246–60.

Ludlow, P. (1998) 'The 1998 UK Presidency: A View from Brussels', *Journal of Common Market Studies*, 36: 573–83.

Lyons, M. (2004) *Well Placed to Deliver? Shaping the Pattern of Government Service: Independent Review of Public Sector Relocation*, London: Stationery Office.

McConnell, A. (2000) 'Governance in Scotland, Wales and Northern Ireland', in R. Pyper and L. Robins (eds), *United Kingdom Governance*, London: Macmillan.

Mackintosh, J. (1976), 'The Problems of Devolution: The Scottish Case', in J. A. G. Griffith (ed.), *From Policy to Administration: Essays in Honour of William A. Robson*, London: George Allen & Unwin, 99–114.

McMillan, J. and Massey, A. (2004) 'Central Government and Devolution', in M. O'Neill (ed.), *Devolution and British Politics*, Harlow: Pearson Longman, 231–50.

Maor, M. and Stevens, H. (1997) 'Measuring the Impact of New Public Management and European Integration on Recruitment and Training in the UK Civil Service', *Public Administration*, 75: 531–51.

Marr, A. (1996) *Ruling Britannia: The Failure and Future of British Democracy*, Harmondsworth: Penguin.

Marsh, D. and Rhodes, R. A. W. (eds) (1992) *Policy Networks in British Government*, Oxford: Clarendon Press.

Marshall, G. (1989a) (ed.) *Ministerial Responsibility*, Oxford University Press.

Marshall, G. (1989b) 'Introduction', in G. Marshall (ed.), *Ministerial Responsibility*, Oxford University Press, 1–13.

Massey, A. and Pyper, R. (2005) *Public Management and Modernisation in Britain*, Basingstoke: Palgrave Macmillan.

Maxwell Fyfe, D. (1954) 'Crichel Down Debate', *HC Debs*, 5s, 530, cc. 1285–7, London: HMSO.

Mellon, E. (2000) 'Executive Agency Chief Executives: Their Leadership Values', in K. Theakston (ed.), *Bureaucrats and Leadership*, Basingstoke: Macmillan, 200–221.

Mény, Y. (1992) *La Corruption de la République*, Paris: Fayard.

Ministry of Defence (2001) *Dstl Framework Document*, London: Ministry of Defence.

Minogue, M. (1998) 'Changing the State: Concepts and Practice in the Reform of the Public Sector', in M. Minogue, C. Polidano and D. Hulme (eds), *Beyond the New Public Management*, Cheltenham, UK and Lyme, USA: Edward Elgar, 17–37.

Minogue, M., Polidano, C. and Hulme, D. (eds) (1998) *Beyond the New Public Management: Changing Ideas and Practices in Governance*, Cheltenham, UK and Lyme, USA: Edward Elgar.

Mitchell, J. (2003) 'Politics in Scotland', in P. Dunleavy, A. Gamble, R. Heffernan and G. Peele (eds), *Developments in British Politics 7*, Basingstoke: Palgrave Macmillan, 161–80.

Montin, C. (2000) 'Flexibility in Personnel Policies in International Organisations', in D. Farnham and S. Horton (eds), *Human Resources Flexibilities in the Public Services*, London: Macmillan, 298–312.

Morrison, H. (1933) *Socialisation and Transport*, London: Constable.

Mottram, R. (2005) 'Professional Skills for Government: Death of the Generalist', *Public Management and Policy Association Review*, 30 (August) 6–9.

Mountfield, R. (2000), 'Civil Service Change in Britain', Paper for the Political Studies Association 50th Annual Conference, 10–13 April, London School of Economics.

Murray, R. (2000) 'Human Resources Management in Swedish Central Government', in D. Farnham and S. Horton (eds), *Human Resources Flexibilities in the Public Services*, Basingstoke: Macmillan, 169–88.

NAO (National Audit Office) (1986) *The Rayner Scrutiny Programmes 1979 to 1983*, HC 322, London: HMSO.

NAO (1997) *The PFI Contracts for Bridgend and Fazakerley Prisons*, HC 253, London: Stationery Office.

NAO (2002) *Dealing with Pollution from Ships*, HC 879, Stationery Office.

NAO (2006a) *Progress in Improving Government Efficiency*, HC 802, London: Stationery Office.

NAO (2006b) *The Delays in Administering the 2005 Single Farm Payment in England*, HC 1631, London: Stationery Office.

NAO (2007) *The Efficiency Programme: A Second Review of Progress*, HC 156, London: Stationery Office.

Nelson, B. F. and Stubb, A. (2003) *The European Union: Readings on the Theory and Practice of European Integration*, Basingstoke: Palgrave Macmillan.

Newman, J. (1999) 'The New Public Management, Modernisation and Organisational Change: Disruptions, Disjunctures and Dilemmas', Paper presented to ESRC Seminar on 'Recent Developments in the New Public Management', Aston University, November.

Newman, J. (2001) *Modernising Governance. New Labour, Policy and Society*, London: Sage.

Nicolson, I. F. (1986) *The Mystery of Crichel Down*, Oxford: Clarendon.

Niskanen, W. A. (1971) *Bureaucracy and Representative Government*, Chicago: Aldine-Atherton.

Nugent, N. (2003) *The Government and Politics of the European Union*, Basingstoke: Palgrave Macmillan.

Oborne, P. (1999) *Alistair Campbell: New Labour and the Rise of the Media Class*, London: Aurum Press.

Oborne, P. and Walters, S. (2004) *Alistair Campbell*, London: Aurum Press.

OECD (Organisation for Economic Co-operation and Development) (1990) *Public Management Developments: Survey 1990* (and subsequent years), Paris: OECD.

OECD (2002) *Public Service as an Employer of Choice*, Paris: OECD.

OECD (2003) *Managing Senior Management: Senior Civil Service Reform in OECD Member Countries*, Paris: OECD.

OECD (2004) *Public Sector Modernisation: Modernising Public Employment*, Paris: OECD.

OECD (2005a) *Paying for Performance: Policies for Government Employees*, Paris: OECD.

OECD (2005b) *Public Sector Modernisation: The Way Forward*, Paris: OECD.

OECD (2006) *Application of the Convention on Combating Bribery*, Paris: OECD.

O'Neill, M. (2004) 'Challenging the Centre: Home Rule Movements', in M. O'Neill (ed.), *Devolution and British Politics*, Harlow: Pearson Longman, 32–64.

ONS (Office for National Statistics) (2005) 'Trends in Public Sector Employment', *Labour Market Trends*, 113: 477–89 (Palgrave Macmillan).

ONS (2006) *Civil Service Quarterly Public Sector Employment Statistics, Quarter 4, 2005*, London: ONS.

OPSR (Office of Public Service Reform) (2002) *Better Government Services: Executive Agencies in the 21st Century*, London: Cabinet Office.

OPSR (2005) *Choice and Voice in the Reform of Public Services*, Cm 6630, London: Stationery Office.

Osborne, D. and Gaebler, T. (1992) *Reinventing Government*, Reading, Mass.: Addison-Wesley.

Osborne, R. (2002) 'Making a Difference? The Role of Statutory Committees in the Northern Ireland Assembly', *Public Administration*, 80: 283–99.

Osmond, J. (2005) 'Provenance and Promise', in J. Osmond (ed.), *Welsh Politics Comes of Age: Responses to the Richard Commission*, Cardiff: Institute of Welsh Affairs, 5–21.

O'Toole, B. (1993) 'Permanent Secretaries, Open Competition and the Future of the Civil Service', *Public Policy and Administration*, 8/3: 1–3.

O'Toole, B. (1997) 'The Concept of Public Duty', in P. Barberis (ed.), *The Civil Service in an Era of Change*, Aldershot: Dartmouth, 82–94.

O'Toole, B. (2004) 'The Challenge of Change in the Civil Service: 2004 in Retrospect', *Public Policy and Administration*, 19/4: 1–16.

O'Toole, B. (2006) 'The Emergence of a "New" Ethical Framework for Civil Servants', *Public Money & Management*, 26/1: 39–46.

Page, E. C. (1997) *People Who Run Europe*, Oxford: Clarendon Press.

Page, E. C. (2005) 'Joined-up Government and the Civil Service', in Bogdanor, V. (ed.), *Joined-up Government*, Oxford University Press.

Page, E. C. and Jenkins, B. (2005) *Policy Bureaucracy: Government with a Cast of Thousands*, Oxford University Press.

Parry, R. and MacDougal, A. (2005) 'Civil Service Reform Post-Devolution: The Scottish and Welsh Experience', *ESRC Devolution Briefings*, 37.

Peters, B. G. (1989) *The Politics of Bureaucracy*, 3rd edn, New York: Longman.

Phillips, N. (2000) *The Inquiry into BSE and Variant CJD in the United Kingdom*, HC 887, London: Stationery Office.

Phillis, B. (2004) *An Independent Review of Government Communications*, London: Cabinet Office.

PHSO (Parliamentary and Health Service Ombudsman) (2005) *A Debt of Honour: the ex gratia Scheme for British Groups Interned by the Japanese during the Second World War*, HC 324, London: Stationery Office.

PHSO (2006) *Annual Report 2005–06*, HC 1363, London: Stationery Office.

Pickering, C. (2002) 'Sir Douglas in Euroland: Treasury Officials and the European Union', *Public Administration*, 80: 583–99.

Pierre, J. (2000) *Debating Governance*, Oxford University Press.

Pierre, J. and Peters, B. G. (2000) *Governance, Politics and the State*, London: Macmillan.

Pierre, J. and Stoker, G. (2000) 'Towards Multilevel Governance', in P. Dunleavy, A. Gamble, I. Holliday and G. Peele (eds), *Developments in British Politics 6*, London: Macmillan, 29–46.

PIU (Performance and Innovation Unit) (2000) *Adding It Up: Improving Analysis and Modelling in Central Government*, London: Cabinet Office.

Plowden, W. (1994) *Ministers and Mandarins*, London: Institute of Public Policy Research.

Pollitt, C. (2003) *The Essential Public Manager*, Maidenhead: Open University Press.

Ponting, C. (1985) *The Right to Know: The Inside Story of the Belgrano Affair*, London: Sphere.

Ponting, C. (1990) *Secrecy in Britain*, Oxford: Basil Blackwell.

Popper, K. (1945) *The Open Society and its Enemies*, London: Routledge.

Prime Minister (2004) 'Modernisation of the Civil Service'; www.number-10.gov.uk.

Prime Minister's Delivery Unit (2006) *Capability Reviews: The Findings of the First Four Reviews*, London: Central Office of Information.

Public Accounts Committee of the House of Commons (1987) *The Financial Management Initiative*, HC 61, London: HMSO.

Public Administration Committee (1998a) *The Government Information and Communication Service*, HC 770, London: Stationery Office.

Public Administration Committee (1998b) *Ministerial Accountability and Parliamentary Questions*, HC 820, London: Stationery Office.

Public Administration Committee (2001) *Special Advisers: Boon or Bane?*, HC 293, London: Stationery Office.

Public Administration Committee (2002) *'These Unfortunate Events': Lessons of Recent Events at the Former DTLR*, HC 303, London: Stationery Office.

Public Administration Committee (2004a) *Civil Service Issues*, HC 423, London: Stationery Office.

Public Administration Committee (2004b) *A Draft Civil Service Bill: Completing the Reform*, HC 128, London: Stationery Office.

Public Administration Committee (2004c) *Ministerial Accountability and Parliamentary Questions*, HC 355, London: Stationery Office.

Public Administration Committee (2005a) *Choice, Voice and Public Services*, HC 49, London: Stationery Office.

Public Administration Committee (2005b) *Ministerial Accountability and Parliamentary Questions*, HC 449, London: Stationery Office.

Public Administration Committee (2006) *Skills for Government*, HC 93, London: Stationery Office.

Public Administration Committee (2007) *Politics and Administration: Ministers and Civil Servants*, HC 122, London: Stationery Office.

Public Finance Foundation (1996) *Government Accountability: Beyond the Scott Report*, London: CIPFA.

Public Service Committee (1996) *Ministerial Accountability and Responsibility*, HC 313, London: HMSO.

Public Service Committee of the House of Lords (1998), *Report*, HL 55, London: Stationery Office.

Pyper, R. (1983) 'The FO Resignations: Individual Ministerial Responsibility Revived?', *Teaching Politics*, 12, 200–10.

Pyper, R. (1985) 'Sarah Tisdall, Ian Willmore and the Civil Servant's "Right to Leak"', *Political Quarterly*, 56/1: 72–81.

Pyper, R. (1987a) 'The Doctrine of Individual Ministerial Responsibility in British Government: Theory and Practice in a new Regime of Parliamentary Accountability', Unpublished PhD thesis, University of Leicester.

Pyper, R. (1987b) 'The Westland Affair', *Teaching Politics*, 16/3: 346–63.

Pyper, R. (1991) *The Evolving Civil Service*, Harlow: Longman.

Pyper, R. (1992) 'Apportioning Responsibility or Passing the Buck? The Cases of Mr Baker, Mr Prior and the Disappearing Prisoners', *Teaching Public Administration*, 12/2: 33–6.

Pyper, R. (1995a) *The British Civil Service*, Hemel Hempstead: Prentice Hall/Harvester Wheatsheaf.

Pyper, R. (1995b) 'Ministerial Responsibility and Next Steps Agencies', in P. Giddings (ed.), *Parliamentary Accountability. A Study of Parliament and Executive Agencies*, London: Macmillan, 19–32.

Pyper, R. (1996) (ed.) *Aspects of Accountability in the British System of Government*, Eastham: Tudor.

Pyper, R. (1999) 'The Civil Service: A Neglected Dimension of Devolution', *Public Money & Management*, 19/2: 45–9.

Pyper, R. (2003) 'Ministers, Civil Servants and Advisors', in J. Fisher, D. Denver and J. Benyon (eds), *Central Debates in British Politics*, Harlow: Pearson, 239–62.

Pyper, R. (2004) 'Civil Service Management and Policy,' in B. Jones, D. Kavanagh, M. Moran and P. Norton (eds), *Politics UK*, Harlow: Pearson Longman, 518–39.

Pyper, R. and Fingland, L. (2006) 'Remote or Responsive? MSPs' Views of the Civil Service', *The Scotsman*, 8 September.

Rao, N. (2006) 'Introducing the New Government of London', *Local Government Studies*, 32/3: 215–22.

Rhodes, R. A. W. (1990) 'Policy Networks: A British Perspective', *Journal of Theoretical Politics*, 2: 293–317.

Rhodes, R. A. W. (1994) 'The Hollowing Out of the State: The Changing Nature of the Public Services in Britain', *Political Quarterly*, 65/2: 138–51.

Rhodes, R. A. W. (1997) *Understanding Governance: Policy Networks, Governance, Reflexivity and Accountability*, Buckingham: Open University Press.

Rhodes, R. A. W., Carmichael, P., McMillan, J. and Massey, A. (2003) *Decentralizing the Civil Service: From Unitary State to Differentiated Polity in the United Kingdom*, Buckingham: Open University Press.

Richard, I. (2004) *Report of the [Richard] Commission on the Powers and Electoral Arrangements of the National Assembly of Wales*, London: Stationery Office.

Richards, D. (1997) *The Civil Service Under the Conservatives 1979–1997*, Brighton: Sussex University Press.

Richards, D. and Smith, M. (2002) *Governance and Public Policy in the UK*, Oxford University Press.

Richards, S. (2000) 'The Special Advisers Are Here to Stay', *New Statesman*, 17 January.

Richardson, J. J. and Jordan, A. G. (1979) *Governing Under Pressure: The Policy Process in a Post-Parliamentary Democracy*, Oxford: Martin Robertson.

Rieger, E. (2000) 'The Common Agricultural Policy', in H. Wallace and W. Wallace (eds), *Policy-Making in the European Union*, Oxford University Press, 179–210.

Rogers, R. and Walters, R. (2004) *How Parliament Works*, 5th edn, Harlow: Pearson Longman.

Saward, M. (1997) 'In Search of the Hollow Crown', in P. Weller, H. Bakvis and R. A. W. Rhodes (eds), *The Hollow Crown*, London: Macmillan.

Scott, R. (1996) *Report of the Inquiry into the Export of Defence Equipment and Dual-Use Goods to Iraq and Related Prosecutions*, HC 115, London: HMSO.

Scottish Office (1997) *Scotland's Parliament*, Cm 3658, London: Stationery Office.

Sedgemore, B. (1980) *The Secret Constitution*, London: Hodder & Stoughton.

Seely, A. (2004) 'Commissioners for Revenue and Customs Bill', *House of Commons Research Paper 04/90*, London: House of Commons Library.

Seldon, A. (1997) *Major: A Political Life*, London: Weidenfeld & Nicolson.

Siedentopf, H. and Ziller, J. (eds) (1988) *Making European Policies Work, I*, London: Sage.

Smith, J. (2001) 'Cultural Aspects of Europeanization: The Case of the Scottish Office', *Public Administration*, 79: 147–65.

Smith, M. J. (2004) 'Mad Cows and Mad Money: Problems of Risk in the Making and Understanding of Policy', *British Journal of Politics and International Relations*, 6: 312–32.

Smith, M. J. and Richards, D. (2002) *Governance and Public Policy in the UK*, Oxford University Press.

Southgate, C. (1994) *Fundamental Review of HM Treasury's Running Costs*, London: HM Treasury.

Stern, N. (2007) *The Economics of Climate Change: The Stern Review*, Cambridge University Press.

Stevens, H. (2004) *Transport Policy in the European Union*, Basingstoke: Palgrave Macmillan.

Talbot, C. (1996) 'The Prison Service: A Framework of Irresponsibility?', *Public Money and Management*, 5–7.

Talbot, C. (2005) 'The Future of the Civil Service: A Growing Debate', *Public Management and Policy Association Review*, 31, November.

Theakston, K. (1995) *The Civil Service since 1945*, Oxford: Basil Blackwell.

Theakston, K. (1999) *Leadership in Whitehall*, London: Macmillan.

Tomlin Commission (1931) *Report of the Royal Commission on the Civil Service, 1929–31*, Cmnd 3909, London: HMSO.

Toynbee, P. and Walker, D. (2001) *Did Things Get Better? An Audit of Labour's Successes and Failures*, Harmondsworth: Penguin.

Transport Committee (1993) *The Future of the Railways in the Light of the Government's White Paper Proposals*, HC 375, London: HMSO.

Transport Committee (2002) *London Underground*, HC 387, London: Stationery Office.

Transport Committee (2003) *Ports*, HC 783, London: Stationery Office.

Travers, T., Jones, G., Hebbert, M. and Burnham, J. (1991) *The Government of London*, York: Joseph Rowntree Foundation.

Travers, T., Jones, G. and Burnham, J. (1997) *The Role of the Local Authority Chief Executive in Local Governance*, York: Joseph Rowntree Foundation.

Treasury and Civil Service Committee (1986) *Civil Servants and Ministers: Duties and Responsibilities*, HC 92, London: HMSO.

Treasury and Civil Service Committee (1994) *The Role of the Civil Service*, HC 27, London: HMSO.

Treasury Sub-Committee of the House of Commons (2006) *Independence for Statistics*, HC 1111, London: Stationery Office.

Varin, K. (1997) 'Les services publics au Royaume Uni', in C. Quin and G. Jeannot, *Un service public pour les Européens?*, Paris: La Documentation française, 185–214.

Verheijen, T. (ed.) (1999) *Civil Service Systems in Central and Eastern Europe*, London: Edward Elgar.

Vincent, D. (1998) *The Culture of Secrecy in Britain: 1832–1998*, Oxford University Press.

Virtanen, T. (2000) 'Flexibility, Commitment and Performance', in D. Farnham and S. Horton (eds), *Human Resources Flexibilities in the Public Services*, London: Macmillan, 39–58.

Waldegrave, W. (1993) *Public Service and the Future: Reforming Britain's Bureaucracies*, London: Conservative Political Centre.

Wallace, H. (2000) 'The Institutional Setting', in H. Wallace and W. Wallace (eds), *Policy-making in the European Union*, Oxford University Press, 3–37.

Ward, L. (2002) 'Press Chief Accused Over Resignation', *Guardian*, 26 February.

Weller, P., Bakvis, H. and Rhodes, R. A. W. (eds) (1997) *The Hollow Crown*, London: Macmillan.

Welsh Office (1997) *A Voice for Wales*, Cm 3718, London: Stationery Office.

Wilford. R. (2004) 'Northern Ireland: Resolving an Ancient Quarrel?', in M. O'Neill (ed.), *Devolution and British Politics*, Harlow: Pearson Longman, 135–67.

Wilson, R. (1999) 'The Civil Service in the New Millennium', Speech to City University Business School, May; www.cabinet-office.gov.uk/1999/senior/rw_speech.htm.

Wilson, R. (2000) *Diversity in the Civil Service: Report to the Prime Minister on Progress 1999–2000*, London: Cabinet Office.

Winstone, R. (2003) 'Whither the Civil Service?', *House of Commons Research Paper 03/49*, London: House of Commons Library.

Woodhouse, D. (1994) *Ministers and Parliament: Accountability in Theory and Practice*, Oxford: Clarendon Press.

Work and Pensions Committee of the House of Commons (2006) *The Efficiency Savings Programme in Jobcentre Plus*, HC 834, London: Stationery Office.

Work Foundation (2004) *Efficiency, Efficiency, Efficiency: The Gershon Review*, London: The Work Foundation.

Young, H. (1976) 'How Whitehall's Mandarins Tamed Labour's 38 Special Advisers', *The Sunday Times*, 19 September.

Young, H. (1993) *One of Us*, London: Pan.

Ziegler, P. (1993) *Wilson*, London: Weidenfeld & Nicolson.

Zifcak, S (1994) *New Managerialism. Administrative Reform in Whitehall and Canberra*, Buckingham: Open University Press.

Index